2ND EDITION

THE Options WORKBOOK

Fundamental Spread Concepts and Strategies for Investors and Traders

ANTHONY J. SALIBA
and the Staff at
International Trading Institute

Dearborn™
Trade Publishing
A Kaplan Professional Company

Senior Acquisitions Editor: Jean Iversen
Senior Project Editor: Trey Thoelcke
Interior Design: Lucy Jenkins
Cover Design: DePinto Studios
Typesetting: the dotted i

Published by Dearborn Trade, a Kaplan Professional Company

Printed in the United States of America

02 03 04 10 9 8 7 6 5 4 3 2 1

Library of Congress Cataloging-in-Publication Data

Saliba, Anthony J.
The options workbook : fundamental spread concepts and strategies for investors and traders / Anthony J. Saliba.—2nd ed.
p. cm.
Includes index.
ISBN 0-7931-5388-3 (8.5x11 pbk)
1. Stock options. 2. Options (Finance) I. Title.
HG6042 .S25 2002
332.63'228—dc21

2001007548

Contents

Acknowledgments

I would like to thank the entire staff of International Trading Institute for their contributions to this project. The second edition of this book was a collaborative effort among Karen Johnson, Chris Hausman, Scott Mollner, Denise Hubbard, Gavin Roe, Terri Raisch, and Jim Kallimani. I would also like to thank William Winger, president of ITI, and Kristine Kallimani, communications liasion, for using the feedback we received from our readers of the first edition to make the second edition more user friendly.

I think the biggest lesson we all took away from this experience is that teaching options strategies in a written form requires a completely different skill set than classroom instruction. Our staff's enthusiasm for taking the mystery out of options and sharing our knowledge with the individual investor was the driving force behind this book.

In addition, I would like to give special thanks to Karen Johnson, former president of International Trading Institute, for making this book possible. She is responsible for the curriculum selection as well as for managing the writing and layout of this book. Karen's dedication to this project allowed my wish to share our options expertise with the masses to become a reality.

Anthony J. Saliba
Founder and CEO
International Trading Institute

Introduction

The investing public's acceptance level of listed options, which hovered at 2.5 percent for the first 20 years of trading, more than doubled between 1993 and 1998. Whether the interest in options continues to grow at this accelerated rate remains to be seen, but I believe it will.

This jump can be attributed to a number of factors, primarily the relentless informational campaigns by the Chicago Board Options Exchange (CBOE), Options Clearing Corporation (OCC), Options Industry Council (OIC), and the extended bull market in equities during the '90s. The amount of assistance offered by these industry organizations is remarkable. It is hard to find another industry that puts such effort into educating its customers.

While general usage of puts and calls has more than doubled, the growth in participation has been limited predominantly to straight purchases and sales. There is no doubt that a straight order (to buy or to sell) is the easiest instruction to manage. Clearly the most leveraged use of this relatively new vehicle, being long a call (or short a call) brings the greatest level of excitement to an individual playing the market. In the late '90s, pure excitement, it seemed, was a governing force in the investing decisions of many.

Put/call purchases and sales are the easiest and most leveraged strategies. These straight orders, however, miss the biggest advantages of options strategy. The combination of options called spreads allows investors to tailor a more sophisticated risk/reward profile, increasing their earning potential to a much greater degree. Options professionals build their positions from a spread viewpoint.

In *The Options Workbook,* we emphasize these fundamentally sound spread relationships, and their composition and effectiveness as surrogates for straight equity transactions. We'll take you through the construction of these combinations one step at a time and reinforce the risk/reward profiles that each carries. There are exercises and quizzes reinforcing the concepts discussed.

We cover the topics of put and call purchases and sales; however, with more brokerage firms streamlining their ability to handle spreads and lowering fees to do two sides of a transaction, we emphasize the value of being spread, a concept being missed by millions of options users today.

You also will see some examples of technology used to price, execute, and manage complex option positions. Although you are only beginning your options education, it is important to be exposed to the sophisticated tools of the pros, as access to similar software is becoming readily available to the common investor.

After completing the following lessons, feel free to e-mail us at options@salibaco.com with any questions you may have about the topics covered. We will do our best to respond in a timely manner.

IMPORTANT DISCLOSURES

Following are several important disclosures we are required to make according to the rules of the CBOE, by which we are governed. Many would call them the *fine print,* but we refer to them as the beginning of wisdom. For that reason we encourage you to read and ponder them.

- Prior to buying or selling an option, a person must receive a copy of the booklet, "Characteristics and Risks of Standardized Options." Copies of this document are available at <www.theocc.com/publications/risks/riskchap1.jsp> or Pat Dajani, Salibaco, 311 S. Wacker Drive, Suite 3800, Chicago, IL 60606, 312-986-5033.
- Options involve risk and are not suitable for all investors.
- In order to trade strategies discussed in the book, a broker/dealer must first approve the customer's account for that specific trading level.
- No statement in this book should be construed as a recommendation to purchase or sell a security or provide investment advice.
- Writers of uncovered calls or puts will be obligated to meet applicable margin requirements for certain options strategies discussed in this book.
- For transactions that involve buying and writing multiple options in combination, it may be impossible at times to simultaneously execute transactions in all of the options involved in the combination.
- There is increased risk exposure when you exercise or close out of one side of a combination while the other side of the trade remains outstanding.
- Because all options transactions have important tax considerations, you should consult your tax advisor as to how taxes affect the outcome of contemplated options transactions.
- The examples in this book do not include commissions and other costs. Transaction costs may be significant, especially in option strategies calling for multiple purchases and sales of options, such as spreads and straddles.
- Note: Most spread transactions must be done in a margin account.

CHAPTER 1

Basic Concepts

Options Vernacular

Founder Anthony Saliba's awareness of the need for education in the derivatives industry was the impetus for the creation of International Trading Institute (ITI). The cornerstone of ITI's training curriculum is disciplined trading and risk management. During the past 12 years, ITI has trained more than 3,000 market professionals, mostly staff members of major financial institutions, from more than 20 countries. ITI's workshops address the needs of pit and screen-based traders as well as new online investors who have recently emerged as the most active in the trading arena.

The Options Workbook is designed to attempt to meet the educational needs of nonprofessional traders and investors wishing to incorporate options into investment strategies in order to enhance their returns by taking advantage of the additional opportunities that options offer. This workbook also will attempt to teach you to view the market from a different perspective and capitalize on a more refined assessment of risk/reward.

The strategies that we have chosen to teach in *The Options Workbook* offer numerous possibilities that may complement your investment objectives. You will be introduced to foundational concepts taught in its basic workshop, *Options for the Professional.* These concepts are the essential building blocks to understand the more advanced strategies that professionals use.

Chapters 2 to 7 provide a concept review of the basic knowledge required for those chapters before proceeding to a thorough discussion of the strategy, including its appropriate market conditions, risks, and profit potential.

Following the discussion are several examples of executing the strategy. At the end of each chapter you will find exercise answers and a quiz that will test your comprehension of the material covered. Our illustrations will use QRx, a proprietary options trading system developed for hybrid markets (outcry and electronic) by

First Traders Analytical Solutions, LLC. By using a professional state-of-the-art system, we hope to provide a realistic learning experience.

The Options Workbook was developed in a collaborative effort by ITI's staff and instructors. Each chapter is presented by a different staff member (or members). In the same way that our "hands-on" workshops are delivered by instructors having varying trading styles, experiences, and expertise, each chapter offers an instructor's personal perspective on how best to present the material being covered.

The following is a quick summary of this book's contents:

- Chapter 1 introduces you to the essential options concepts and vocabulary you'll need to know prior to learning options strategies, and tests you on them before you delve into the lessons.
- Chapter 2 explains the basic building blocks of options: calls and puts.
- Chapter 3 explores synthetic relationships between calls, puts, and the underlying security.
- Chapter 4 covers directional strategies, specifically verticals. You will go into the different categories of verticals including debit and credit spreads, and further break them down according to market bias: bull spread (call), bear spread (put), bull spread (put), and bear spread (call).
- Chapter 5 presents nondirection dependent strategies. Coverage of straddles and strangles will show you how you can attempt to be profitable, regardless of the direction of the market.
- Chapter 6 presents several strategies that potentially can be used to capitalize on directionless or range bound markets, including the butterfly, condor, and iron butterfly.
- Chapter 7 teaches an approach to trading ratio spreads and backspreads, as well as delta-neutral spreads. Similar to straddles and strangles, these spreads also are considered volatility strategies.
- Chapter 8 introduces current technology available to professional options traders, and an update on the industry's evolution. Because we believe it is only a matter of time before nonprofessionals will have the opportunity to compete with the professionals, we thought it would be of interest to our readers to see some of the sophisticated tools available to help professional traders manage their trading portfolios today.
- Appendix A provides a final examination covering the material presented in the lessons. The exam will prove to be a good test of your comprehension of the various strategies taught throughout the text. You have the option to log on to our Web site and take it electronically. If you do not have access to the Internet, you can send us your completed answer sheet via U.S. mail (our address is included at the top of the answer sheet) and we will send you your results.
- Appendix B provides background information on Tony Saliba, founder of International Trading Institute, and offers a discussion with Tony concerning the industry and his trading experiences.
- Appendix C profiles the contributors of *The Options Workbook.*
- Appendix D is Anthony Saliba's recommendations for options Web sites.

- As a quick reference tool, Appendix E provides profit and loss profiles of the strategies presented in the text.

At the end of each chapter you will see the ITI icon. This indicates that you can log on to ITI's Web site <www.itichicago.com> to attempt to improve your trading expertise with more exercises, further reading, drills, simulations, and links to other options sites.

As the old saying goes, "You must learn to walk before you run." Before you even think about incorporating options into your portfolio, you need to understand the basics—including the terminology. Let's get started!

Adjusted option: An option created as the result of a special event such as a stock split, stock dividend, merger, or spinoff taking place during the life of an option. An adjusted option may cover more than the usual one hundred shares. For example, after a 3-for-2 stock split, the adjusted option will represent 150 shares. For such options, the premium must be multiplied by a corresponding factor. Example: buying 1 call (covering 150 shares) at $4 would cost $600. *See also* Strike price interval.

All-or-none order (AON): An order that is designated to be executed only if the entire order can be executed.

American-style options: Options that may be exercised on or before the expiration date.

Analytics: Calculations performed on updated prices.

AON: *See* All-or-none order.

Arbitrage: A trading technique that involves the simultaneous purchase and sale of identical assets traded on two different exchanges with the intention of profiting by a difference in price between exchanges.

Ask/ask price: The lowest price at which a dealer or trader is willing to sell a tradable instrument at a particular time.

Assigned: Received notification of an assignment by The Options Clearing Corporation. *See also* Assignment.

Assignment: Notification by The Options Clearing Corporation to a clearing firm member and to the writer of an option that the owner of the option has exercised the option and that the terms of settlement must be met. Assignments are made on a random basis by The Options Clearing Corporation. The process by which the seller of an option is notified of the buyer's intention to exercise that option.

ATM: *See* At-the-money.

At-the-money (ATM): An option whose exercise price is equal to the current market price of the underlying security. An ATM option may or may not have intrinsic value.

Automatic exercise: A procedure used by The Options Clearing Corporation to exercise in-the-money (ITM) options at expiration. This procedure protects the owner from losing the intrinsic value of the option because of failure to exercise. Unless instructed not to do so, the Options Clearing Corporation will exercise all expiring equity options that are held in customer accounts if they are in-the-money by 75 cents or more. There is also an automatic exercise limit for index options. *See also* In-the-money.

Backspread: A delta-neutral spread composed of more long options than short options on the same underlying instrument. This position generally profits from a large movement in either direction in the underlying instrument.

Bear: An individual with the opinion that a security, or the market in general, will decline in price; someone having a negative or pessimistic outlook.

Bear market: A prolonged period of falling prices. A bear market in stocks is usually brought on by the anticipation of declining economic activity.

Bear spread: A strategy involving two or more options of the same type that will profit from a decline in the underlying stock. Consists of buying an option with a higher strike and selling an option with a lower strike. The maximum risk will be realized if the underlying stock rises in price.

Bear spread (call): A credit spread in which a decline in the price of the underlying security will theoretically increase the value of the spread. For example: the simultaneous purchase of the one call option with a higher strike price and the writing of another call option with a lower strike price. For example, buying 1 XYZ Jan 55 call and writing 1 XYZ Jan 50 call.

Bear spread (put): A debit spread in which a decline in the price of the underlying security will theoretically increase the value of the spread. For example: the simultaneous writing of the one put option with a lower strike price and the purchase of another put option with a higher strike price. For example, writing 1 XYZ Jan 50 put and buying 1 XYZ Jan 55 put.

Bid/bid price: The highest price a dealer is willing to pay for a security at a particular time.

Black-Scholes formula: A widely used model for option pricing developed by Fischer Black and Myron Scholes. This formula can be used to calculate a theoretical value for an option using current stock prices, expected dividends, the option's strike price, expected interest rates, time to expiration, and expected stock volatility. While the Black-Scholes model does not perfectly describe real-world options markets, it still is often used in the valuation and trading of options.

Box spread: A four-sided option spread that involves a long call and a short put at one strike price as well as a short call and a long put at another strike price. For example, buying 1 LMN Jan 50 call, and writing (selling) 1 LMN Jan 55 call; simultaneously buying 1 LMN Jan 55 put, and writing 1 Jan 50 put.

Break-even point(s): The stock price(s) at which an option strategy results in neither a profit nor a loss. An option strategy's break-even point(s) are normally stated as of the option's expiration date; a theoretical option-pricing model can be used to determine the strategy's break-even point(s) for other dates as well.

Breaking: A market drop in the price of a security.

Broker loan rate: Interest rate at which brokerage firms borrow from banks to finance their clients' security positions. The call loan rate is sometimes used because the loans can be called on a 24-hour notice.

Broker/Dealer: In the broadest sense, an agent who facilitates trades between a buyer and a seller and receives a commission for services. Brokers acting in a dealer capacity may buy and sell for their own account and keep their own inventory of securities on which they can profit or incur losses. Some stock brokerage firms act as brokers and dealers. Brokers are also classed as full service or discount, the former using a commission-based sales force and the latter using salaried brokers only.

Bull: A person who believes that a security, or the market in general, will rise in price; a positive or optimistic outlook.

Bull (or bullish) spread: A strategy involving two or more options of the same type (or options combined with an underlying stock position) that will profit from a rise in the price of the underlying stock. Consists of selling an option with a higher strike, and buying an option with a lower strike. The maximum risk will be realized if the underlying stock falls in price.

Bull spread (call): A debit spread in which a rise in the price of the underlying security will theoretically increase the value of the spread. For example, the simultaneous purchase of one call option with a lower strike price and the writing of another call option with a higher strike price. For example, buying 1 XYZ Jan 50 call and writing 1 XYZ Jan 55 call.

Bull spread (put): A credit spread in which a rise in the price of the underlying security will theoretically increase the profit value of the spread. For example, the simultaneous writing of one put option with a higher strike value and the purchase of another put option with a lower strike price. For example, writing 1 XYZ Jan 55 put and buying 1 XYZ Jan 50 put.

Butterfly spread: A strategy involving four options of the same type that span three strike prices. The strategy has both limited risk and limited profit potential. For example: a long call butterfly is created by buying one call at the lowest strike price, selling two calls at the middle strike price, and buying one call at the highest strike price. A long put butterfly is established by buying one put at the lowest strike price, writing two puts at the middle strike price, and buying one put at the highest strike price. For example: A long call butterfly might be buying 1 ABC Jan 40 call, writing 2 ABC Jan 45 calls, and buying 1 ABC Jan 50 call.

Calendar spread: The simultaneous purchase and sale of options of the same class (call or put, having same underlying) at the same strike prices, but with different expiration dates, selling the short-term option and buying the long-term option.

Call option: A contract between a buyer and a seller whereby the buyer acquires the right, but not the obligation, to buy a specified underlying instrument at a fixed price on or before a specified date should the buyer of the call option wish to exercise the option. The seller of the call option assumes the obligation of delivering the instrument should the buyer wish to exercise the option. Investors profit by buying calls before an increase in the price of the underlying stock. For example, the owner (or holder) of an ITI Jun 60 call would have the right to purchase 100 shares of ITI at $60 (strike price) per share, between now and the third Friday in June (expiration date).

Carry/Carrying charge: The interest expense on money borrowed to finance a margined securities position.

Cash-settled American index options (cash index): These options can be exercised on any business day prior to expiration and the settlement value will be based on the index close that day, settled in the cash equivalent of the amount in-the-money.

Chicago Board Options Exchange (CBOE): The largest and oldest listed options exchange.

Class of options: A term referring to all options of the same type—either calls or puts—having the same underlying instrument.

Clearinghouse: A facility that compares and reconciles both sides of a trade in addition to receiving and delivering payments and securities.

Collar: An option strategy that involves an out-of-the-money call and an out-of-the-money put. This is normally used as a long stock protective strategy when the call is sold and the put is purchased. The opposite of this strategy, called a "fence," could be applied as a protective measure in a short stock position.

Combination: An option position that involves the purchase/sale of a call and the sale (purchase) of a put on the same underlying strike with the same expiration. Can also be referred to as any set of multiple purchases and sales of options.

Condor spread: A strategy involving four options and four strike prices, and that has both limited risk and limited profit potential. A long call condor spread is established by buying one call at the lowest strike, writing one call at the second strike, writing another call at the third strike, and buying one call at the fourth (highest) strike with the same expirations.

Contract size: The number of underlying shares covered by one option contract. This is 100 shares for one equity option unless adjusted for a special event, such as a stock split or a stock dividend.

Conversion: An investment strategy in which a long put and a short call with the same strike price and expiration are combined with long stock to lock in a nearly risk-less profit. For example, by purchasing 100 shares of XYZ stock at 50, writing 1 XYZ Jan 50 call, and buying 1 XYZ Jan 50 put at desirable prices. The process of executing these three-sided trades is also called conversion arbitrage. *See also* Reverse conversion.

Covered call/Covered call writing: An option strategy in which call options are sold against equivalent amounts of long stock; for example, writing 2 XYZ Jan 50 calls while owning 200 shares of XYZ stock.

Covered option: An open short option position that is offset by a corresponding stock position on a share-for-share basis. This ensures that if the owner of the option exercises, the writer of the option will not have a problem fulfilling the delivery requirements. Note: A cash-secured put is also a covered option. *See also* Uncovered option.

Credit spread: The difference in the premium prices of two options, where the credit premium of the one sold exceeds the debit premium of the one purchased. A bull spread with puts and a bear spread with calls are examples of credit spreads.

CTA: Commodity trading advisor.

Dealer: *See* Broker/Dealer.

Debit spread: A spread in which the difference in the long and short options premiums results in a net debit.

Delta: The sensitivity (rate of change) of an option's theoretical value (assessed value) for a one dollar change in price of the underlying instrument. Expressed as a percentage, it represents an equivalent amount of underlying at a given moment in time. Calls have positive deltas; puts have negative deltas.

Diagonal spread: The combination of a vertical and a calendar spread, wherein the investor buys and sells options of the same class at different expiration dates and different strike prices.

DPM: Designated primary market maker.

Early exercise: A feature of American-style options that allows the owner to exercise an option at any time prior to its expiration date.

Edge: In a customer transaction, edge refers to the markup or markdown price that a market maker generates in the deal. It can be thought of as a tax charged by the market maker for services rendered.

Equity option: An option on shares of an individual common stock.

Equivalent strategy: Investment strategy that has a similar risk/reward profile as another investment strategy. For example, a long May 60-65 call vertical spread is equivalent to a short May 60-65 put vertical spread. *See also* Synthetics.

European-style option: An option that can be exercised only at expiration. European-style options usually expire the third Friday of every month. *See also* American-style options.

Exercise: The process by which the holder of an option notifies the seller of intention to take delivery of the underlying in the case of a call, or make delivery in the case of a put, at the specified exercise price.

Exercise price: The price at which the underlying will be delivered in the event the option is exercised. For example, a call contract may allow the buyer to purchase 100 shares of ITI stock at any time in the next three months at an exercise (or strike) price of $70. The exercise price is referred to as the strike price. These prices usually are expressed in numbers divisible by $5, or—in some cases—$2.50 or $10, depending on the price of the underlying. When a stock has split, strike prices may be stated in fractions. *See also* Strike price.

Expiration: The date an option contract becomes void. All holders of options must indicate their desire to exercise by the business day preceding the expiration date. It is the last day on which an option can be exercised. If not exercised, the option may become worthless. Options that close $0.75 in-the-money are automatically exercised at expiration.

Expiration cycle: The cycle of expiration dates used in short-term options trading. For example, contracts may be written for one of three cycles: January, April, July, October; February, May, August, November; or March, June, September, December. Because options (with the exception of LEAPS®) are traded in contracts for three, six, and nine month contracts, only three of the four months in the set are traded at once. In our example, when the January contract expires, trading begins in the October contract.

Expiration date: The date on which an option and the right to exercise it cease to exist. Listed stock options expire the Saturday following the third Friday of every month.

Expiration month: The month during which the expiration date occurs.

Expiration time: The time of day by which all exercise notices must be received on the expiration date. Check with your account executive regarding your brokerage firm's deadline for submitting exercise notices on expiration Friday.

Extrinsic value: The price of an option less its intrinsic value. The entire premium of an out-of-the-money option consists of extrinsic value. This is often referred to as the time value portion of option premiums.

Fences: *See* Collar.

Fill-or-kill order (FOK): A type of order that requires that the order be executed completely or not at all. A fill-or-kill order is similar to an all-or-none (AON) order. The difference is that if the order cannot be completely executed (i.e., filled in its entirety) as soon as it is announced in the trading crowd, it is to be "killed" (i.e., canceled) immediately. Unlike an AON order, a FOK order cannot be used as part of a GTC order.

Flat spread: *See* Neutral spread.

Floor broker: Liaison between customers and pit traders.

FOK: *See* Fill-or-kill order.

Future: A contract to buy or sell a predetermined quantity of a commodity or financial product for a specific price on a given date.

Gamma: The sensitivity (rate of change) of an option's delta at a given moment in time. It is the change in delta with respect to a 1-point change in the underlying. For example, let's say a call option with a 100 strike price has a 50 delta. If the underlying moves from 100 to 101, the option premium (price) will increase by .50 (50 percent). Now that the call is in-the-money by $1, we know that the delta would be more than 50. If now with the underlying at 101 and the gamma at 10, then the new delta would be 60.

Good til cancel (GTC) order: An order to buy or sell a security that will remain in effect until the order is executed or canceled.

GTC: *See* Good til cancel order.

Hedge/Hedged position: A position established with the specific intent of protecting an existing position. For example, an owner of common stock may buy a put option to hedge against a possible stock price decline.

Hedging: An investment strategy that attempts to lower risk by buying securities that have offsetting risk characteristics. A perfect hedge eliminates risk entirely. Hedging strategies lower the return because there is a cost involved in reducing risk.

Historic volatility: A measure of actual stock price changes over a specific period of time. *See also* Standard deviation.

Horizontal spread: *See* Calendar spread.

Implied volatility: A measure of the volatility of the underlying security, derived by applying current prices rather than historical prices.

Index: A compilation of the prices of several common entities into a single number; for example, the S&P 100 Index.

Indexing: Constructing a portfolio to match the performance of a broad-based index, such as the S&P 500. Individuals can do this by purchasing shares in an index mutual fund.

Index option: An option whose underlying asset is an index. Generally, index options are cash-settled.

Interest: Charge levied for the privilege of borrowing money.

Interest rate risk: The risk that a change in the interest rates will negatively affect the value of an investor's holdings; generally associated with bonds, but applying to all investments.

In-the-money (ITM) option: An option that has intrinsic value. A call is in-the-money if its strike (strike price, or exercise price) is lower than the market price of the underlying. A put is in-the-money if its strike price is higher than the market price of the underlying. A call option on XYZ having a strike price of 100 would be in-the-money if XYZ were selling for 102, for instance, and a put option with the same strike price would be in-the-money if XYZ were selling for 98.

Intrinsic value (*also called* parity): The amount by which an option is in-the-money (ITM). Out-of-the-money (OTM) options have no intrinsic value. Intrinsic value is the difference between the exercise price or strike price of an option and the market value of the underlying security. For example, if the strike price is 55 on a call option to purchase a stock with a market price of $57, the option has an intrinsic value of $2. Or, in the case of a put option, if the strike price were 55 and the market price of the underlying stock were $53, the intrinsic value of this option also would be $2.

Investment: The use of money to create more money through an appreciating or income-producing asset.

Iron butterfly: An option strategy with limited risk and limited profit potential that involves both a long (or short) straddle, and a short (or long) strangle. For example, a short iron butterfly might be: buying 1 ABC May 90 call and 1 ABC May 90 put, and writing 1 ABC May 95 call and writing 1 ABC May 85 put.

ITM: *See* In-the-money option.

Last trading day: The last business day prior to the option's expiration date during which purchases and sales of options can be made. For equity options, this is generally the third Friday of the expiration month. Note: If the third Friday of the month is an exchange holiday, the last trading day will be the Thursday immediately preceding the third Friday.

LEAPS®: Long-term equity anticipation securities (also known as long-dated options) are calls and puts with expirations as long as two to three years. Typically, equity LEAPS® have two series at any time with January expiration.

Leg: A term describing one side of a spread position. A trader who legs into a spread establishes one side first, hoping for a favorable price movement so the other side can be executed at a better price. This is, of course, a higher-risk method of establishing a spread position. A leg also can be defined as a sustained trend in the stock market.

Leverage: A means of increasing return or worth without increasing investment. For example, using borrowed funds to increase one's investment return by buying stocks on margin. Option contracts are leveraged because they provide the prospect of a high return with little investment. Of course, options are a risky investment and there is no guarantee that the investor would not lose the entire premium.

Listed option: An exchange-approved put or call trading on a national options exchange with standardized terms. In contrast, over-the-counter options usually have nonstandard or negotiated terms.

Long: The position resulting from the purchase of a contract or instrument.

Long position: Term used to describe the ownership of a security, contract, or commodity that grants the owner the right to transfer ownership by sale or gift.

Margin: The amount deposited into a brokerage account, if planning to borrow funds from the brokerage houses to buy securities. A margin call is a requirement for more funds to be deposited into one's account when the marketable value of the underlying asset falls below the minimum level required by federal regulations and the investor's brokerage house.

Market on close (MOC): An order to buy or sell at the last price on the close.

MM: Market maker.

MOC: *See* Market on close.

Naked option: *See* Uncovered option.

Neutral: An adjective describing the belief that a stock or the market in general will neither rise nor decline significantly.

Neutral spread: A position that will perform best if there is little or no net change in the price of the underlying stock. Also known as flat or square.

Neutral strategy: An option strategy (or stock and option position) that is neither bullish nor bearish.

Offer/Offer price: In the securities business this means the same as the ask/ask price, or the price at which a seller is offering to sell an option or a stock.

Open interest: The total number of outstanding (contracts that are still open) option contracts in a given series.

Open outcry: The trading method by which competing market makers and floor brokers representing public orders shout their bids and offers on the trading floor.

Option: A contract that gives the owner the right, if exercised, to buy or sell a security at a specific price within a specific time limit. Options may be traded as securities themselves, with buyers and sellers trying to profit from price changes or used as an investment hedge. They are generally available for one to nine months, with some longer term options (LEAPS®) also available for selected securities. Each stock option contract generally carries the right to buy or sell 100 shares of the underlying stock (100 is the multiplier), although as a result of a merger, acquisition, stock split, or spin off, it can be different.

Option chain: A list of the options available for the underlying stock symbols in which you are interested.

Option cycle: The time from when an option contract is listed by the exchange; sometimes referred to as an option's "lifetime." *See also* Expiration cycle.

Option pricing curve: A graphical representation of the estimated theoretical value of an option at one point in time, at various prices of the underlying stock.

Option pricing model: Evaluating an option's value through the use of a pricing model allows one to determine the theoretical value (TV) of the option; i.e., the price you would expect to pay in order to break even in the long run.

Option writer: The seller of an option contract who is obligated to meet the terms of delivery if the option is exercised. This seller has made an opening sale transaction, and has not yet closed that position.

Options Clearing Corporation (OCC): The issuer of all listed options contracts trading on national options exchanges. The OCC makes possible secondary markets in options while not guaranteeing the liquidity or availability of those markets. Exchange closures or periods of severe illiquidity could prevent the timely liquidation of an option position.

OTC: *See* Over-the-counter option.

OTM: *See* Out-of-the-money option.

Out-of-the-money (OTM) option: An option that has no intrinsic value. A call is out-of-the-money if its strike price is higher than the current market price of the underlying. A put is out-of-the-money if its strike price is lower than the current price of the underlying. A December 60 call option would be out-of-the-money when XYZ stock is selling for $55 a share. Similarly, an XYZ December 60 put option would be out-of-the-money when XYZ stock is selling for $65 a share.

Over the counter (OTC): A security that is traded via a telephone and computer network rather than on the floor of an organized exchange. There is a direct link between the buyer and seller of the securities, and there is no secondary market available.

Over-the-counter (OTC) option: An option that is negotiated in the over-the-counter market, is not listed on an options exchange, and has nonstandardized (negotiated) terms.

Parity: A term used to describe an in-the-money option contract's total premium when that premium is the same amount as its intrinsic value. For example, when an option's value is equal to its intrinsic value, it is said to be "worth parity." When an option is trading for only its intrinsic value, it is said to be "trading for parity." Parity may be measured against the stock's last sale, bid, or offer.

Pin risk: The risk to an investor (option seller) that the stock price will exactly equal the strike price of a written option at expiration; i.e., that option will be exactly at-the-money. The investor will not know how many written (short) options will be assigned. The risk is that on the Monday following expiration, the investor might have an unexpected long (in the case of a written put) or short (in the case of a written call) stock position, and thus be subject to the risk of an adverse price move.

Position: The combined total of an investor's open option contracts (calls and/or puts) and long or short stock. It is an investor's stake in a particular security or market.

Premium: The total price of an option: intrinsic value plus extrinsic value.

Put option: A put option gives the owner the right, but not the obligation, to sell the underlying stock at a given price (the strike price) by a given time (the expiration date). The owner is speculating that the option will go up in value and the underlying stock will go down in value. The purpose can be to either speculate with the option (hope it goes up and sell for a profit) or sell the underlying stock at a locked-in price if the stock price goes down enough. For example, one ITI MAR 65 put would give the owner the right to sell 100 shares of ITI at $65 (strike price) per share between now and the third Friday in March (expiration date).

Put-call ratio: The ratio of trading volume in put options to the trading volume in call options. The ratio provides a quantitative measure of the bullishness or bearishness of investors. A high volume of puts relative to calls indicates investors are bearish, whereas a high ratio of calls to puts shows bullishness. Often used as an indicator of market sentiment.

Quote: The bid and ask prices of a specific security.

Ratio spread: Most commonly used to describe the purchase of an option(s), call or put, and the writing of a greater number of the same type of options that are out-of-the-money with respect to those purchased. All options involved have the same expiration date. For example, buying 5 XYZ May 60 calls and writing 6 XYZ May 65 calls. *See also* Ratio write.

Ratio write: An investment strategy in which stock is purchased and call options are written on a greater than one-for-one basis; i.e., more calls written than the equivalent number of shares purchased. For example, buying 500 shares of XYZ stock and writing 6 XYZ May 60 calls. *See also* Ratio spread.

Reverse conversion: An investment strategy used by professional option traders in which a short put and long call with the same strike price and expiration are combined with short stock to lock in a price. For example, selling short 100 shares of XYZ stock, buying 1 XYZ May 60 call, and writing 1 XYZ May 60 put at favorable prices. The process of executing these three-sided trades is sometimes called reversal arbitrage. *See* Conversion.

Rho: The sensitivity of theoretical option prices with regard to small changes in interest rates. Increases in interest rates lead to higher call values and lower put values. Lower interest rates do the opposite.

Selling short: Opening sale of a security.

Series of options: Option contracts on the same class having the same strike price and expiration month. For example, all XYZ May 60 calls constitute a series.

Settlement: The transfer of the security (for the seller) or cash (for the buyer) in order to complete a security transaction.

Settlement date: The date on which an executed order must be settled. Buyers pay for securities with cash, and sellers deliver certificates of sold securities.

Settlement price: The official price at the end of a trading session. Buyers pay for securities with cash, and sellers deliver certificates of sold securities. This price is established by the Options Clearing Corporation and is used to determine changes in account equity, margin requirements, and for other purposes.

Short: A position resulting from the sale of a contract or instrument that you do not own. For example: If you are short XYZ, this means you sold XYZ.

Short option position: The position of an option writer that represents an obligation on the part of the option's writer to meet the terms of the option if it is exercised by its owner. The writer can terminate this obligation by buying back (cover or close) the position with a closing purchase transaction.

Short sale: A trade where the investor borrows a security from the broker, sells it at market price, and receives the proceeds of the sale, less commission. The short seller then hopes that the security will go down in price in order to be bought to cover the security and return it to the broker. However, if the price goes up, the seller will eventually receive a margin call and be expected to either buy at the current price and take the loss or add more cash or marginable securities to the seller's account, and be vulnerable to further risk. When you are long a security, the worst you can do is lose an amount equal to the cost of the security. When you are short, theoretically, your risk is unlimited as a security's price can keep rising.

Short stock position: A strategy that profits from a stock price decline. It is initiated by borrowing stock from a broker-dealer and selling it in the open market. This strategy is closed (covered) at a later date by buying back the stock and returning it to the lending broker-dealer.

Specialist: A member of the floor of an exchange who is responsible for a given stock. Specialists can place contingency orders for a customer on the book, and can then execute these orders for the customers (as an agent), or buy and sell for their own accounts (as a principal). Specialists incur some obligations for this privileged position. For example, specialists must be prepared to buy stock when there is active interest in selling, and sell when there is active interest in buying, in order to maintain a fair and orderly market.

Spread option: A position involving the purchase of an option and the simultaneous sale of an option of the same type (put or call) on the same underlying security.

Spread order: A position consisting of two parts, each of which alone would profit from opposite directional price moves. As orders, these opposite parts are entered and executed simultaneously in the hope of limiting risk, or benefiting from a change of price relationship between the two parts. *See also* Leg.

Square spread: *See* Neutral spread.

Straddle: The purchase or sale of an equal number of puts or calls with the same underlying, strike price, and expiration.

Strangle: The purchase or sale of an equal number of puts or calls with the same underlying and expiration, but different strike prices.

Strike/Strike price: The price that an owner of an option can purchase (call) or sell (put) the underlying stock. Used interchangeably with striking price, strike, or exercise price.

Strike price interval: The normal price differential between option strike prices. Equity options generally have $2.50 strike price intervals (if the underlying stock price is below $25), $5.00 intervals (from $25 to $200), and $10 intervals (above $200). LEAPS® generally start with one at-the-money, one in-the-money, and one out-of-the-money strike price. The latter two are usually set 20–25 percent away from the former. Strike price intervals occasionally vary when there has been a stock split or company merger/takeover.

Synthetics: Two or more trading vehicles packaged to emulate another trading vehicle or spread. Because the package involves different components, price is also different, but the risk is the same (there are exceptions, however).

Synthetic long call: A long stock position and a long put position.

Synthetic long put: A short stock position and a long call position.

Synthetic long stock: A long call position and a short put position.

Synthetic short call: A short stock position and a short put position.

Synthetic short put: A long stock position and a short call position.

Synthetic short stock: A short call position and a long put position.

Theoretical option pricing model: *See* Black-Scholes formula.

Theoretical value (TV): The estimated value of an option derived from a mathematical model. *See also* Black-Scholes formula.

Theta: The sensitivity of theoretical option prices with regard to small changes in time. Theta measures the rate of decay in the time value of options. *See also* Time decay.

Time decay: A term used to describe how the theoretical value of an option "erodes" or reduces with the passage of time. Time decay is specifically quantified by theta.

Time spread: An option strategy that generally involves the purchase of a farther-term option (call or put) and the selling (writing) of an equal number of nearer-term options of the same type and strike price. For example, buying 1 ITI May 60 call (far-term portion of the spread) and selling 1 ITI March 60 call (near-term portion of the spread). Also known as calendar spread or horizontal spread.

Time value: The part of an option's total price that exceeds its intrinsic value. The price of an out-of-the-money option consists entirely of time value.

Trader: A person or company that buys and sells, for this book's purposes, securities such as stocks, mutual funds, and options.

TV: *See* Theoretical value.

Types of options: Options can be of two types, calls or puts.

Uncovered option (*also called* Naked option): A short option position that is not fully collateralized if notification of assignment is received. A short call position is uncovered if the writer does not have a long stock or long call position. A short put position is uncovered if the writer is not short stock or long another put.

Underlying: The instrument (stock, future, or cash index) to be delivered when an option is exercised. The amount of underlying for each option contract depends on the security traded. For example, in stock options, each contract typically represents 100 shares of the underlying stock. An underlying security must be delivered if a put option or call option contract is exercised.

Underlying security (stock): The stock subject to being purchased or sold upon exercise of an option contract.

Vega: The sensitivity of an option's theoretical value to a change in implied volatility. *See* Implied volatility.

Vertical spread: The simultaneous purchase and sale of options of the same class at different strike prices, but with the same expiration date. For example: ABC April 150/155 call spread. You purchase the ABC Apr 150 call and sell the ABC Apr 155 call. Similar to the outright purchase of a call, your maximum loss is the amount that you paid for the spread (debit). If the underlying closes below the 150 strike, on expiration, then both calls expire worthless and you only lose the debit. The break-even in this example is the lower strike plus the debit amount.

Volatility: The degree to which the price of an underlying tends to fluctuate over time. This variable, which the market implies to the underlying, may result from pricing an option through a model. Volatility is viewed from the historical side, which applies to the underlying, and from the implied side, which applies to the option at any given moment in time.

CHAPTER ONE QUIZ

Now test your options vocabulary with this quiz.

1. *Call Option*

   A contract between a buyer and a seller whereby the ________ acquires the right, but not the obligation, to ________ a specified underlying instrument at a fixed price on or before a specified date, should the _________ of the call option wish to exercise the option. The seller of the call option assumes the obligation of _________ the instrument should the buyer wish to exercise the option.

2. *Put Option*

   A contract between a buyer and a seller whereby the ________ acquires the right, but not the obligation, to _________ a specified underlying instrument at a fixed price on or before a specified date should the ________ of the put option wish to exercise the option. The seller of the put option assumes the obligation of taking ________ of the instrument should the buyer wish to exercise the option.

3. *Underlying*

   The instrument (stock, future, or cash index) to be ________ when an option is exercised. The amount of underlying for each option contract depends on the security traded. For example, in stock options, each contract represents 100 shares of the underlying stock.

4. *Exercise Price*

   The ________ at which the underlying will be ________ in the event the option is exercised.

5. *Exercise*

   The process by which the ________ of an option notifies the ________ of an intention to *take* delivery of the underlying, in the case of a ________, or *make* delivery, in the case of a ________, at the specified exercise price.

6. *Assignment*

   The process by which the _________ of an option is notified of the ________ intention to exercise the option.

7. *Expiration*

   The date an option contract becomes ________. All ________ of this option must indicate their desire to exercise by this date.

8. *American-Style Options*

   Options that may be exercised ___________ the expiration date.

9. *European-Style Options*

   Options that may be ________ the expiration date only.

10. *In-the-Money (ITM)*

    A call is in-the-money if its strike is ________ than the market price of the underlying. A put is in-the-money if its strike price is ________ than the market price of the underlying.

11. *At-the-Money (ATM)*

    An option whose exercise price is ____________________ to the current market price of the underlying security.

12. *Out-of-the-Money (OTM)*

    An option that has no ________ value. A call is out-of-the-money if its strike price is _________ than the current market price of the underlying. A put is out-of-the-money if its strike price is ________ than the current price of the underlying.

13. *Intrinsic Value (also called* Parity)

    The amount by which an option is ___________. Out-of-the-money (OTM) options have ________ intrinsic value.

14. *Extrinsic Value*

    The price of an option less its ________________. The entire premium of an ______________ option consists of extrinsic value.

15. *Long*

    Position resulting from the ________ of a contract or instrument.

16. *Short*

    A position resulting from the ___________ of a contract or instrument. To _________ a contract without, or prior to, buying it.

17. *Spread*

A ________ market position and an offsetting ________ market position in contracts with the same underlying.

18. *Bull Spread*

Any spread in which a _________ in the price of the underlying security will theoretically increase the value of the spread.

19. *Bear Spread*

Any spread in which a ________ in the price of the underlying security will theoretically increase the value of the spread.

20. *Neutral Spread*

A position that has virtually ________ exposure to the conditions of a market. Also known as *flat* or *square.*

21. *Delta*

The sensitivity (rate of change) of an option's theoretical value (assessed value) to changes in ________ of the underlying instrument. Expressed as a percentage, it represents an equivalent amount of __________ at a given moment in time. ________ have positive deltas; ________ have negative deltas.

22. *Gamma*

The sensitivity (rate of change) of an option's ________ at a given moment in time.

23. *Vega*

The sensitivity of an option's theoretical value to a 1 percent change in ________________.

24. *Theta*

The _________ of an option's theoretical value over one day in time.

25. *Synthetics*

Two or more trading vehicles ___________ to emulate another vehicle or a spread. Because the package involves different components, price is also different, but the risk profile is the same (there are exceptions, however).

26. *Volatility*

The degree to which the price of an underlying tends to _________ over time. Volatility is viewed from the _________ side—which applies to the underlying, and from the ________ side—which applies to the option at any given moment in time. Or, in mathematical terms, the annualized standard deviation of a given underlying instrument over a specific period of time.

CHAPTER ONE QUIZ ANSWER KEY

1. *Call Option*

A contract between a buyer and a seller whereby the *buyer* acquires the right, but not the obligation, to *buy* a specified underlying instrument at a fixed price on or before a specified date, should the *buyer* of the call option wish to exercise the option. The seller of the call option assumes the obligation of *delivering* the instrument should the buyer wish to exercise the option.

2. *Put Option*

A contract between a buyer and a seller whereby the *buyer* acquires the right, but not the obligation, to *sell* a specified underlying instrument at a fixed price on or before a specified date should the *buyer* of the put option wish to exercise the option. The seller of the put option assumes the obligation of taking *delivery* of the instrument should the buyer wish to exercise the option.

3. *Underlying*

The instrument (stock, future, or cash index) to be *delivered* when an option is exercised. The amount of underlying for each option contract depends on the security traded. For example, in stock options, each contract represents 100 shares of the underlying stock.

4. *Exercise Price*

The *price* at which the underlying will be *delivered* in the event the option is exercised.

5. *Exercise*

The process by which the *holder* of an option notifies the *seller* of an intention to *take* delivery of the underlying, in the case of a *call*, or *make* delivery, in the case of a *put*, at the specified exercise price.

6. Assignment

   The process by which the <u>*seller*</u> of an option is notified of the <u>*buyer's*</u> intention to exercise the option.

7. *Expiration*

   The date an option contract becomes <u>*void*</u>. All <u>*holder(s)*</u> of this option must indicate their desire to exercise by this date.

8. *American-Style Options*

   Options that may be exercised <u>*on or before*</u> the expiration date.

9. *European-Style Options*

   Options that may be <u>*exercised on*</u> the expiration date only.

10. *In-the-Money (ITM)*

    A call is in-the-money if its strike is <u>*lower*</u> than the market price of the underlying. A put is in-the-money if its strike price is <u>*higher*</u> than the market price of the underlying.

11. *At-the-Money (ATM)*

    An option whose exercise price is <u>*approximately equal*</u> to the current market price of the underlying security.

12. *Out-of-the-Money (OTM)*

    An option that has no <u>*intrinsic*</u> value. A call is out-of-the-money if its strike price is <u>*higher*</u> than the current market price of the underlying. A put is out-of-the-money if its strike price is <u>*lower*</u> than the current price of the underlying.

13. *Intrinsic Value* (*also called* Parity)

    The amount by which an option is <u>*in-the-money*</u>. Out-of-the-money (OTM) options have <u>*no*</u> intrinsic value.

14. *Extrinsic Value*

    The price of an option less its <u>*intrinsic value*</u>. The entire premium of an <u>*out-of-the-money*</u> option consists of extrinsic value.

15. *Long*

    Position resulting from the <u>*purchase*</u> of a contract or instrument.

16. *Short*

Position resulting from the ____*sale*____ of a contract or instrument. To ____*sell*____ a contract without, or prior to, buying it.

17. *Spread*

A ___*long*___ market position and an offsetting ___*short*___ market position in contracts with the same underlying.

18. *Bull Spread*

Any spread in which a ____*rise*____ in the price of the underlying security will theoretically increase the value of the spread.

19. *Bear Spread*

Any spread in which a ___*decline*___ in the price of the underlying security will theoretically increase the value of the spread.

20. *Neutral Spread*

A position that has virtually ____*no*____ exposure to the conditions of a market. Also known as *flat* or *square.*

21. *Delta*

The sensitivity (rate of change) of an option's theoretical value (assessed value) to changes in ___*price*___ of the underlying instrument. Expressed as a percentage, it represents an equivalent amount of ___*underlying*___ at a given moment in time. ____*Calls*____ are expressed as positive deltas; ____*puts*____ are expressed as negative deltas.

22. *Gamma*

The sensitivity (rate of change) of an option's ___*delta*___ at a given moment in time.

23. *Vega*

The sensitivity of an option's theoretical value to a 1 percent change in *implied volatility.*

24. *Theta*

The ___*erosion*___ of an option's theoretical value over one day in time.

25. *Synthetics*

Two or more trading vehicles _*packaged*_ to emulate another vehicle, or a spread. Because the package involves different components, price is also different, but the risk profile is the same (there are exceptions, however).

26. *Volatility*

The degree to which the price of an underlying tends to _*fluctuate*_ over time. Volatility is viewed from the _*historical*_ side—which applies to the underlying, and from the _*implied*_ side—which applies to the option at any given moment in time. Or, in mathematical terms, the annualized standard deviation of a given underlying instrument over a specific period of time.

CHAPTER 2

The Building Blocks of Options

Introduction to Calls and Puts

CONCEPT REVIEW

Stock

Underlying: The instrument (stock, future, or cash index) to be delivered when an option is exercised. The amount of underlying for each option contract depends on the security traded. For example, in stock options, each contract typically represents an agreement concerning 100 shares of the underlying stock. An underlying security must be delivered if a put option or call option contract is exercised.

Long position: Ownership of a security contract or commodity that grants the owner the right to transfer ownership by sale or gift.

Short position: A position resulting from the sale of a contract or instrument.

Calls

Bid: The bid is the highest price a buyer is willing to pay for the purchase of a security.

Ask: The ask is the lowest price a seller of a security is willing to accept.

Bid/ask spread: The difference between the bid and the ask prices is the spread.

Quote: The bid and the ask prices of a specific security.

Long call: A contract between a buyer and a seller whereby the buyer acquires the right, but not the obligation, to buy a specified underlying instrument at a fixed price on or before a specified date (expiration), should the buyer of the call option wish to exercise the option.

Exercise price or strike price: The price at which the underlying will be delivered in the event that the option is exercised. Exercise or strike prices occur at regular intervals, routinely in $2.50, $5, or $10 increments.

"K": Abbreviation for strike.

P&L: Abbreviation for profit and loss.

Intrinsic value: The amount by which a call option is in-the-money.

Extrinsic value: The remaining portion of an option after subtracting its intrinsic value. The entire premium of an out-of-the-money option consists of extrinsic value.

At-the-money (ATM): An option with an exercise price is approximately equal to the current market price of the underlying security.

In-the-money (ITM) call options: A call is in-the-money if its strike price is less than the market price of the underlying. This call premium is composed of both intrinsic and extrinsic value.

Out-of-the-money (OTM) call options: A call is out-of-the-money if its strike price is greater than the market price of the underlying. Therefore, the call has no intrinsic value.

Exercise: The process by which the holder of an option notifies the seller of intention to take delivery of the underlying in the case of a call, or make delivery in the case of a put, at the specified strike price.

Expiration: The last day that the owner can exercise an option; the business day preceding the expiration date.

American-style options: Options that may be exercised on or before the expiration date.

Premium: The total price of the option contract; intrinsic value plus time value. Often used as a contrary indicator of market sentiment.

Theoretical value: An option value generated by a mathematical model, which provides an estimation of the price one would expect to pay for the option, or receive from the sale of the option, in order to break even in the long run.

Short call option position: The seller of the short call option assumes the obligation to sell the underlying at a specified price to the buyer, should the buyer choose to exercise the option.

Assigned: Received notification of an assignment by The Options Clearing Corporation.

Puts

Long put option position: A contract between a buyer and a seller whereby the buyer acquires the right, but not the obligation, to sell a specified underlying instrument at a fixed price on or before a specified date (expiration), should the buyer of the put option wish to exercise the option.

Margin call: A request from brokerage houses for additional equity to be deposited to meet the minimum margin requirement when the marketable value of the underlying asset falls below the minimum level required by federal regulations and the investor's brokerage house.

Intrinsic value (parity) of an option: The amount by which a put option is in-the-money. OTM options have no intrinsic value.

Extrinsic value of an option: The price of a put option after subtracting its intrinsic value. The entire premium of an OTM option consists of extrinsic value.

In-the-money (ITM) put options: A put is in-the-money if its strike price is greater than the market price of the underlying. This put is composed of both intrinsic and extrinsic value.

Out-of-the-money (OTM) put options: A put is out-of-the-money if its strike price is less than the market price of the underlying. Therefore, the put has no intrinsic value.

Option exercise: The process by which the owner of the put notifies the seller of the intention to make delivery of the underlying at the specified strike price. The result is a net short position in the underlying.

Short put option position: The seller of the put option assumes the obligation to buy the underlying at a specified price from the buyer, should the buyer choose to exercise the option.

Option assignment: The process by which the seller of the put is notified by the buyer of the intention to exercise the long put option. The net result is a long position in the underlying for the seller.

LONG STOCK (UNDERLYING)

Cashflow note. *The purchase of the underlying for options (common stock in this example), involves paying cash for shares, either by a direct cash outlay or by borrowing money (margin) to pay for the stock. In other words, you can either borrow cash from a financial institution in order to finance the stock purchase, or simply use money from an existing account (such as your savings account). In either case, you pay a price for buying the stock. If you borrow the money to finance your purchase, you must pay interest on your loan. If you use money that you have in savings, you experience an opportunity cost, as you are sacrificing the interest that you would be earning on this money.*

If you are using a margin account, you currently would be required to deposit 50 percent of the total price of the shares you are going to purchase.

A long stock position is bullish because you earn a profit as the stock price rises and suffer a loss as the stock price falls. The maximum reward or profit that you can make is unlimited to the upside, meaning the higher the stock climbs, the more profit you realize. However, your risk, or maximum loss, is limited to the downside all the way to zero.

Let's look at a P&L graph of a long underlying. Take a moment to familiarize yourself with the graph. Graphing the underlying is straightforward, and being comfortable reading P&L charts is essential as we begin to explore options.

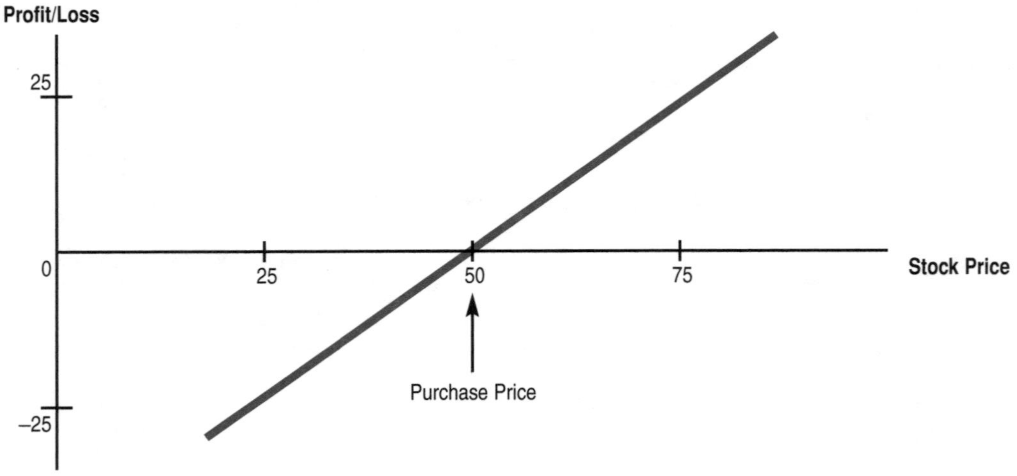

If you purchased stock at $50 and sold it at $75 you would have a $25 profit. Your purchase price of stock—or your break-even—is the point on the graph where the underlying passes through the *x* axis. With every $1 move up in the underlying you would net a $1 profit per share.

SHORT STOCK (UNDERLYING)

Cashflow note. *Margining short stock positions differs from long positions. Typically, a brokerage firm will require a deposit consisting of the entire stock price and an additional 50 percent or more. If the short position goes against you (stock begins to rise), you may be required to deposit additional funds into your margin account to cover your position. As the short seller of the stock, you would also be responsible for payment of dividends.*

When you short a stock, you are basically borrowing the stock and then turning around and selling it. Your hope is that the price of the stock will fall prior to the date you are required to return it. This will allow you to buy it back in the open market at a lower price than you sold it for initially. A short stock position is bearish, because you profit from a decrease in the price of the stock and suffer a loss as the stock price rises. A short stock position has limited profit potential and unlimited loss potential.

Let's say you borrowed shares of XYZ stock from your brokerage firm and shorted them at $30 per share. If the stock falls to $20 per share, you could buy them back at the new market price and repay your loan. However, your total net profit is not $10 per share. You have other considerations that affect your net profit, such as cost-of-carry and interest received. You must remember to subtract the cost-of-carry (interest paid to borrow the stock) and add the interest you earned on the money that you received for the short sale of the stock (assuming you invested it).

Your maximum reward for a short stock position is limited to the downside, meaning if the stock falls anywhere below the purchase price, you will profit all the way until the stock hits zero. Losses, however, can be unlimited, because the stock price could rise to the moon. Take a look at the P&L graph of the short stock below.

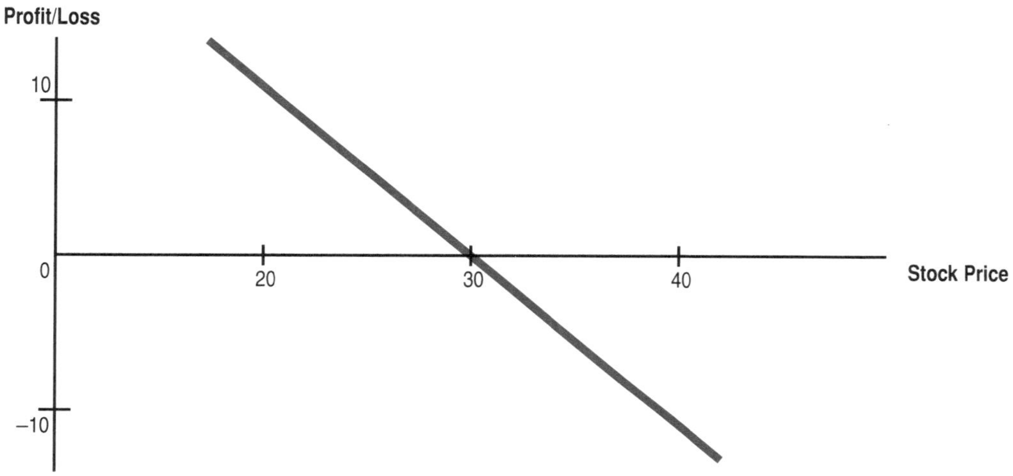

Again, your break-even is where the line crosses the *x* axis (30). Because you are short the stock, you are hoping for it to fall in price so that when you have to repay your stock loan, you can purchase it somewhere below your break-even.

LONG CALL

Owning an equity call option contract gives you the right, but not the obligation, to buy 100 shares of underlying at a specific price during a certain period. A price, or premium, is paid for this right. A long call option offers you unlimited profit potential and limited risk.

With prices constantly rising or falling, owning a call option would allow you to guarantee that you could purchase the underlying at a specific price, should the stock rise above the strike price of the option sometime in the future. Because your right to purchase only lasts a specific amount of time, typically less than nine months with equity options, the option contract's value tends to decrease over time, because you theoretically have less time or opportunity for the option to go in-the-money (have some intrinsic value).

Should the stock decrease in price, you would not exercise your option and your contract would simply expire worthless. The only loss you would experience is the amount you paid for the option (the option premium).

With equity options, each option contract typically represents 100 shares of the underlying equity. If you purchase one XYZ call, this represents 100 shares of XYZ. Therefore if you purchase 5 XYZ calls, and XYZ is trading at $50 per share, you have control over $25,000 worth of XYZ stock. As you can see, a major advantage of trading options is the amount of leverage they can exert.

Let's look at an actual call option contract and its components:

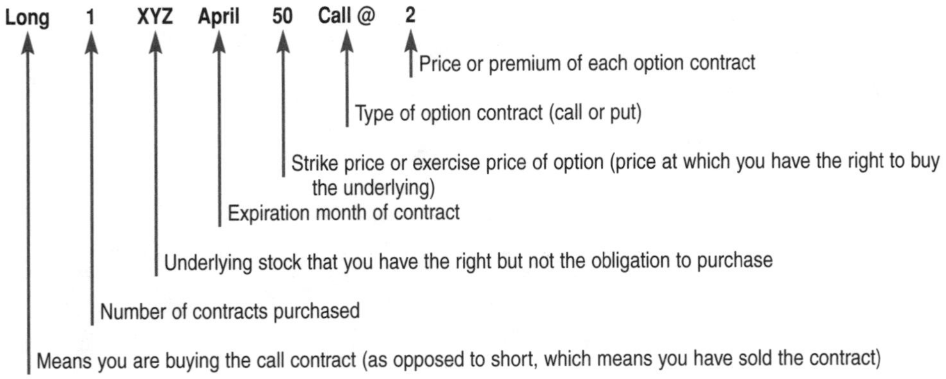

Let's review: This contract would allow the owner or buyer of the call to buy XYZ stock for $50 per share until April expiration for a total premium of $200 ($2 per share of stock × 100 shares).

ITI 29.80 - 30.20				
CALLS			PUTS	
bid	*ask*		*bid*	*ask*
		MAR		
4.80	5.30	**25**	0.05	0.10
3.00	3.50	**27.5**	0.25	0.40
1.00	1.40	**30**	0.60	0.90
0.80	1.10	**32.5**	2.70	3.10
0.60	0.90	**35**	4.90	5.40
		APR		
5.90	6.40	**25**	0.50	0.75
4.00	4.40	**27.5**	0.90	1.30
2.20	2.50	**30**	1.50	1.90
1.10	1.50	**32.5**	2.90	3.20
0.80	1.10	**35**	5.00	5.40
		JUL		
6.40	6.90	**25**	0.55	0.85
4.90	5.40	**27.5**	1.50	1.80
3.60	4.10	**30**	2.50	3.00
2.80	3.20	**32.5**	4.00	4.50
2.30	2.60	**35**	5.90	6.40

Purchase Price of March 35 Call (0.90, circled)

Purchase Price of July 25 Call (6.90, circled)

As a call buyer you must address a matrix of options that may be purchased and that are grouped according to price and time. Options are organized by strike prices that rise sequentially in $2.50, $5, or $10 increments; call option prices decrease as strike prices rise, as the options change from being ITM (having intrinsic value) to being OTM (not having any intrinsic value). Further, options in the United States are available that expire in at least four different calendar months.

As is shown in the example of an electronic option trading screen, you must make a strategic decision about which call is best to buy. Such a decision must be based on how you estimate the underlying will behave, on the amount of risk you deem acceptable, and on the potential reward that is desired.

Notice that if stock is trading at 30.00, the 25 calls regardless of the month are ITM by 5.00. The 35 calls are OTM. The price of the ITM Jul 25 call is 6.90, considerably greater than the Mar 35 call that is trading with only .90 extrinsic value. The difference between the amount the Jul 25 call is ITM and the price of that call (6.90 – 5.00 = 1.90) is the extrinsic value. Extrinsic value is explained in detail in the next section.

To make an informed decision when considering stocks for investment, you should think about the following:

- Historical performance and data available
- Current and future economic trends
- Industry trends
- Product trends
- Volatility

The Parts of an Option's Price (Intrinsic and Extrinsic Value)

Any option that is considered in-the-money (ITM) has a price composed of two elements: (1) intrinsic value (or parity) and (2) extrinsic value. A call's intrinsic value is equal to the amount by which the underlying's market price is greater than the option's strike price; and the option's extrinsic value equals the amount that the option's price exceeds its intrinsic value. For example, the July 25 call is an ITM call because the current stock price, $30, is greater than the $25 strike price.

Stock Price	= $30.00	Option Price	= $6.90
Strike Price	= $25.00	Intrinsic Value	= $5.00
Difference	= $ 5.00 (Intrinsic Value)	Extrinsic Value	= $1.90

Of the $6.90 price, $5.00 is intrinsic value; and the remainder, $1.90, is considered extrinsic value.

A key concept concerning intrinsic and extrinsic value involves the speed with which each type changes when the underlying stock price changes. Because intrinsic value represents the amount by which the option is ITM, it will move on a one-to-one, or linear, basis with the price of the stock. Extrinsic value has a much more complicated relationship with price movement in the underlying. Subsequent chapters describe the relationship in greater detail. They will address issues such as volatility and will describe the mathematical formulas that define option pricing. However, the essence of the idea is that extrinsic value does not move on a one-to-one basis with the price of the underlying, and it must be treated differently as a result.

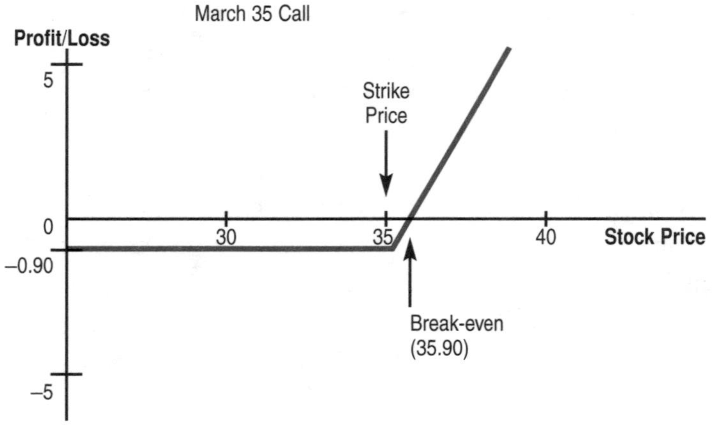

An OTM option is composed of extrinsic value only. An example would be the March 35 call at $.90. Because the market price of the underlying ($30) is less than the option's strike price (35), the full price of the option cannot contain any intrinsic value.

EXERCISE ONE

Take a look at quotes of DEF calls. (Calls are located to the left of strike prices and puts are to the right of strike prices.) Assume you wish to purchase the calls at the strikes located in the box. Determine which calls are ITM, OTM, or ATM. Also try to determine intrinsic (IV) and extrinsic values (EV) based on the ask price. Notice the stock

K	ITM/ATM/OTM	IV	EV
35	________	___	___
57.50	________	___	___
70	________	___	___
72.50	________	___	___
90	________	___	___

CALLS				PUTS		
Bid	**Theo**	**Ask**	**Strike**	**Bid**	**Theo**	**Ask**
64.88	**64.91**	64.94	**DEF**			
			Sep00			
			Oct00			
34.75	**35.32**	35.75	**30.00**	0.00	**0.07**	0.19
29.88	**30.42**	30.88	**35.00**	0.00	**0.11**	0.19
25.00	**25.56**	26.00	**40.00**	0.06	**0.20**	0.25
20.38	**20.79**	21.38	**45.00**	0.31	**0.37**	0.50
18.25	**18.46**	18.75	**47.50**	0.50	**0.52**	0.69
16.00	**16.20**	16.50	**50.00**	0.69	**0.73**	0.88
13.88	**14.01**	14.38	**52.50**	1.00	**1.02**	1.19
11.75	**11.93**	12.25	**55.00**	1.38	**1.40**	1.56
9.88	**9.96**	10.25	**57.50**	1.88	**1.93**	2.06
8.00	**8.15**	8.38	**60.00**	2.50	**2.60**	2.75
6.38	**6.52**	6.75	**62.50**	3.38	**3.45**	3.50
4.88	**5.08**	5.25	**65.00**	4.25	**4.50**	4.63
3.63	**3.84**	4.00	**67.50**	5.50	**5.77**	5.88
2.63	**2.82**	2.88	**70.00**	7.00	**7.27**	7.38
1.81	**2.01**	2.00	**72.50**	8.63	**8.97**	9.00
1.19	**1.38**	1.31	**75.00**	10.50	**10.88**	11.00
0.75	**0.93**	0.94	**77.50**	12.63	**12.97**	13.13
0.50	**0.61**	0.63	**80.00**	14.88	**15.23**	15.38
0.25	**0.39**	0.44	**82.50**	17.38	**17.61**	17.88
0.13	**0.25**	0.31	**85.00**	19.88	**20.09**	20.38
0.13	**0.11**	0.19	**90.00**	24.63	**25.09**	25.63
0.00	**0.09**	0.19	**95.00**	29.63	**30.09**	30.63
0.00	**0.05**	0.13	**100.00**	34.63	**35.09**	35.63
0.00	**0.01**	0.19	**105.00**	39.63	**40.09**	40.63

is currently trading at $64.94 (current market bid/ask will always be located in upper left-hand corner of the trading screen).

The Profit and Loss Profile of a Long Call Position

The next step in understanding option price behavior is establishing the profit or loss patterns for a long call. In a volatile market, option traders frequently see rapid price changes in their positions so that the position can be closed for a profit before expiration becomes an issue. Yet, standard practice involves examining how a position would need to behave before expiration in order to assess risk and reward accurately.

Using the July 25 call example again, the call buyer initially incurs a loss (or a debit) equal to the amount of the price paid (premium) for the option. In this case, the buyer incurs a loss of $6.90 (or $690.00) by buying the July 25 call with the stock price at $30. In contrast to simply owning the stock, the call buyer has limited his or her financial risk to $6.90 (or $690.00), rather than $30 (or $3,000), in the event that the stock price drops to zero.

In terms of profit, however, the call buyer can realize a financial gain only if the stock price rises more than the amount of premium paid for the option. As a tradeoff for limiting the downside risk, the call buyer does not begin to realize a profit until after the option's break-even point has been passed ($31.90). As can be seen in the following graph, the call's P&L turns positive not at the $25 strike price but at $31.90 ($25 + $6.90) (the option's strike price plus its premium).

To summarize, the long call position is bullish and involves a cash outlay similar to owning the underlying. However, its profit and loss profile is significantly different because it has considerably less risk, and costs less to initiate the position. (Long calls will always involve some risk.)

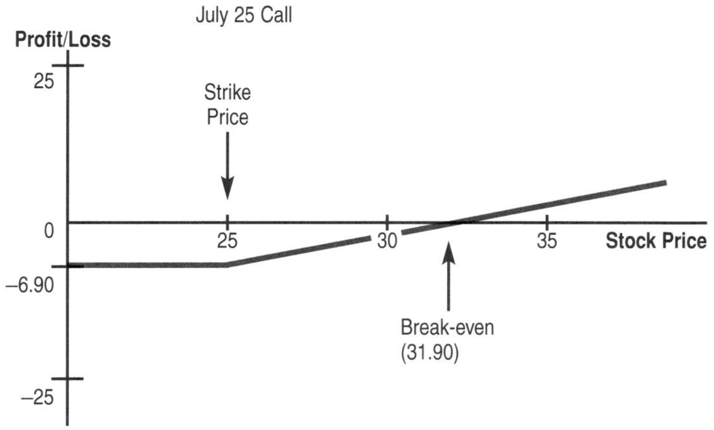

EXERCISE TWO

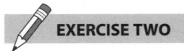

CALLS				PUTS		
Bid	**Theo**	**Ask**	**Strike**	**Bid**	**Theo**	**Ask**
64.88	**64.91**	64.94	**DEF**			
			Oct 00			
34.75	**35.32**	35.75	**30.00**	0.00	**0.07**	0.19
29.88	**30.42**	30.88	**35.00**	0.00	**0.11**	0.19
25.00	**25.56**	26.00	**40.00**	0.06	**0.20**	0.25
20.38	**20.79**	21.38	**45.00**	0.31	**0.37**	0.50
18.25	**18.46**	18.75	**47.50**	0.50	**0.52**	0.69
16.00	**16.20**	16.50	**50.00**	0.69	**0.73**	0.88
13.88	**14.01**	14.38	**52.50**	1.00	**1.02**	1.19
11.75	**11.93**	12.25	**55.00**	1.38	**1.40**	1.56
9.88	**9.96**	10.25	**57.50**	1.88	**1.93**	2.06
8.00	**8.15**	8.38	**60.00**	2.50	**2.60**	2.75
6.38	**6.52**	6.75	**62.50**	3.38	**3.45**	3.50
4.88	**5.08**	5.25	**65.00**	4.25	**4.50**	4.63
3.63	**3.84**	4.00	**67.50**	5.50	**5.77**	5.88
2.63	**2.82**	2.88	**70.00**	7.00	**7.27**	7.38
1.81	**2.01**	2.00	**72.50**	8.63	**8.97**	9.00
1.19	**1.38**	1.31	**75.00**	10.50	**10.88**	11.00
0.75	**0.93**	0.94	**77.50**	12.63	**12.97**	13.13
0.50	**0.61**	0.63	**80.00**	14.88	**15.23**	15.38
0.25	**0.39**	0.44	**82.50**	17.38	**17.61**	17.88
0.13	**0.25**	0.31	**85.00**	19.88	**20.09**	20.38
0.13	**0.11**	0.19	**90.00**	24.63	**25.09**	25.63
0.00	**0.09**	0.19	**95.00**	29.63	**30.09**	30.63
0.00	**0.05**	0.13	**100.00**	34.63	**35.09**	35.63
0.00	**0.01**	0.19	**105.00**	39.63	**40.09**	40.63

Using the prices given here, plot the P&L graphs and try to determine the premium, break-even (B/E), and the maximum risk associated with each call. Remember, calls are on the left of the strike column and puts are on the right. Recall also, buyers must pay the ask price, sellers will receive the bid price.

long DEF 50 call

PREMIUM:
B/E:
MAX RISK:

long DEF 70 call

PREMIUM:
B/E:
MAX RISK:

Effect of Option Decay

The insurance against unlimited loss provided by an option does not last forever. Options expire at regular intervals, at which point either they are equal to their intrinsic value or are worthless if they expire out-of-the-money.

Consequently, the option buyer must realize a move above the call's break-even point before expiration. The size of the underlying's move is no longer the only factor, but timing must be considered as well. As time passes, the value of the extrinsic component of the call will erode. The decay does not occur at a steady rate but increases in speed as expiration approaches. Time decay, also referred to as theta, is explained in greater detail later in this chapter.

If an OTM call expires worthless, meaning that the stock could be bought cheaper in the open market than at the option's strike price, then the entire value of the call will have collapsed to nothing. The option buyer could try to sell the call before expiration in order to recoup some of the initial investment (premium paid).

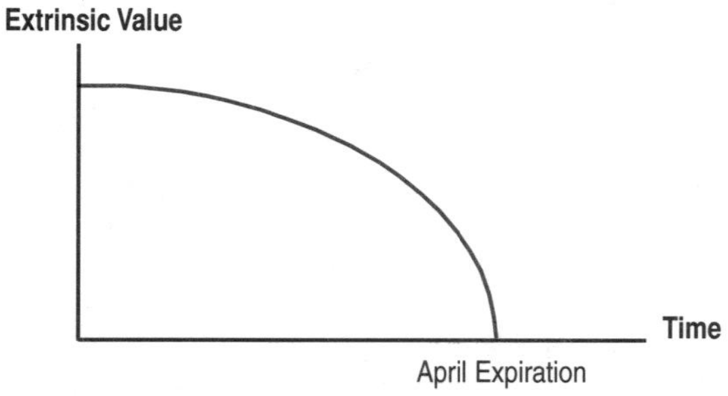

In the previous case, let's assume that the stock price is frozen at $30.00. The ITM call's value will gradually deteriorate from $6.90 to $5.00; as time passes getting closer to expiration, its extrinsic value disappears. The $5.00 price equals the 25 call's intrinsic value as it is left with no extrinsic value. The call buyer could choose to sell the call before expiration in order to capture what little extrinsic value remains.

Option Exercise as It Relates to the Holder of a Call

American-style options offer the call buyer the opportunity to exercise the option in advance of the option's eventual expiration. Doing so indicates that the call buyer wishes to buy the underlying stock at the option's strike price.

SHORT CALL

Selling a call option contract is a bearish move. Contrary to being long a call, selling a call offers unlimited risk and limited reward. If you are a call seller, you will profit if the stock price either falls or stays the same. In other words, you sell the call, receive the premium (your maximum profit), and hope that the stock either stays the same or drops. Assuming the sale of an at-the-money call, then if the stock price stays the same or falls, the holder of the call (the investor you sold it to) will not exercise it. There is no reason, because the investor can just as easily buy the stock outright in the marketplace. You (the call seller) are betting the opposite of the call option buyer. You hope that the cash received from the sale of the call (the premium) is not offset by a move in the underlying in the wrong direction.

As we see, the price (bid) of the March 32.50 call is .80 even though technically it is OTM. This .80 is all extrinsic value, because extrinsic value equals time value. With the April 27.50 call, there is also extrinsic value embedded in the price. Its intrinsic value is only 2.50 (30.00 – 27.50 = 2.50); however, the price is 4.00. This means there is 1.50 of extrinsic value.

A reduction in the call option's value will result from a drop in

ITI
29.80 - 30.20

CALLS			PUTS	
bid	*ask*		*bid*	*ask*
		MAR		
4.80	5.30	**25**	0.05	0.10
3.00	3.50	**27.5**	0.25	0.40
1.00	1.40	**30**	0.60	0.90
0.80	1.10	**32.5**	2.70	3.10
0.60	0.90	**35**	4.90	5.40
		APR		
5.90	6.40	**25**	0.50	0.75
4.00	4.40	**27.5**	0.90	1.30
2.20	2.50	**30**	1.50	1.90
1.10	1.50	**32.5**	2.90	3.20
0.80	1.10	**35**	5.00	5.40
		JUL		
6.40	6.90	**25**	0.55	0.85
4.90	5.40	**27.5**	1.50	1.80
3.60	4.10	**30**	2.50	3.00
2.80	3.20	**32.5**	4.00	4.50
2.30	2.60	**35**	5.90	6.40

Sale Price of March 32.5 Call → 0.80 (circled)

Sale Price of April 27.5 Call → 4.00 (circled)

the stock price and/or from the time decay of the option's contract. In terms of cash flow and directional bias, selling calls has many of the same characteristics of short selling the underlying. However, the risk and reward profile of the short call position differs substantially as will be shown later.

Selling ITM and OTM Calls (Intrinsic and Extrinsic Value)

Two types of calls can be sold: (1) ITM calls or (2) OTM calls. ATM options consist only of extrinsic value. For the sake of simplicity, we will treat them as OTM options. Though selling both types of calls has the same basic principles, selling ITM calls has a slightly different implication for the preferred behavior of the stock than does selling OTM calls. As was discussed originally in this chapter's section on long calls, an ITM option's price contains both intrinsic and extrinsic value. As intrinsic value will rise and fall on a one-to-one basis with the price of the underlying, the seller of the ITM call will benefit directly from a stock price decline. Of course, the ITM call's extrinsic value would diminish with a downward move in the stock price, providing a gain for the call seller. The majority of the profit, however, would be generated by the change in the option's intrinsic value because extrinsic value does not move linearly with the price of the underlying.

Sellers of OTM calls benefit less from a downward move in the price of the underlying than the ITM call seller. Such is the case because OTM calls have no intrinsic value that will decline linearly with the stock price. The OTM call seller will benefit as the option's extrinsic value drops, but in less than a one-to-one fashion. Instead, the OTM seller will rely more heavily on the premium's decay over time than the ITM seller.

The Profit/Loss Profile of a Short Call Position

As with our discussion of long options positions, the next step in understanding options price behavior involves establishing the profit/loss patterns for a short call. For example, a seller of the April 27.50 call with the stock price at $30 will receive $4.00 (or $400.00) in premium ($2.50 in intrinsic value + $1.50 in extrinsic value ×

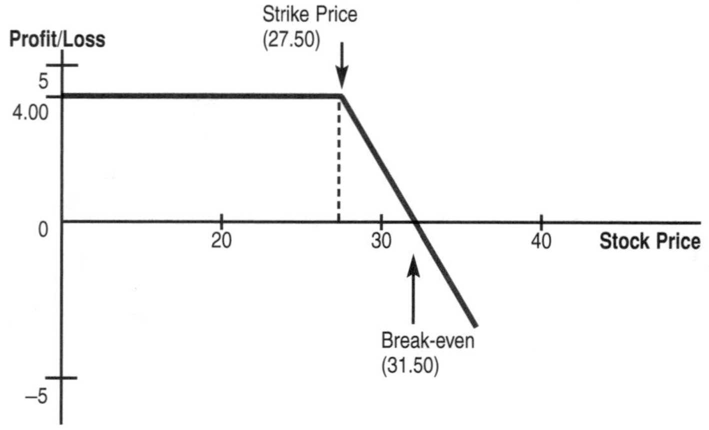

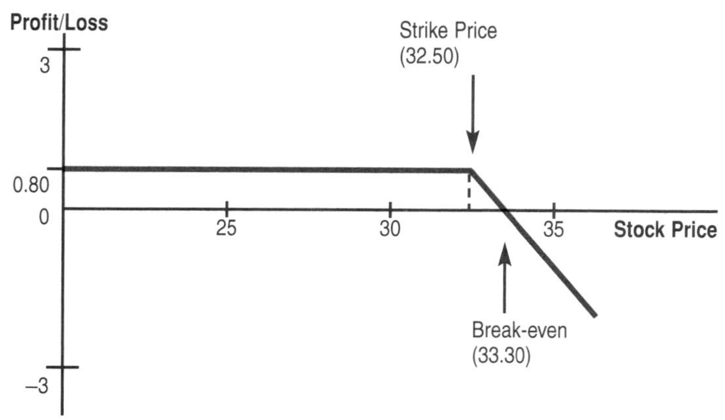

100, the multiplier for each option contract). Such a seller would benefit greatly by a downward move in the stock price below $27.50 so that the option's intrinsic value drops to zero linearly, and its extrinsic value falls to zero nonlinearly. On the other hand, as the stock price moves upward through the option's break-even level of $31.50 ($27.50 strike price + $4.00 in option premium), losses are unlimited.

Similarly, the seller of the March 32.5 call receives $.80 (or $80.00) in premium, none of which represents intrinsic value. The option's break-even level equals $33.30 ($32.50, strike price + $.80 in option premium). Losses are unlimited should the stock move upward through the break-even level.

EXERCISE THREE

Using these prices for DEF, plot the P&L graphs and determine the premium, break-even (B/E), and the maximum risk associated with each call. Remember, you are selling the calls, so you would sell on the bid (what someone is willing to bid or pay for the call).

CALLS				PUTS		
Bid	**Theo**	**Ask**	**Strike**	**Bid**	**Theo**	**Ask**
64.88	**64.91**	64.94	**DEF**			
			Oct00			
34.75	**35.32**	35.75	**30.00**	0.00	**0.07**	0.19
29.88	**30.42**	30.88	**35.00**	0.00	**0.11**	0.19
25.00	**25.56**	26.00	**40.00**	0.06	**0.20**	0.25
20.38	**20.79**	21.38	**45.00**	0.31	**0.37**	0.50
18.25	**18.46**	18.75	**47.50**	0.50	**0.52**	0.69
16.00	**16.20**	16.50	**50.00**	0.69	**0.73**	0.88
13.88	**14.01**	14.38	**52.50**	1.00	**1.02**	1.19
11.75	**11.93**	12.25	**55.00**	1.38	**1.40**	1.56
9.88	**9.96**	10.25	**57.50**	1.88	**1.93**	2.06
8.00	**8.15**	8.38	**60.00**	2.50	**2.60**	2.75
6.38	**6.52**	6.75	**62.50**	3.38	**3.45**	3.50
4.88	**5.08**	5.25	**65.00**	4.25	**4.50**	4.63
3.63	**3.84**	4.00	**67.50**	5.50	**5.77**	5.88
2.63	**2.82**	2.88	**70.00**	7.00	**7.27**	7.38
1.81	**2.01**	2.00	**72.50**	8.63	**8.97**	9.00
1.19	**1.38**	1.31	**75.00**	10.50	**10.88**	11.00
0.75	**0.93**	0.94	**77.50**	12.63	**12.97**	13.13
0.50	**0.61**	0.63	**80.00**	14.88	**15.23**	15.38
0.25	**0.39**	0.44	**82.50**	17.38	**17.61**	17.88
0.13	**0.25**	0.31	**85.00**	19.88	**20.09**	20.38
0.13	**0.11**	0.19	**90.00**	24.63	**25.09**	25.63
0.00	**0.09**	0.19	**95.00**	29.63	**30.09**	30.63
0.00	**0.05**	0.13	**100.00**	34.63	**35.09**	35.63
0.00	**0.01**	0.19	**105.00**	39.63	**40.09**	40.63

short DEF 47.50 call

PREMIUM:
B/E:
MAX RISK:

short DEF 60 call

PREMIUM:
B/E:
MAX RISK:

short DEF 70 call

PREMIUM:
B/E:
MAX RISK:

Effect of Option Decay

In contrast to the long option positions in which time decay is an obstacle to be overcome, time decay in the short option position is a benefit. Of course, any factor that would reduce the price of options once they have been sold provides a benefit for the seller. Therefore if you keep in mind that the extrinsic value is composed of "time value" (the more time the option has to end up ITM), as a short seller you want the option to expire as soon as possible. It is crucial to remember that time decay affects only the extrinsic component of the option price. In terms of intrinsic value, the amount by which the option is in-the-money would not be affected by time.

The end result is dramatic when considering whether to sell ITM or OTM calls. Clearly, selling ITM calls provides a more direct profit from a decline in the price of the stock. However, selling OTM calls often provides greater protection against unexpected underlying price increases by having higher associated break-even points.

Option Assignment as It Relates to a Short Call Seller

Any option seller must address the risk of being assigned on the short option position. In the case of a short call position, the call seller would take a short position in the stock if assigned. Remember, a call is the right to buy, and the trader has sold that right to another party. Consequently, the trader now has an obligation to sell at the strike price if the opposite party chooses to exercise the right to buy.

LONG PUT

Similar to buying a call, buying a put involves a cash outlay. However, the put buyer is hoping to profit from a drop in the price of the underlying stock. Owning a put gives you the right but not the obligation to sell the underlying security for a predetermined price within a certain time frame. Put buying is similar to taking a short position in the underlying in terms of directional view; except, the put buyer pays for this right, taking a long option position rather than receiving money for short selling of the stock.

There are several reasons why owning a put may be more appealing than shorting stock. First, you have limited risk. The maximum amount you can lose is the amount (premium) that you paid for the purchase of the put. Another advantage is that you don't risk the chance of having a margin call, as you can maintain your long put position all the way through its expiration, with no chance of any other cash outlays. Conversely, when you short stock, you may be required to meet a margin call to cover your position for a period of time, even though ultimately the position could be profitable.

Owning a put option contract gives you the right, but not the obligation, to sell 100 shares of underlying at a specific price during a certain period of time. Just as with a call, a premium is paid for this right. A long put option offers you substantial profit potential to the downside and limited risk.

With prices constantly rising or falling, owning a put option guarantees that you sell the underlying at a specific price, should the stock fall below the strike price of the option sometime in the future. Because your right to exercise only lasts a specific amount of time, typically less than nine months with equity options, the option contract's value tends to decrease over time, as you theoretically have less time or opportunity for the options to go in-the-money, or rather, be worth something as we explained with the call options.

Should the stock increase in price, you would not exercise your options, as your contract would simply expire worthless. Therefore, the only loss you would experience is the amount you paid for the options.

If you purchase 1 XYZ put, this actually represents 100 shares of XYZ, the same as the call contract. Therefore if you purchase 5 XYZ puts, and XYZ is trading at $50 per share, you have control over $25,000 worth of XYZ stock. This would give you leverage for sale of the stock.

Let's look at an actual put options contract and its components:

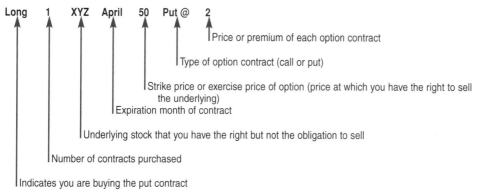

Long 1 XYZ April 50 Put @ 2

- **2**: Price or premium of each option contract
- **Put**: Type of option contract (call or put)
- **50**: Strike price or exercise price of option (price at which you have the right to sell the underlying)
- **April**: Expiration month of contract
- **XYZ**: Underlying stock that you have the right but not the obligation to sell
- **1**: Number of contracts purchased
- **Long**: Indicates you are buying the put contract

ITI 29.80 - 30.20				
CALLS			**PUTS**	
bid	*ask*		*bid*	*ask*
		MAR		
3.00	3.50	**27.5**	0.25	0.40
1.00	1.40	**30**	0.60	0.90
0.80	1.10	**32.5**	2.70	3.10
0.60	0.90	**35**	4.90	5.40
		APR		
5.90	6.40	**25**	0.50	0.75
4.00	4.40	**27.5**	0.90	1.30
2.20	2.50	**30**	1.50	1.90
1.10	1.50	**32.5**	2.90	3.20
0.80	1.10	**35**	5.00	5.40
		JUL		
6.40	6.90	**25**	0.55	0.85
4.90	5.40	**27.5**	1.50	1.80
3.60	4.10	**30**	2.50	3.00
2.80	3.20	**32.5**	4.00	4.50
2.30	2.60	**35**	5.90	6.40

Purchase Price for April 25 Put (0.75)

Purchase Price for April 35 Put (5.40)

Let's review: This contract would allow the owner of the put to sell XYZ stock for $50 per share until April expiration for the price of $2, for a total premium cost of $200 ($2 per share of stock × 100 shares).

As a put buyer, you confront a similar matrix of options that you do as a call buyer. Puts also are organized by strike prices that change sequentially, such as in $2.50, $5, or $10 increments; but put prices decrease as strike prices decline. Viewing the same electronic option trading screen that was presented in the long call section, you must strategically choose which option you think will have the greatest profit potential.

Again, to make an informed decision, you should consider the same data as we covered in the call section.

The Parts of an Option's Price (Intrinsic and Extrinsic Value)

As with the calls, any put that is considered in-the-money has a price composed of two elements: (1) intrinsic value (or parity) and (2) extrinsic value. The put's intrinsic value is equal to the amount by which the option's strike price is greater than the underlying's market price; and the put's extrinsic value equals the amount of the option's price that exceeds its intrinsic value. For example, the April 35 put is an ITM put because the strike price is greater than the current stock price of $30. As the owner of the put, you have the right to sell the stock at $35 when the underlying is trading at $30 on the open market.

Strike Price	= $35.00	Option Price	= $5.40
Stock Price	= $30.00	Intrinsic Value	= $5.00
Difference	= $ 5.00 (Intrinsic Value)	Extrinsic Value	= $0.40

With an ITM put option, you actually have two choices to consider. Let's say the underlying stock (ITI) was trading at $20 and you bought a June 20 ITI put for $2, for a total cash outlay of $200. If the stock price falls to $15 prior to June expiration, and the premium on the put rises to $6 (as the put is now even further in-the-money), then you have a decision to make.

You can buy 100 shares of ITI at $15 and simultaneously exercise your put, allowing you to sell those shares for $20 per share. This would net you a $300 profit ($5 × 100 shares = $500 – $200; premium or price you paid for the purchase of the put. Or, you can choose not to exercise your option, and simply sell it for a $400 profit. Think about it. You paid $200 for the put ($2 × 100 shares) and now that it is even further in-the-money and is trading for $6, you can sell it for $600 ($6 × 100 shares). You benefit by selling the remaining extrinsic value.

Any out-of-the-money put is composed of extrinsic value only. An example would be the April 25 put at $.75, because the option's strike price is less than the market price of the underlying.

EXERCISE FOUR

CALLS				PUTS		
Bid	**Theo**	**Ask**	**Strike**	**Bid**	**Theo**	**Ask**
64.88	**64.91**	64.94	**DEF**			
			Oct00			
34.75	**35.32**	35.75	**30.00**	0.00	**0.07**	0.19
29.88	**30.42**	30.88	**35.00**	0.00	**0.11**	0.19
25.00	**25.56**	26.00	**40.00**	0.06	**0.20**	0.25
20.38	**20.79**	21.38	**45.00**	0.31	**0.37**	0.50
18.25	**18.46**	18.75	**47.50**	0.50	**0.52**	0.69
16.00	**16.20**	16.50	**50.00**	0.69	**0.73**	0.88
13.88	**14.01**	14.38	**52.50**	1.00	**1.02**	1.19
11.75	**11.93**	12.25	**55.00**	1.38	**1.40**	1.56
9.88	**9.96**	10.25	**57.50**	1.88	**1.93**	2.06
8.00	**8.15**	8.38	**60.00**	2.50	**2.60**	2.75
6.38	**6.52**	6.75	**62.50**	3.38	**3.45**	3.50
4.88	**5.08**	5.25	**65.00**	4.25	**4.50**	4.63
3.63	**3.84**	4.00	**67.50**	5.50	**5.77**	5.88
2.63	**2.82**	2.88	**70.00**	7.00	**7.27**	7.38
1.81	**2.01**	2.00	**72.50**	8.63	**8.97**	9.00
1.19	**1.38**	1.31	**75.00**	10.50	**10.88**	11.00
0.75	**0.93**	0.94	**77.50**	12.63	**12.97**	13.13
0.50	**0.61**	0.63	**80.00**	14.88	**15.23**	15.38
0.25	**0.39**	0.44	**82.50**	17.38	**17.61**	17.88
0.13	**0.25**	0.31	**85.00**	19.88	**20.09**	20.38
0.13	**0.11**	0.19	**90.00**	24.63	**25.09**	25.63
0.00	**0.09**	0.19	**95.00**	29.63	**30.09**	30.63
0.00	**0.05**	0.13	**100.00**	34.63	**35.09**	35.63
0.00	**0.01**	0.19	**105.00**	39.63	**40.09**	40.63

Take a look at the quotes for DEF puts. Assume you wish to purchase the puts at the strikes located in the box. Determine which puts are ITM, OTM, or ATM. Also try to determine intrinsic and extrinsic values based on the ask price (remember you are buying again).

K	ITM/ATM/OTM	IV	EV
100			
90			
82.50			
65			
55			
40			

Once you've finished this exercise, read on to the next section.

The Profit and Loss Profile of a Long Put Position

The next step is establishing the profit or loss patterns for a long put. As with calls, options traders frequently see quick price changes in their positions, so that put positions can be closed for a profit before expiration becomes an issue. Standard practice examines how a position would need to behave before expiration in order to assess risk and reward accurately.

Let's use the same April 35 put that was discussed earlier. As a put buyer, you would initially incur a loss equal to the amount of the premium of the option. In this case, the buyer incurs a loss of $5.40 if buying the April 35 put with the stock price at $30. In contrast to simply shorting the stock, the put buyer has limited the financial risk to $5.40 per share in the event that the stock price rises.

As a short seller of stock, you realize a gain as soon as the stock price falls below the sale price. However, as a put owner, you don't realize a profit until after the option's break-even point has been passed. As can be seen in the following graph, the put's P&L turns positive not at the $35 strike price, nor the current stock price of $30, but at $29.60 ($35.00 – $5.40; the option's strike price less its premium). As

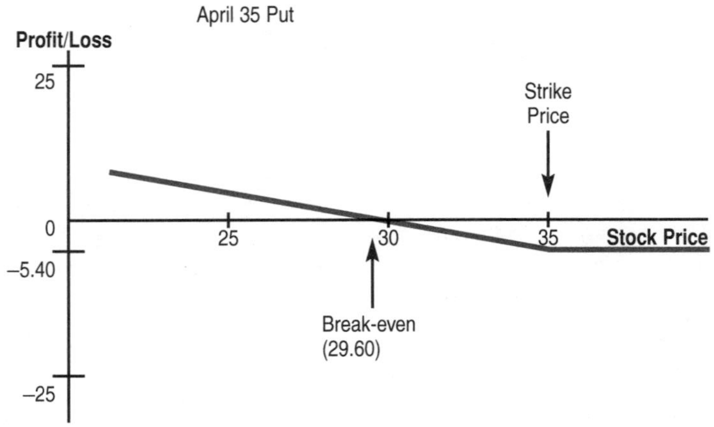

seen with the call buyer, the put buyer must wait until after the underlying has passed through its strike by an amount equal to its premium, delaying financial gains in exchange for a sort of insurance against greater financial loss.

To summarize, the long put position has a bearish directional bias. It involves a cash outlay in contrast to short selling the underlying. Furthermore, its P&L profile differs significantly from the naked short sale of stock because there is limited risk.

EXERCISE FIVE

CALLS				PUTS		
Bid	**Theo**	**Ask**	**Strike**	**Bid**	**Theo**	**Ask**
64.88	**64.91**	64.94	**DEF**			
			Oct00			
34.75	**35.32**	35.75	**30.00**	0.00	**0.07**	0.19
29.88	**30.42**	30.88	**35.00**	0.00	**0.11**	0.19
25.00	**25.56**	26.00	**40.00**	0.06	**0.20**	0.25
20.38	**20.79**	21.38	**45.00**	0.31	**0.37**	0.50
18.25	**18.46**	18.75	**47.50**	0.50	**0.52**	0.69
16.00	**16.20**	16.50	**50.00**	0.69	**0.73**	0.88
13.88	**14.01**	14.38	**52.50**	1.00	**1.02**	1.19
11.75	**11.93**	12.25	**55.00**	1.38	**1.40**	1.56
9.88	**9.96**	10.25	**57.50**	1.88	**1.93**	2.06
8.00	**8.15**	8.38	**60.00**	2.50	**2.60**	2.75
6.38	**6.52**	6.75	**62.50**	3.38	**3.45**	3.50
4.88	**5.08**	5.25	**65.00**	4.25	**4.50**	4.63
3.63	**3.84**	4.00	**67.50**	5.50	**5.77**	5.88
2.63	**2.82**	2.88	**70.00**	7.00	**7.27**	7.38
1.81	**2.01**	2.00	**72.50**	8.63	**8.97**	9.00
1.19	**1.38**	1.31	**75.00**	10.50	**10.88**	11.00
0.75	**0.93**	0.94	**77.50**	12.63	**12.97**	13.13
0.50	**0.61**	0.63	**80.00**	14.88	**15.23**	15.38
0.25	**0.39**	0.44	**82.50**	17.38	**17.61**	17.88
0.13	**0.25**	0.31	**85.00**	19.88	**20.09**	20.38
0.13	**0.11**	0.19	**90.00**	24.63	**25.09**	25.63
0.00	**0.09**	0.19	**95.00**	29.63	**30.09**	30.63
0.00	**0.05**	0.13	**100.00**	34.63	**35.09**	35.63
0.00	**0.01**	0.19	**105.00**	39.63	**40.09**	40.63

Using the prices for DEF, plot the P&L graphs and determine the premium, break-even (B/E), and the maximum risk associated with each put. Remember you are buying, so you will want to purchase on the "ask."

long DEF 72.50 put

PREMIUM:
B/E:
MAX RISK:

long DEF 40 put

PREMIUM:
B/E:
MAX RISK:

long DEF 60 put

PREMIUM:
B/E:
MAX RISK:

Effect of Option Decay for Long Puts

As a put buyer you are looking for a move below the put's break-even point before expiration. The size of the underlying's move is no longer the only factor to consider as timing plays an important role as well. As time passes, the value of the extrinsic component of the put will erode. The decay does not occur at a steady rate, but increases in speed as expiration approaches.

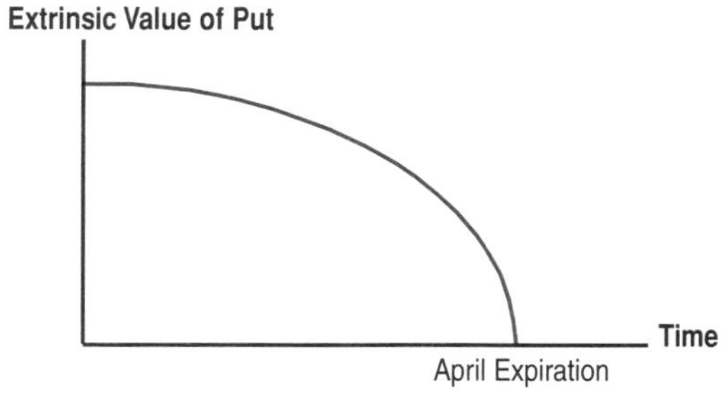

If an OTM put expires worthless—meaning that the stock did not fall below the option's strike price, then the entire value of the put will have collapsed to nothing. However, as the options buyer, you could try to sell the put before expiration in order to recoup some of your initial investment in the put's purchase price (extrinsic value).

Options Exercise as It Relates to the Holder of a Put

American-style options also offer the put buyer the opportunity to exercise the options in advance of their eventual expiration. Doing so indicates that the put buyer wishes to sell the underlying stock at the option's strike price.

SHORT PUT

The sale of a put offers limited reward and substantial risk to the downside (all the way to $0). Similar to the sale of a call, an option premium is received for the sale of the put. As the seller, you are hoping for the stock to stay above the strike price, which would result in the holder (buyer) of the options never exercising it. If, however, the stock price falls below the strike price, then you risk being assigned. Being assigned would require you to buy stock from the holder of the options at the strike price. This would mean you now own stock at a price greater than it can be sold in the open market.

In terms of directional bias, selling puts has many of the same characteristics as buying the underlying. However, the risk/reward profile and the cash flow of the short put position differ substantially.

Selling ITM and OTM Puts (Intrinsic and Extrinsic Value)

Identical to calls, three types of puts can be sold: ITM, OTM, and ATM. The sale of both types share the same basic characteristics. By selling ITM puts, you hope to capitalize on the linear relationship between the put's intrinsic value and the stock price. As a seller of ITM puts, you benefit on a one-to-one basis from a stock price rise. Of course, as was discussed in previous sections, the ITM put's extrinsic value

ITI 29.80 - 30.20				
CALLS			PUTS	
bid	*ask*		*bid*	*ask*
		MAR		
4.80	5.30	**25**	0.05	0.10
3.00	3.50	**27.5**	0.25	0.40
1.00	1.40	**30**	0.60	0.90
0.80	1.10	**32.5**	2.70	3.10
0.60	0.90	**35**	4.90	5.40
		APR		
5.90	6.40	**25**	0.50	0.75
4.00	4.40	**27.5**	0.90	1.30
2.20	2.50	**30**	1.50	1.90
1.10	1.50	**32.5**	2.90	3.20
0.80	1.10	**35**	5.00	5.40
		JUL		
6.40	6.90	**25**	0.55	0.85
4.90	5.40	**27.5**	1.50	1.80
3.60	4.10	**30**	2.50	3.00
2.80	3.20	**32.5**	4.00	4.50
2.30	2.60	**35**	5.90	6.40

Sale Price for March 32.5 Put (2.70)

Sale Price for July 25 Put (0.55)

would diminish with an upward move in the stock; but the majority of the profit would be generated by the change in the option's intrinsic value because extrinsic value does not move linearly with the price of the underlying.

The trading screen shows that with the underlying at 30.00, the March 32.50 put is 2.50 ITM. However, because the price is 2.70, we know it has .20 of extrinsic value. The OTM July 25 put has no intrinsic value; therefore, its premium is entirely composed of extrinsic value.

Similar to the calls, as a seller of OTM puts, you will benefit less from an upward move in the price of the underlying than as an ITM put seller. The OTM put seller will benefit as the option's extrinsic value drops—its sole source of value, but in less than a one-to-one fashion. As with call selling, the OTM seller will rely more heavily on time decay than the ITM seller.

The Profit and Loss Profile of a Short Put Position

Short put price behavior is similar to that of the short call except that the short put position takes an opposing, bullish directional view. For example, a seller of the March 32.50 put with the stock price at \$30 will receive \$2.70 (or \$270.00) in premium (\$2.50 in intrinsic value + \$0.20 extrinsic value × 100 per contract). Such a seller would benefit greatly from an upward move in stock price above \$32.50 so that the option's intrinsic value drops to zero linearly, and its extrinsic value falls to zero nonlinearly. Losses for short puts are not unlimited but can be substantial on the downside.

Similarly, the seller of the July 25 put receives \$0.55 (or \$55.00), none of which represents intrinsic value. The option's break-even level equals \$24.45 (\$25.00 strike price – \$0.55 in option premium). Again, losses for short puts can be substantial on the downside.

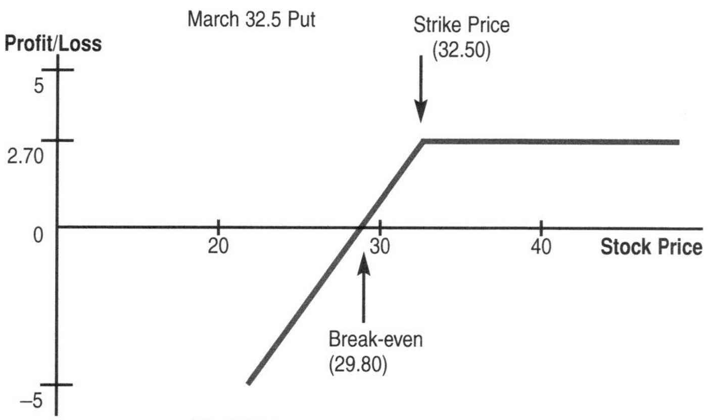

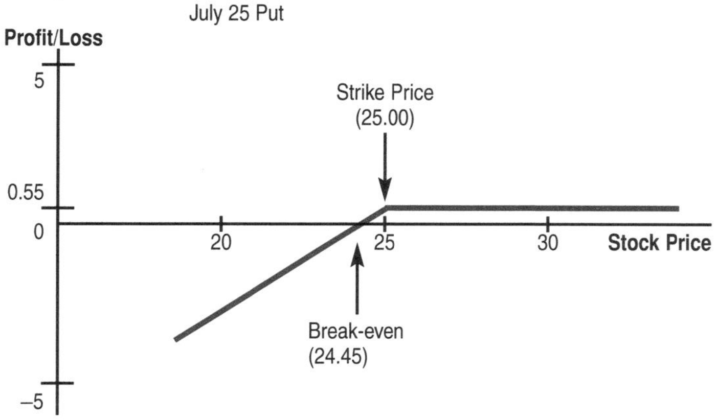

EXERCISE SIX

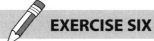

Using the prices for DEF in the trading screen, plot the P&L graphs and try to determine the premium, break-even (B/E), and the maximum risk associated with each put. Remember you're selling, so you will sell on the bid.

CALLS				PUTS		
Bid	**Theo**	**Ask**	**Strike**	**Bid**	**Theo**	**Ask**
64.88	**64.91**	64.94	**DEF**			
			Oct00			
34.75	**35.32**	35.75	**30.00**	0.00	**0.07**	0.19
29.88	**30.42**	30.88	**35.00**	0.00	**0.11**	0.19
25.00	**25.56**	26.00	**40.00**	0.06	**0.20**	0.25
20.38	**20.79**	21.38	**45.00**	0.31	**0.37**	0.50
18.25	**18.46**	18.75	**47.50**	0.50	**0.52**	0.69
16.00	**16.20**	16.50	**50.00**	0.69	**0.73**	0.88
13.88	**14.01**	14.38	**52.50**	1.00	**1.02**	1.19
11.75	**11.93**	12.25	**55.00**	1.38	**1.40**	1.56
9.88	**9.96**	10.25	**57.50**	1.88	**1.93**	2.06
8.00	**8.15**	8.38	**60.00**	2.50	**2.60**	2.75
6.38	**6.52**	6.75	**62.50**	3.38	**3.45**	3.50
4.88	**5.08**	5.25	**65.00**	4.25	**4.50**	4.63
3.63	**3.84**	4.00	**67.50**	5.50	**5.77**	5.88
2.63	**2.82**	2.88	**70.00**	7.00	**7.27**	7.38
1.81	**2.01**	2.00	**72.50**	8.63	**8.97**	9.00
1.19	**1.38**	1.31	**75.00**	10.50	**10.88**	11.00
0.75	**0.93**	0.94	**77.50**	12.63	**12.97**	13.13
0.50	**0.61**	0.63	**80.00**	14.88	**15.23**	15.38
0.25	**0.39**	0.44	**82.50**	17.38	**17.61**	17.88
0.13	**0.25**	0.31	**85.00**	19.88	**20.09**	20.38
0.13	**0.11**	0.19	**90.00**	24.63	**25.09**	25.63
0.00	**0.09**	0.19	**95.00**	29.63	**30.09**	30.63
0.00	**0.05**	0.13	**100.00**	34.63	**35.09**	35.63
0.00	**0.01**	0.19	**105.00**	39.63	**40.09**	40.63

short DEF 47.50 put

PREMIUM:
B/E:
MAX RISK:

short DEF 70 put

PREMIUM:
B/E:
MAX RISK:

short DEF 85 put

PREMIUM:
B/E:
MAX RISK:

Options Assignment

Comparable to the short call position, a put option seller must address the risk of being assigned on the short option position. In the case of a short put position, the put seller must take a long position in the stock. Remember, a put is the right to sell, and the writer has sold that right to sell to another party. Consequently, the trader now has an obligation to buy if the opposite party chooses to exercise his or her right to sell.

A FEW OTHER BASICS YOU NEED TO KNOW . . .

Options Pricing Models

Evaluating an option's value through the use of a pricing model allows one to determine the theoretical value (TV) of the option. The TV of an option is the price one would expect to pay in order to break even in the long run, given the assumptions of the model. Once the TV is known, one can then evaluate whether the option's current market price is overpriced or underpriced.

An options pricing model generates only a prediction, or an "estimate" of how an option might perform. Because the inputs can be inaccurate, there is no assurance that the model's price will be accurate.

The Black-Scholes model introduced in 1973 is uncomplicated and practical. Although many other pricing models are used, Black-Scholes is the most commonly used theoretical pricing model.

The following are six factors that must be input into the Black-Scholes model in order to derive an option's TV:

1. Price of underlying contract
2. Exercise price
3. Time left until expiration
4. Volatility of underlying
5. Interest rates
6. Dividends

For the purpose of this book, reference these six points when pricing an option. Keep in mind, though, that every pricing model has its limitations.

The Greeks

The Greeks—delta, gamma, theta, and vega—are measurements of options prices with respect to movements in the underlying, time until expiration, and volatility. Options can be traded not only for profits attributable to movements in the underlying, but changes in other factors such as the amount of time left in the life of the options, and movements in supply and demand. Having a thorough understanding of how options can change in value from changes in these inputs allows the trader to make profitable trades and also may provide insights for nonprofitable trades.

Delta. The first derivative we discuss is the delta of the options. The delta is the sensitivity of an option's value with respect to changes in the underlying. We will first define the delta of the underlying using stock as our underlying in the following examples. The delta of the stock can be considered 1 (100 percent). This makes sense because if the stock moves up $1 higher from the price that we purchased it, we make $1, or 100 percent of the movement (not including any possible transaction costs or tax implications). If the stock that we are long moves against us, we will lose exactly the amount of the adverse movement. A trader who is long stock can be said to have long (or positive) delta. A positive delta simply expresses the direction you wish the underlying to move. Anyone who has purchased stock is bullish and thus has a positive delta. In other words, a trader wants the stock to move up in order to profit. Conversely, a trader who has sold stock short incurs a negative delta. This trader is bearish and anticipates a drop in the stock so it can be purchased back at a cheaper price.

Options, like stock, can have either negative or positive deltas. However, options deltas can never be greater than 1, or 100 percent, of the movement of the underlying. Keep in mind, options premiums are derived from the underlying and thus, by definition, could never have a delta greater than the underlying itself. Long calls have a bullish market exposure and have positive deltas. The deltas can range from 0 to 100. For example, the ITI June 100 calls have a delta of 50. Any trader who has purchased one call currently has a positive 50 delta. This means for every $1 of movement in the ITI stock, the June 100 calls will change by $0.50, or 50 percent of the movement of the stock. If the June ITI 100 calls had a premium of $10 with the stock at $100, the option premium would increase by $0.50 to $10.50 with a movement in the stock from $100 to $101. Long calls, because they give the holder the right to purchase stock, have a positive market exposure and therefore positive deltas. If the trader decides that the stock will not move up and sells calls, the position incurs a negative delta. This trader now believes that the price of the call will decrease and thus be able to purchase it back at a lower price. If ITI stock decreases from $100 to $99, the new value of the ITI June 100 calls will be $0.50 less, or $9.50.

As we discussed, call option deltas range from 0 to 100. At-the-money options have roughly a 50 delta. The 50 delta basically says that the option has a 50 percent chance of finishing in-the-money at expiration. In-the-money options will have a delta of greater than 50 and out-of-the money options will have a delta of less than 50. Options that are more in-the-money will have higher deltas because they obviously have a higher probability of finishing in-the-money at expiration. The ITI June 90 call will have a greater delta than the June 100 call because of its greater chance of finishing in-the-money at expiration because they are already ITM, and the June 110 call will have a lower delta being $10 OTM. The higher the call's strike, the lower the delta relative to lower strike calls.

Put deltas will range from 0 to negative 100. Puts are bearish positions and will have negative deltas. As the underlying moves down in value, put options will increase in value because of their negative delta exposure. A Dec 25 put with a delta of –70 will move $0.70 with a one point move in the underlying. If the stock moves from $22 to $21, the option premium will increase by $0.70. If the underlying moves up $1, the option premium would decrease by $0.70. It is helpful to know that the sum of the delta for a call and the absolute value of the delta for a put for the same strike, expiration date, and underlying will always be equal to 100.

Options deltas can be affected by other factors such as time and volatility. In-the-money options expand toward 100 the closer expiration nears. Remember that all in-the-money options at expiration will have a delta of 100. At expiration, options that are in-the-money are considered stock. As the in-the-money options expand to 100, the out-of-the-money options' deltas decrease to 0. Options with longer maturities and the same strike will have deltas closer to 50. For example, a call option with a strike of 90 and 20 days until expiration has a delta of 99. A call with the same strike of 90 but with 200 days until expiration could have a delta of 78, closer to 50. With more time until expiration, the 90 put with 200 days has a higher chance of finishing in-the-money than the shorter-term option. It makes sense that the out-of-the-money option's delta with more time until expiration will have higher probability of finishing out-of-the-money so the deltas are lower than shorter-term options.

The same rules apply to volatility. As volatility increases, out-of-the-money option deltas have a higher probability of finishing in-the-money and their deltas increase toward 50. In-the-money options now have a lower chance of finishing in-the-money and they decrease toward 50. The opposite is true if volatility decreases. Now, in-the-money options will more than likely expire in-the-money and their deltas increase toward 100 while the out-of-the-money options decrease toward 0.

Understanding delta is essential if you want to establish a stock equivalent hedge. Stock always has a delta of 100, so to determine your stock equivalent, you simply divide the underlying's delta (100) by the option's delta. For example, if your option's delta is at 25, your result would be a 4:1 ratio. This indicates that you would need to sell one underlying for every four options contracts you purchased.

For example:

Sell 1 underlying having 100 positive deltas = –100 deltas
Buy 4 options having positive 25 deltas = +100 deltas

Puts would be exactly the opposite. Because we know puts have negative deltas, you would purchase one underlying as opposed to selling it.

You can also hedge options with options. For example, if you purchase 10 OTM calls, each call having a delta of +40, your delta position is +400. You could hedge your delta risk by purchasing 8 ATM puts, each having deltas of –50, or –400 deltas total, netting you a delta position of 0.

Any position—regardless of the number of calls, puts, and underlying—can be delta neutral if the positive and negative deltas of the entire position offset each other.

Gamma. The second Greek we will discuss is gamma. Gamma is the change in delta with respect to a 1 point change in the underlying. The deltas of options cannot stay unchanged as the underlying moves up or down. We have seen how delta affects the premiums of options and it is important to understand that the delta itself changes. Let's look at an at-the-money June 100 call with a delta of 50. If we have purchased this call, we are bullish and have a positive delta of 50. What happens to the delta itself as the underlying moves? If the underlying moves up from 100 to 101, we know the option premium increases by $0.50. Now that this call is slightly in-the-money, our delta should be greater than 50. If the gamma were 10 for this option, the new delta would be 60. Now the option will increase more in value as the underlying moves up because of its larger delta.

We can apply the same principal to long puts. A long put is a bearish position that has a negative delta. Even though this has a negative delta, it still has positive gamma because we are long options. If the underlying moves down, an at-the-money put will become more in-the-money and increase in delta. A June 50 put with a delta of –50 and a gamma of +5 will have a new delta of –55 if the underlying moves down 1 point. It should also be noted that a call and a put with the same underlying, strike, and time until expiration will have the same gamma. If a call delta increases because of the gamma, then the delta of the put must fall by the same amount. As one can see, long options produce favorable deltas and are thus considered long gamma positions.

Short gamma positions are ones in which we are short options. If options that we are short move in-the-money (or less out-of-the-money), they increase in delta and we begin to lose money at an increasing rate. At this point you might ask, "Whyever be short options?" Remember, one of the advantages of being short options is the ability to benefit from time decay. However, if the underlying moves adversely, any decay collected could be wiped out because the position will produce unfavorable deltas. Conversely, long options positions must pay out decay for the opportunity to create favorable deltas.

So where exactly is the greatest gamma with respect to the underlying? We can demonstrate that at-the-money options have the greatest gammas with an extreme example. Let's consider an at-the-money option right before expiration. The at-the-money option will have a delta of 50, however, it will move to either 100 or 0 as soon as the stock ticks up or down. In-the-money options right before expiration have deltas of 100 and will have no gamma. Out-of-the-money options have no deltas and have no gamma right before expiration. As a general rule, the at-the-money options will always have the greatest gamma. As the underlying moves away from a strike, the gamma decreases, and as the underlying moves toward a strike, the gamma increases. It is not possible to give numerical rules governing gammas as there are for deltas (for example 0–100) because of the different inputs into models that can produce very distinct gammas for different underlying. The important point is knowing how the gamma affects the delta of the position.

Gammas further out in time will be less than gammas closer to expiration. The closer an option gets to expiration, the more or less chance it has of finishing in-the-money or out-of-the-money, and the deltas move toward 0 or 100 at a faster rate. Options with longer maturities have deltas that are less sensitive to changes in the underlying and thus have lower gammas.

Theta. The next Greek we will examine is theta. Theta is the erosion in option premium for one day in time passing. Options are wasting assets. As they approach expiration, they will either be worth parity or nothing. The decay from day to day is theta. It makes sense that out-of-the-money options have a lower chance of finishing in-the-money with less time to expiration and thus will erode in value every day closer to expiration. Like gamma and vega, the at-the-money options will have the most theta. Because they are composed entirely of time value, they will have the maximum amount of theta. The erosion in options increases as they approach expiration. A July 30 call with a theta of –0.20 will erode in value by $0.20 with one day in time passing. If the option value is $3.00 today, with all other factors unchanged, the option premium will be $2.80 tomorrow. The theta will increase the closer the option gets to expiration. The same July 30 call with a value of $2.80 would now have a theta greater than $0.20, say $0.25. The theta will increase until all extrinsic value of the option has eroded at expiration.

Vega. The last Greek we will consider is vega. Vega is the sensitivity of an option's value with respect to changes in volatility. Volatility, in its simplest sense, is supply and demand. When there is more demand for options, prices increase; when demand decreases, prices fall. Vega measures the change in options premiums when volatility changes. Long options positions, whether they are calls or puts, will be long vega and increase in value as demand increases. Short options positions will have a negative vega exposure and will profit from a decline in volatility. A call and put on the same underlying with the same strike and same time-until-expiration will have the same vega. This must be the case because of the synthetic relationships we have discussed earlier, and are discussed in detail in Chapter 3.

Let's look at a Dec 75 call with a vega of $0.25. The vega number will be the change in the option premium for a 1 point change in implied volatility. If the premium of the option is $10 and volatility increases by 1 point, then the new option premium will be $10.25. If the volatility decreases by 1 point, the option premium will be $9.75. The Dec 75 put would change by the same amount. So which strikes in relation to the underlying have the most vega? Because at-the-money options consist entirely of time and volatility value, they will be most sensitive to changes in volatility and thus have the greatest vega. As the underlying moves away from a strike, the vega decreases; and as the underlying moves toward a strike, the vega increases.

An out-of-the-money call and an equally out-of-the-money put will have approximately the same vega. If the underlying were at $100, the Jan 80 put and the Jan 120 call would have similar, but not identical, vegas.

Next, we should discuss the differences in vegas between option maturities. Options that approach expiration will be less sensitive to volatility changes than longer dated options. As an option nears expiration, its value will depend on whether it is in-the-money or out-of-the-money. All out-of-the-money options will be worthless and thus have no sensitivity to volatility. In-the-money options will be worth intrinsic value and also will have no sensitivity to changes in volatility. However, longer dated options will be very sensitive to swings in volatility. In general, the longer the maturity of the option, the more vega it will have. The premiums of longer maturity options consist of more time and volatility value.

Introduction to Volatility and Its Role in Pricing Options

Because *The Options Workbook* is meant to be an introduction to options, we will only touch on volatility as it relates to understanding the basic building blocks of options.

Volatility is a measurement of a stock's tendency to move up and down in price. Typically, it is the only variable in an option pricing model not known with certainty in advance. There are multiple types of volatility to consider:

- *Historical.* Estimates based on past market value fluctuations. Expressed as an annual percentage of the underlying. Calculated for any instrument for which historical data is available. It is calculated by using the standard deviation of an underlying's closing price change from day to day.
- *Implied.* Derived from applying current option prices to an options' pricing model. A measure of the volatility of the underlying security, this number is required in order for an option pricing formula to calculate the current market price of an option. Implied volatility is used to help predict the future volatility, while historical measures past volatility.
- *Future.* A prediction of volatility based on a specified time period in the future.
- *Seasonal.* Underlying markets with strong seasonal tendencies; for example, "the January effect" in equities, weather markets in commodities, etc.
- *Directional.* Volatility in some markets seems sensitive to price and general trend of the underlying. Equities and interest rate futures tend to experience increasing volatility in a declining market, while commodities tend to experience increasing volatility in a rising market.

Understanding historical (statistical) and implied volatility is especially important. Calculating the volatility ratio allows us to compare historical and implied volatility levels. The following describes each ratio and tells why it is useful:

- *90-day volatility ratio* (divide 1-day implied volatility by 90-day historical volatility): This calculation is used to determine if an option is overpriced or undervalued.
- *High-volatility ratio* (implied volatility is greater than historical): Indicates options tend to be overpriced.
- *Low-volatility ratio* (historical volatility is greater than implied): Indicates options tend to be underpriced.

What can be learned by studying and predicting volatility? Knowing and studying the tendencies of volatility, a trader should be able to construct strategies to take advantage of the fluctuations between implied and historical volatilities. Other points to consider about volatility's role in the pricing of options are:

- Volatility helps determine whether an option is overvalued or undervalued, by comparing the theoretical price of the option (model derived) to the current market price of the option.
- Volatility over a given time period is highly correlated to the volatility of the previous identical time period. In other words, the volatility of the next 30 days is likely to be similar to the last 30 days, etc. This is referred to as serial correlation. Short-term volatilities reflect recent market activity and long-term volatilities predict the trend farther into the future.
- Volatility fluctuates inversely with respect to time. As short-term volatility has moved away from the mean by short-term events, it has less chance to return to the mean because of time limitations, whereas longer-term volatility has a greater amount of time to revert to that mean.
- Volatility tends to be mean reverting. Over the short term or intermediate term, when markets become imbalanced, volatility fluctuations can be violent. But when the underlying market finally achieves balance, volatility moves back toward its long-term mean.

In later chapters, we will introduce trading strategies that will allow you to take advantage of varying levels of volatility in the market.

Some Basics to Understand about Banking

Banking, also called cost-of-carry, is used to describe the amount of money it costs to hold stock. In the case of short stock, it is a credit to your account. It is also described as a carrying cost or opportunity cost of holding stock. For example, if you own 1,000 shares of JKL at $100, this is $100,000 that you have invested in the stock that is not in the bank earning interest. In determining the banking for options, the following equation is used:

$$B = K \times \text{days to expiration}/360 \times I$$

In this equation, (B) equals the strike of the option (K), times the number of days to the option's expiration divided by 360 (number of days in a year), times the interest rate (I). In other words, you are calculating the cost of carrying the money it takes to buy the stock at the strike price from now until the option expires at the given interest rate. Keep in mind that your bank or clearing firm is going to give you a different rate for long positions versus short positions. To borrow money to purchase stock, the rate will be higher than when you sell the stock and lend the proceeds of the sale to the bank. For example, the long rate could be 6.25 percent and the short rate could be 5 percent.

Before continuing on to the next lesson, it is essential to have a good understanding of calls and puts, as well as the other concepts introduced in this chapter. Be sure to take the quiz at the end of the chapter to test your comprehension. Also, remember that when you see the ITI logo, this means you can log on to our Web site for further exercises and details.

ANSWERS TO CHAPTER TWO EXERCISES:

EXERCISE ONE

K	ITM/ATM/OTM	IV	EV
35	ITM	29.94	0.94
57.50	ITM	7.44	2.81
70	OTM	0	2.88
72.50	OTM	0	2.00
90	OTM	0	0.19

EXERCISE TWO

long DEF 50 call

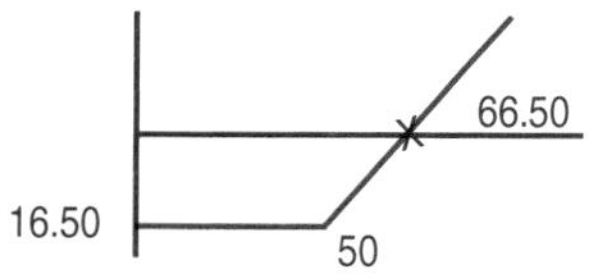

long DEF 70 call

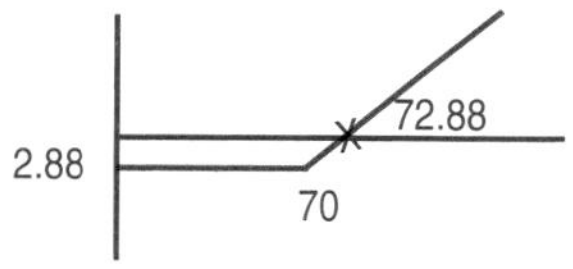

PREMIUM:	16.50	PREMIUM:	2.88
B/E:	66.50	B/E:	72.88
MAX RISK:	16.50	MAX RISK:	2.88

EXERCISE THREE

short DEF 47.50 call

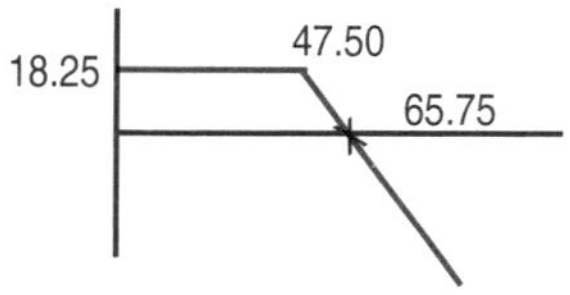

short DEF 60 call

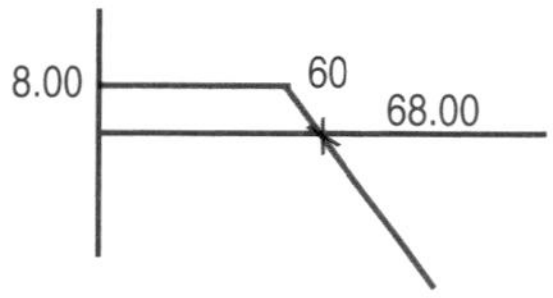

short DEF 70 call

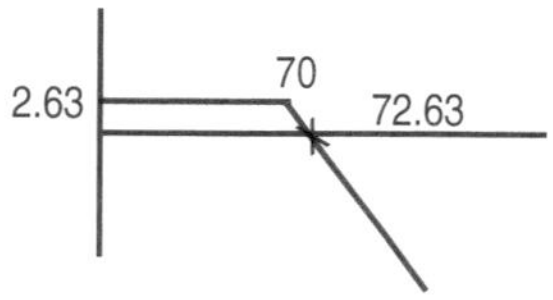

PREMIUM:	18.25	PREMIUM:	8	PREMIUM:	2.63
B/E:	65.75	B/E:	68	B/E:	72.63
MAX RISK:	unlimited to upside	MAX RISK:	unlimited to upside	MAX RISK:	unlimited to upside

EXERCISE FOUR

K	ITM/ATM/OTM	IV	EV
100	ITM	35.06	0.57
90	ITM	25.06	0.57
82.50	ITM	17.56	0.32
65	ITM	0.06	4.57
55	OTM	0	1.56
40	OTM	0	0.25

EXERCISE FIVE

long DEF 72.50 put

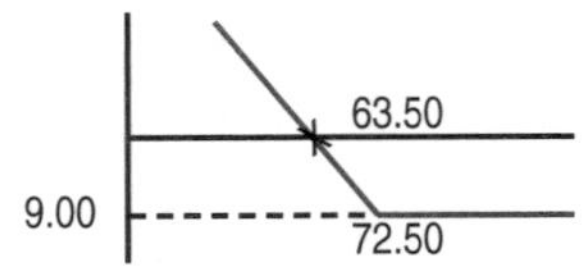

PREMIUM: 9.00
B/E: 63.50
MAX RISK: 9.00

long DEF 40 put

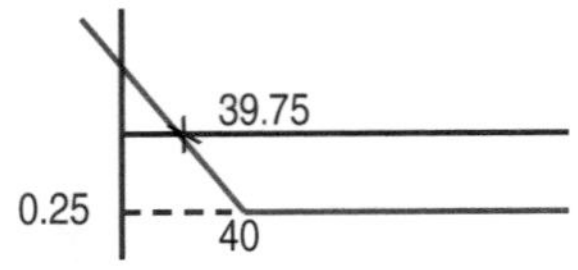

PREMIUM: 0.25
B/E: 39.75
MAX RISK: 0.25

long DEF 60 put

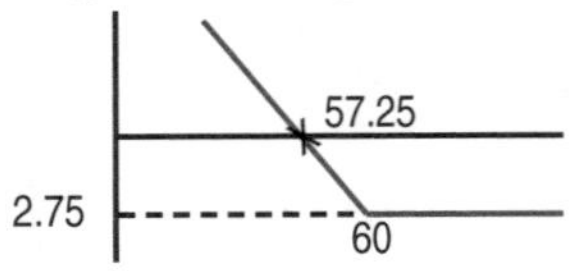

PREMIUM: 2.75
B/E: 57.25
MAX RISK: 2.75

EXERCISE SIX

short DEF 47.50 put

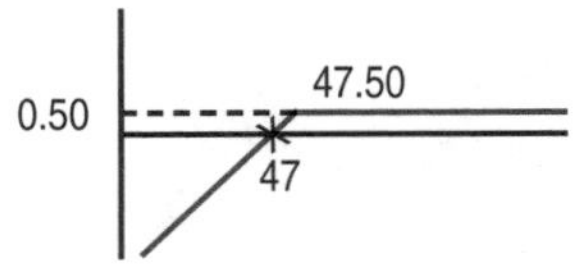

PREMIUM: .50
B/E: 47.00
MAX RISK: unlimited to downside

short DEF 70 put

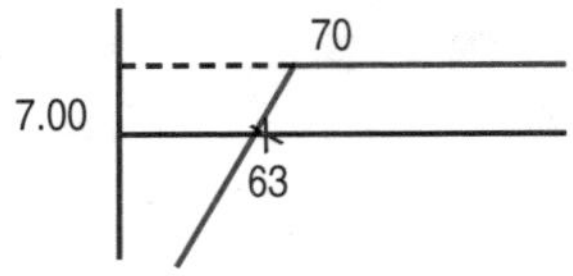

PREMIUM: 7.00
B/E: 63.00
MAX RISK: unlimited to downside

short DEF 85 put

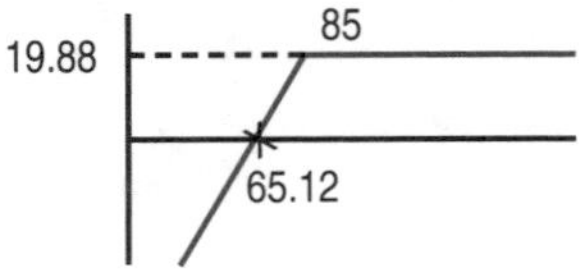

PREMIUM: 19.88
B/E: 65.12
MAX RISK: unlimited to downside

CHAPTER TWO QUIZ

1. You are short one Oct 460 put you sold for 70 with the underlying at 390. Explain your profit or loss if any, at expiration, with the underlying at:
   a. 350
   b. 290
   c. 265

2. True or false? An out-of-the-money (OTM) option has no intrinsic value.

3. True or false? The entire premium of an OTM option consists of extrinsic value.

4. Determine if each option is ITM, OTM, or ATM, if ITI stock is trading at 55.25.
   a. Oct 50 call @ 5.50 ______
   b. Nov 60 call @ 3 ______
   c. Dec 55 put @ 6 ______

5. If a put expires in-the-money, is the underlying above or below the strike price?

6. If a put expires out-of-the-money, is the underlying above or below the strike price?

7. If a call expires in-the-money, is the underlying above or below the strike price?

8. If a call expires out-of-the-money, is the underlying above or below the strike price?

9. If a call expires in-the-money,

   a. the call buyer will ______

   b. their resulting underlying position is ______

   c. the call seller will ______

10. If a put expires in-the-money,

    a. the put buyer will ______

    b. their resulting underlying position is ______

    c. the put seller will ______

11. Immediately after expiration, what is the value of an out-of-the-money option?

12. When an option expires in-the-money, at what price is the underlying instrument exchanged?

13. Immediately after expiration, what is the value of an in-the-money option?

14. A position that is long the underlying (e.g., future, equity, index) has
    a. a bullish or bearish directional bias?
    b. limited or unlimited profit potential?
    c. limited or unlimited loss exposure?

15. A position that is short the underlying (e.g., future, equity, index) has
    a. a bullish or bearish directional bias?
    b. limited or unlimited profit potential?
    c. limited or unlimited loss exposure?

16. A position that is long a call has
    a. a bullish or bearish directional bias?
    b. limited or unlimited profit potential?
    c. limited or unlimited loss exposure?
    d. positive or negative time decay? Does time work for or against you?

17. A position that is short a put has
    a. a bullish or bearish directional bias?
    b. limited or unlimited profit potential?
    c. limited or unlimited loss exposure?
    d positive or negative time decay? Does time work for or against you?

18. A position that is short a call has
    a. a bullish or bearish directional bias?
    b. limited or unlimited profit potential?
    c. limited or unlimited loss exposure?
    d. positive or negative time decay? Does time work for or against you?

19. A position that is long a put has
    a. a bullish or bearish directional bias?
    b. limited or unlimited profit potential?
    c. limited or unlimited loss exposure?
    d. positive or negative time decay? Does time work for or against you?

20. Determine the following:
    a. Long 500 shares of ITI @ 60?
       Risk:
       Reward:
       Break-even:
    b. Short 15 ITI Dec 45 puts @ 4.75
       Risk:
       Reward:
       Break-even:
    c. Short 21 ITI Mar 45 calls @ 6.63
       Risk:
       Reward:
       Break-even:

21. True or false? Implied volatility is a measure using real-time prices rather than historical price and applies to the options rather than the underlying.

22. True or false? Implied volatility is based on past market fluctuations.

23. True or false? Different put and call strikes, as well as different expirations, have their own volatilities.

24. True or false? Vega measures the sensitivity of the option premium to an expected change in the volatility of the underlying.

25. Fill in the missing input for the banking equation:

    B = ______ × days to expiration/360 × i

26. Calculate cost of carry for the following: The April 45 options expire in 71 calendar days with the interest rate to finance the underlying at 9.5 percent.

27. Do dividends work for or against you if you are short stock?

28. What are the six inputs that are used in the Black-Scholes model to derive an option's price?

29. True or false? Calls and puts have positive deltas.

30. What does the trader anticipate with long volatility?

31. What does the trader anticipate with short volatility?

QUIZ ANSWER KEY

1. a. $40 × 100 = $4,000 loss
   b. $100 × 100 = $10,000 loss
   c. $125 × 100 = $12,500 loss

2. True

3. True

4. a. ITM
   b. OTM
   c. ATM/OTM

5. Below

6. Above

7. Above

8. Below

9. a. exercise the call.
   b. long underlying.
   c. be assigned on the call, and assume a short position at the strike price.

10. a. exercise the put.
    b. short underlying.
    c. be assigned on the put, and buy the underlying at the strike price.

11. Zero

12. At the exercise or strike price

13. Its intrinsic value

14. a. Bullish
    b. Unlimited
    c. Unlimited to zero

15. a. Bearish
    b. Unlimited to zero
    c. Unlimited

16. a. Bullish
    b. Unlimited
    c. Limited
    d. Negative/Against

17. a. Bullish/Neutral
    b. Limited
    c. Unlimited to zero
    d. Positive/For

18. a. Bearish/Neutral
    b. Limited
    c. Unlimited
    d. Positive/For

19. a. Bearish
    b. Unlimited to zero
    c. Limited
    d. Negative/Against

20. a. \$30,000 (500 shares × \$60/share)
   Unlimited
   60
   b. \$60,375 (15 contracts × 100 multiplier × \$45/share = \$67,500)
   7,125 (15 × 100 × 4.75) – premium received (\$4.75 × 15 contracts × 100 multiplier = \$7,125)
   40.25
   c. Unlimited
   \$13,923 (\$6.63 × 21 contracts × 100)
   51.63

21. True

22. False

23. True

24. True

25. K, or strike price

26. = 45 × .095 × 71/360 = .84

27. Against. If you are short stock then you pay out the dividend.

28. Price of underlying, exercise price, time until expiration, volatility of underlying, interest rates, and dividends

29. False. Calls have positive deltas and puts have negative deltas.

30. That the market will move more than anticipated or that demand for options will increase, raising implied volatility

31. That the market will move less than anticipated and that the demand for options will decrease, lowering implied volatility

CHAPTER 3

Synthetic Relationships

CONCEPT REVIEW

Rolling a position: The process by which a position is closed in one month, frequently the first or "front" month, and a similar position is put on a month in the future.

Leverage: In option terms, leverage refers to the opportunity to participate in a potentially profitable investment or trade by employing derivative products; this allows you to commit less capital to the deal than would be required without leveraging. These are a risky investment and there is no guarantee an investor would not have significant losses.

Over parity for ITM options: The price of an option after subtracting the difference between the option's strike price and the market price of the underlying (in essence, subtracting the option's intrinsic value). In simple terms, the remaining amount equals the option's extrinsic value.

Over parity for OTM options: The price of an option after adding the difference between the option's strike price and the market price of the underlying. Because these options are out-of-the-money, the difference between the strike price and stock price is not considered intrinsic value.

Banking or cost-of-carry: The interest cost or earnings from holding either a long or short position in the actual underlying.

Synthetics: Two or more trading vehicles packaged together to emulate another trading vehicle or spread. Because the package involves different components, price is also different, but the risk is the same (there are exceptions, however).

Synthetic long call: A long stock position with a long put position. Synthetic long call = long put + long stock

Synthetic long put: A short stock position with a long call position. Synthetic long put = long call + short stock

Synthetic long stock: A long call position with a short put position. Synthetic long stock = long call + short put

Synthetic short call: A short stock position with a short put position. Synthetic short call = short stock + short put.

Synthetic short put: A long stock position with a short call position. Synthetic short put = long stock + short call.

Synthetic short stock: A short call position with a long put position. Synthetic short stock = short call + long put.

Trading options can provide both flexibility and versatility through the packaging of several instruments. These "packages," or synthetics, can emulate different stock or option positions without trading the actual instrument. In a sense, synthetic positions can be seen as a substitute for the actual instrument. In certain circumstances, it can be advantageous for a trader to adopt a strategy using synthetics. Using combinations of calls, puts, and/or stock, it is possible to create a position that acts like the one desired. This chapter will discuss both how to create synthetic stock, calls, and puts; and the advantages and disadvantages of synthetic positions.

SYNTHETIC STOCK

Long Synthetic Stock

A long synthetic stock position is created by purchasing a call and selling a put with the same strike price and same expiration date. As the price of the actual stock increases, the call will appreciate in value and the put will depreciate. This change in the price of the call and put will replicate the profit and loss of the true underlying. A decrease in the actual price of the stock would have the opposite effect on the call and put, again simulating the price behavior of the real underlying.

One might wonder why even bother to trade a call and a put to create stock. In fact, the synthetic position can offer several advantages that real stock may not. First, the amount of capital required to purchase (sell) a call and sell (purchase) a put could be substantially less than that required to trade the stock itself. Such an

Synthetic Long Stock

XYZ Spot Stock Price = $100
June 100 Call Premium = $5
June 100 Put Premium = $5

Profit & Loss Scenario

Exercise Price	Stock Price	P&L Long Call @ 5	P&L Short Put @ 5	Net Synthetic Long Stock
$100	$94	–$5	–$1	–$6
100	95	–5	0	–5
100	96	–5	1	–4
100	97	–5	2	–3
100	98	–5	3	–2
100	99	–5	4	–1
100	100	–5	5	0
100	100.25	–4.75	5	0.25
100	100.5	–4.5	5	0.5
100	101	–4	5	1
100	102	–3	5	2
100	103	–2	5	3
100	104	–1	5	4
100	105	0	5	5
100	106	1	5	6
100	107	2	5	7
100	108	3	5	8
100	109	4	5	9
100	110	5	5	10
100	111	6	5	11

Synthetic Long Stock

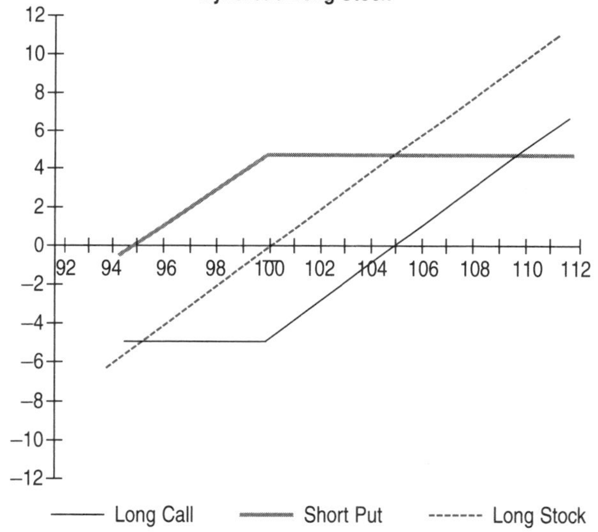

opportunity to trade options in place of the underlying is an example of leverage, the financial equivalent of getting more "bang for your buck."

The example will illustrate the utility of exploiting the leverage available in trading options (of course, derivatives always carry risk as well): XYZ stock is trading at $100. The June 100 call is trading for a premium of $5 and the June 100 put is trading for $4. A synthetic long stock position could be created by purchasing the June 100 call for $5 and selling the June 100 put for $4. As with all options, the call would be paid for in full and the short put would be subject to margin requirements. Nonetheless, the financial commitment to the trade would be considerably less than the $100 per share that the trader would have to pay if required to pay for the stock in full.

Another advantage is the versatility of synthetic positions. If the stock increases in value, a trader could buy back the short put, which will be trading for less, resulting in a profit, and remain long the call. However, the position at this point would no longer be considered synthetic stock. The long call would only mimic the movement of the stock if it were deep in-the-money.

In terms of disadvantages, options have finite lives, and a stock does not, except for total failure of a company. As was discussed in Chapter 2, options expire on a regular basis. If a trader wished to continue to hold synthetic stock after expiration, he or she would have to roll the position to another month. The strike does not have to be the same, however, because a synthetic stock position works at any of the strikes.

Again, an example would help to illustrate the need for rolling the position. The long synthetic stock that the trader purchased for a debit of $1 is now going to expire in one day. XYZ stock is now trading at $108, the value of the June 100 call is $8.50, and the June 100 put is trading at $.50. A trader could sell out the call and purchase the put (short synthetic stock) for a credit of $7. The roll would be accomplished by a simultaneous combination purchase of a further month call and sale of a put with the same expiration and strike. Essentially, the trader has sold synthetic stock in one month and purchased it in another.

Short Synthetic Stock

In terms of creating synthetic short stock, using the same XYZ stock that is now trading at $96, the XYZ May 95 call is valued at $4.50. The matching May 95 put trades at $2.50. A synthetic short stock position could be created by selling the May

Synthetic Short Stock

XYZ Spot Stock Price = $96.00
May 95 Call Premium = $4.50
May 95 Put Premium = $2.50

Profit & Loss Scenario

Exercise Price	Stock Price	P&L Short Call @ 4.5	P&L Long Put @ 2.5	Net Synthetic Short Stock
$95	$82.5	$4.5	$10	$14.5
95	85	4.5	7.5	12
95	87.5	4.5	5	9.5
95	90	4.5	2.5	7
95	92.5	4.5	0	4.5
95	95	4.5	–2.5	2
95	95.5	4	–2.5	1.5
95	96	3.5	–2.5	1
95	96.5	3	–2.5	0.5
95	97	2.5	–2.5	0
95	97.5	2	–2.5	–0.5
95	98	1.5	–2.5	–1
95	98.5	1	–2.5	–1.5
95	99	0.5	–2.5	–2
95	99.5	0	–2.5	–2.5
95	100	–0.5	–2.5	–3
95	102.5	–3	–2.5	–5.5
95	105	–5.5	–2.5	–8
95	107.5	–8	–2.5	–10.5
95	110	–10.5	–2.5	–13
95	112.5	–13	–2.5	–15.5
95	115	–15.5	–2.5	–18

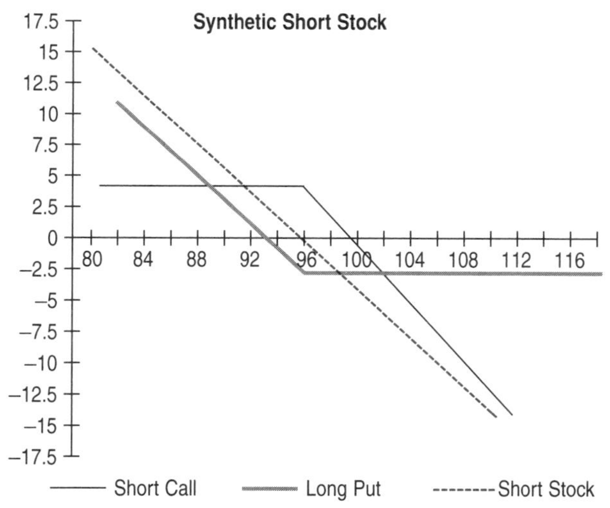

95 call and buying the May 95 put for a $2 credit. As the price of the real underlying falls, the call will depreciate in value and the put will appreciate; the reverse is true should the stock price rise. The combination of changes in the options' values mimics the profit/loss profile of a short stock position.

The $2 credit is certainly less than receipt of the full $96 that would be available from short selling the underlying. However, margin requirements for the short call position are much more manageable than those for short selling the real underlying. Furthermore, the short call position could be closed in the event of a stock price decline, leaving the trader with a long put position acquired originally for a $2 credit, again demonstrating the greater flexibility of the synthetic position.

SYNTHETIC CALL

Long Synthetic Call

With synthetic stock, the trader used a combination of a call and a put to create a risk profile that equaled that of the real underlying. Now, actual stock and a put will be used in combination to create a risk profile that equals a call. A long synthetic call is created by purchasing a put and also purchasing the underlying stock. The strike price of the put would be the equivalent strike price of the synthetic call. If a trader bought the December 50 put and then purchased stock, for example, this would be the equivalent of purchasing the December 50 call.

The profit and loss of synthetic calls mirror those of actual calls. The rules for break-even, maximum loss, and maximum reward are the same for the actual and the synthetic. As demonstrated in Chapter 1, break-even points for long calls always equal the option's strike price plus its premium; and maximum loss for long calls is never more than the premium paid.

This strategy, as with actual calls, provides the possibility of unlimited gains with limited loss. The long stock could increase in value indefinitely. However, the posi-

Synthetic Long Call

XYZ Spot Stock Price = $50
Dec 50 Put Premium = $2

Profit & Loss Scenario

Exercise Price	Stock Price	P&L Long Put @ 2	P&L Long Stock @ 50	Net Synthetic Long Call
$50	$44	$4	–$6	–$2
50	45	3	–5	–2
50	46	2	–4	–2
50	47	1	–3	–2
50	48	0	–2	–2
50	49	–1	–1	–2
50	50	–2	0	–2
50	50.25	–2	0.25	–1.75
50	51	–2	1	–1
50	52	–2	2	0
50	53	–2	3	1
50	54	–2	4	2
50	55	–2	5	3
50	56	–2	6	4
50	57	–2	7	5
50	58	–2	8	6

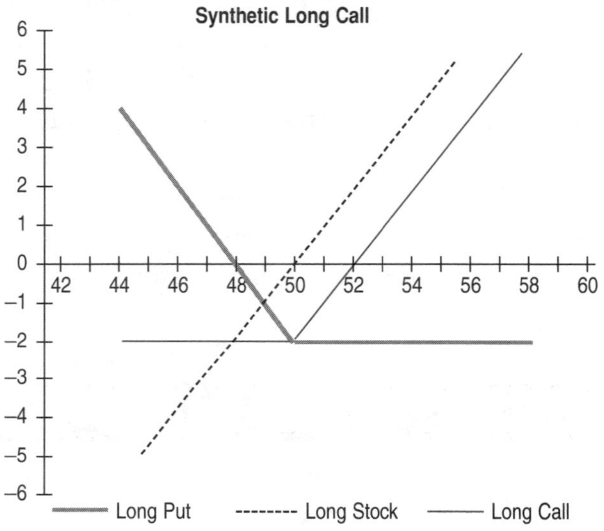

tion's overall profit must take into account the put purchased. For example, a trader could purchase stock at $50 and a December 50 put for $2. The position's potential profit is considered unlimited. As long as the stock increases in value, the holder will gain. What the trader has done here, though, is purchase a measure of downside protection. If the stock should decline in value, in this case below $50, the trader would have protection through the ownership of the December 50 put. In other words, any loss below $50 in the actual stock would be balanced through an appreciation in the value of the put that is owned. Creating long synthetic calls is a popular strategy among fund managers. Fund managers purchase puts to protect their long stock on the downside.

As previously mentioned, such downside protection comes at a premium. The break-even in this strategy equals the strike price plus the cost of the put. The trader does not recover the cost of this protection until the stock is at $52. The $2 gain in the stock offsets the cost of the put. If the stock remains here at expiration, then the trader recoups the full cost of the put. If the stock is any higher, the trader receives a profit from the long stock.

At what point does our protection begin on the downside? The position requires an initial outlay of $2 for the put, so it must be in-the-money by that amount to regain our premium spent. In this case, the put is worth $2 at a stock price of $48 at expiration, and the trader would lose nothing on the put purchase. However, the trader does lose $2 from the stock purchased at $50. At any price below $48, the in-the-money put will act like short stock at expiration and offset any loss from the long stock. The maximum loss of the synthetic call is simply $2, or the premium of the long put.

Short Synthetic Call

The short synthetic call is created by selling a put and selling stock. As with the real short call, this is considered a limited gain strategy with unlimited potential losses. As long as the underlying appreciates, the short stock portion of the position will continue to lose. The potential profit comes from the short put, which would only fully be realized if it finished out-of-the-money at expiration.

Selling synthetic calls is used when one believes that the stock either will decline or remain unchanged. It might seem that "unlimited" gains would be possible from the short stock if the stock's price were to continue to depreciate. However, the synthetic position is short a put, and the gains from the short stock position will be balanced by the losses on the short put.

An example would help to demonstrate the similarities between the synthetic call and the real thing. A trader could sell the April 80 put for $5.25 and sell the underlying at $78. The combination is the synthetic equivalent to selling the April 80 call.

Synthetic Short Call

XYZ Spot Stock Price = $78.00
April 80 Put Premium = $5.25

Profit & Loss Scenario

Exercise Price	Stock Price	P&L Short Put @ 5.25	P&L Short Stock @ 78	Net Synthetic Short Call
$80	$65	–$9.75	$13	$3.25
80	65.5	–9.25	12.5	3.25
80	66	–8.75	12	3.25
80	66.5	–8.25	11.5	3.25
80	68	–6.75	10	3.25
80	70	–4.75	8	3.25
80	72.75	–2	5.25	3.25
80	74	–0.75	4	3.25
80	74.75	0	3.25	3.25
80	76	1.25	2	3.25
80	78	3.25	0	3.25
80	78.25	3.5	–0.25	3.25
80	78.5	3.75	–0.5	3.25
80	80	5.25	–2	3.25
80	82	5.25	–4	1.25
80	83.25	5.25	–5.25	0
80	84	5.25	–6	–0.75
80	86	5.25	–8	–2.75

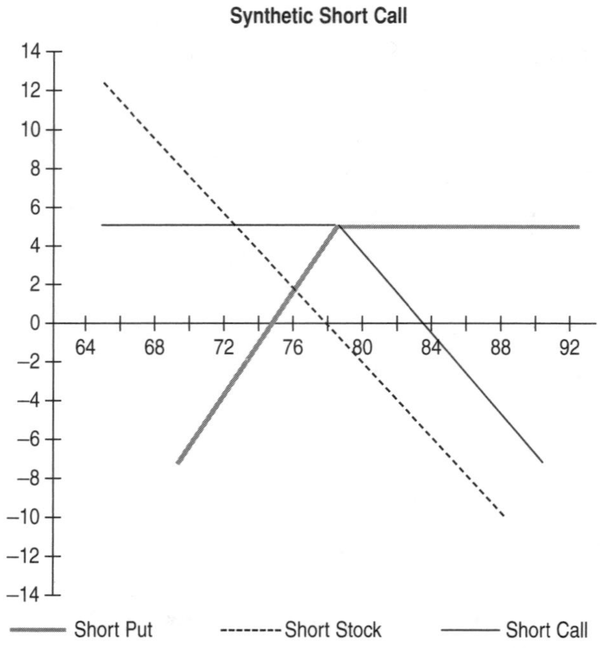

As the stock price falls, the gains from the short stock part of the position are offset by the losses on the short put. However, the extrinsic value portion of the put price will decline to zero, and the trader will be able to realize that profit. The decline in the extrinsic value of the put as the underlying's price falls mirrors the reduction in the value of the real April 80 call.

The upside risk of a synthetic short call position is exactly the same as that of a real short call position. The losses on the short stock position cannot be balanced by gains on the short put because the only gain possible from the short put is the premium collected from its sale. The position's break-even can be determined first by subtracting the difference between the put's strike price and the market price of the underlying—$2 in this example—from the $5.25 in premium collected from the put sale. The remaining $3.25 is added to the put's strike price to define at what point the option's sale no longer helps to offset the losses from the short stock. Consequently, just as with the real call, the synthetic position has unlimited upside risk.

Pricing Synthetic Calls

Creating synthetic calls requires combining puts and the underlying in packages. Yet, a critical question has been left out of the discussion so far. Is there a price advantage to using synthetic options instead of the real things? The answer is sometimes yes and sometimes no. A relatively straightforward process can be used to discover if a price advantage is available. Using simple arithmetic and some concepts from Chapter 2 will open this avenue of possibilities to the burgeoning option trader.

The value of real ITM options is composed of both intrinsic and extrinsic value. For OTM options, the entire price of the put is extrinsic value.

The appropriate starting point is the realization that any put that is considered in-the-money has a corresponding call that is considered out-of-the-money, and any OTM put has an equivalent ITM call. Therefore, the price of any real call should equal the price over parity of the equivalent put with one adjustment that will be described later.

What is price over parity? The concept varies subtly between ITM and OTM options. For an ITM put, the price over parity equals the price of the put after subtracting its intrinsic value. The price over parity of the put, consequently, is its extrinsic value. In regard to an OTM put, however, intrinsic value cannot be subtracted from its price because it is composed entirely of extrinsic value. Therefore, the difference between the market price of the underlying and the put's strike price must be added to the put's value in order to arrive at the price over parity.

A few examples will help to demonstrate the concept. The May 50 put is $5 in-the-money with the stock trading at $45, and the May 40 put is $5 out-of-the-money.

ITM Put:	May 50 put	OTM Put:	May 40 put
Stock Price:	$45	Stock Price:	$45
Put Price	= $7.25	Put Price	= $2.50
Intrinsic Value	= $5.00	Stock – Strike	= $5.00
Price over Parity	= $2.25	Price over Parity	= $7.50

The final step in determining the relative price of the synthetic call to the real call is to adjust the price-over-parity value for the interest cost associated with holding a stock position as part of the synthetic package. As was described previously, committing capital to buying the underlying contains an inherent cost in the sense that the capital is not in a bank safely earning interest. Similarly, any proceeds received from a short sale of stock could be placed in a bank on which interest could be earned during the life of the short position. Such costs or returns are known in the business as either banking or cost-of-carry.

For synthetic option positions, the cost of carry is determined by calculating the interest cost for the strike price level of the option in question. The cost for that level is calculated for the time period beginning on the day of the position's initiation until the option's expiration date. For example, the interest cost for the previous ITM example would be calculated using an interest rate, the strike price of 50 and the number of days remaining between today and May expiration.

When examining synthetic call positions, the cost of carry must be added to the price-over-parity value for the synthetic package. For pedagogical purposes we will assign a banking cost of $.35 to the examples cited previously.

ITM Put:	May 50 put	OTM Put:	May 40 put
Stock Price:	$45	Stock Price:	$45
Price over Parity	= $2.25	Price over Parity	= $7.50
Cost-of-Carry	= $0.35	Cost-of-Carry	= $0.35
Synthetic Call	= $2.60	Synthetic Call	= $7.85

Using the two concepts of price over parity and cost of carry, the trader can assess whether the synthetic or the real call is the better one to purchase or to sell. Factors outside of price clearly influence such a decision. Nevertheless, price is a very important consideration in any financial transaction and will allow a trader to make increasingly intelligent decisions about how to put on a potentially profitable trade.

SYNTHETIC PUT

Synthetic Long Put

A synthetic long put requires the purchase of a call and the simultaneous sale of stock. The strike and expiration date of the call will replicate a put with the same strike price and expiration. A trader purchasing the November 75 call and selling stock would synthetically create a long November 75 put. This strategy has the possibility of "unlimited" gains with limited losses. However, the gains are not unlimited in reality, as is the case with synthetic long calls, because the price of a stock cannot drop below zero.

If the stock decreases in value, the position profits from the short sale of the underlying. By purchasing the call, the trader has purchased upside protection, or insurance against an upward move. A drastic move to the upside will be protected by the long call in the strategy because any loss in the short stock will be offset by gains from the long call.

For example, a trader sells 100 shares of XYZ stock at $77 and purchases the November 75 call for $3. The trader makes money as the stock decreases and is pro-

Synthetic Long Put

XYZ Spot Stock Price = $77
Nov 75 Call Premium = $3

Profit & Loss Scenario

Exercise Price	Stock Price	P&L Long Call @ 3	P&L Short Stock @ 77	Net Synthetic Long Put
$75	65	–$3	$12	$9
75	66	–3	11	8
75	67	–3	10	7
75	68	–3	9	6
75	69	–3	8	5
75	70	–3	7	4
75	72	–3	5	2
75	74	–3	3	0
75	76	–2	1	–1
75	77	–1	0	–1
75	77.25	–.75	–.25	–1
75	77.5	–0.5	–0.5	–1
75	78	0	–1	–1
75	79	1	–2	–1
75	80	2	–3	–1
75	81	3	–4	–1
75	82	4	–5	–1
75	83	5	–6	–1
75	84	6	–7	–1
75	85	7	–8	–1

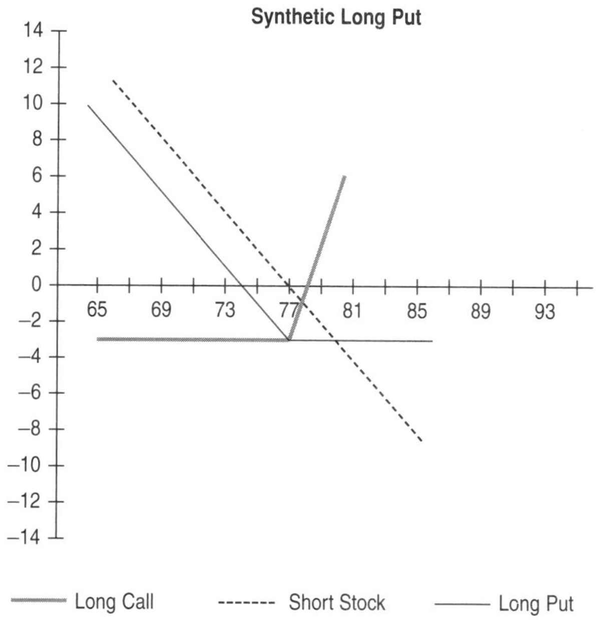

tected above a stock price of $75. Here, he or she purchases an in-the-money call valued at $3. The break-even for this strategy is the stock price less the premium of the call, or $74. At this point the trader has gained $3 from the short stock, which covers the premium paid for the November 75 call.

If the stock were to increase in value, the trader could exercise the call giving him or her the right to purchase stock at $75. At $75 or any price above, the trader will only lose $1. If the stock finishes at $80, the trader would lose $3 from the short sale and gain a net profit of $2 on the long call.

Synthetic Short Put

The synthetic short put is replicated by selling a call and buying stock. This is considered a limited gain strategy with potentially substantial losses on the downside. The risk in the position lies in the long stock part of the position if the underlying were to drop in value. The possible gain comes from the short call, which would be realized fully only if it finished out-of-the-money.

Selling a synthetic put is used when one believes that the stock either will increase or remain unchanged. It is not an unlimited gain strategy because as the stock increases in value, the value of the short call increases and thus caps the profit in the position. Selling synthetic puts is a popular strategy with people who own stock at lower prices and now want to receive a little extra premium. An investor who purchased stock at $50 could sell calls with higher strike prices. The belief is that if the stock goes through a higher strike, then obviously the stock has made money. If it does not, then the investor has made money from the short sale of the call. Using the same November 75 call, the trader could sell the call for $3 and buy the underlying at $77. As the price of the underlying rises, the gains from the long stock position

Synthetic Short Put

XYZ Spot Stock Price = $77.00
Nov 75 Call Premium = $3.00

Profit & Loss Scenario

Exercise Price	Stock Price	P&L Short Call @ 3.00	P&L Long Stock @ 77	Net Synthetic Short Put
$75	$65	$3	–$12	–$9
75	66	3	–11	–8
75	67	3	–10	–7
75	68	3	–9	–6
75	69	3	–8	–5
75	70	3	–7	–4
75	72	3	–5	–2
75	74	3	–3	0
75	76	2	–1	1
75	77	1	0	1
75	77.25	0.75	0.25	1
75	77.5	0.5	0.5	1
75	78	0	1	1
75	79	–1	2	1
75	80	–2	3	1
75	81	–3	4	1
75	82	–4	5	1
75	83	–5	6	1
75	84	–6	7	1
75	85	–7	8	1

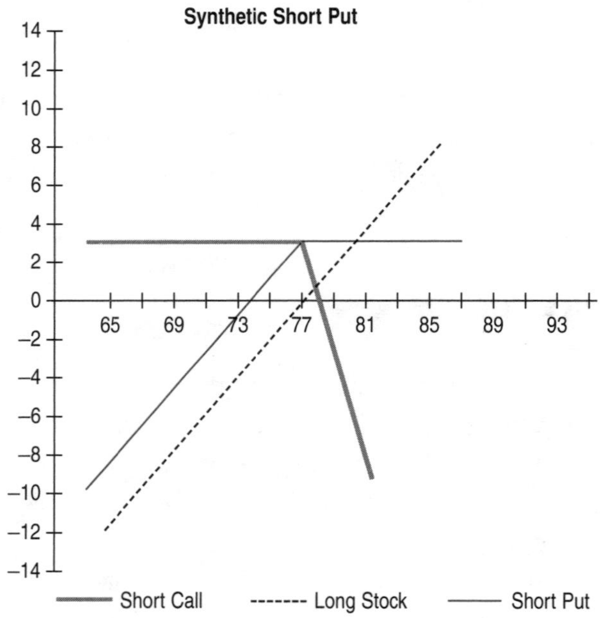

are offset by the losses on the short call. However, the trader does get to collect the premium from the short call sale.

If the price of the underlying were to decline, however, the potential losses for the position are bounded only by the fact that the price of the underlying cannot fall below zero. The short call position is unable to counter the losses generated by the long stock portion of the synthetic package. In order to determine the position's break-even level, the trader must first subtract the difference between the stock price and the option's strike price, $2 in this case, from the premium collected from the sale of the call. The remaining $1 is subtracted from the call's strike price to define the level at which the option's sale no longer helps to offset the losses on the long stock. The profit and loss profile mirrors that of the real short put position.

Pricing Synthetic Puts

As has been described, creating synthetic puts requires combining calls and the underlying in packages. Yet, similar to the discussion of synthetic calls, a critical question has been left out of the discussion so far. Is there a price advantage to using synthetic options instead of the real things? The answer for synthetic puts is also sometimes yes and sometimes no. The same relatively straightforward process can be used to discover if a price advantage is available. The value of real calls is composed of both intrinsic and extrinsic value. For OTM options, the entire price is extrinsic value. Similar to the description of pricing synthetic calls, the price of any real put should equal the price over parity of the equivalent call with the same adjustment for cost of carry.

For an ITM call, the price over parity equals the price of the call after subtracting its intrinsic value. As with the real puts, the price over parity of the real calls equals its extrinsic value. In regard to an OTM call, however, intrinsic value cannot be subtracted from its price because it is composed entirely of extrinsic value. Therefore, the difference between the market price of the underlying and the call's strike price must be added to the call's value in order to arrive at a price-over-parity figure.

A few examples will help to demonstrate the concept. The August 30 calls are $5 in-the-money with the stock at $35, and the August 40 calls are $5 out-of-the-money.

ITM Call:	August 30 call	OTM Call:	August 40 call
Stock Price:	$35	Stock Price:	$35
Call Price	= $6.25	Call Price	= $1.00
Intrinsic Value	= <u>$5.00</u>	Strike – Stock	= <u>$5.00</u>
Price over Parity	= $1.25	Price over Parity	= $6.00

When examining synthetic put positions, banking must be subtracted from the price-over-parity value for the synthetic package. In relation to the examples described previously, the banking figure will be set at $0.25.

As with the synthetic calls, the trader can assess whether the synthetic or the real put is the better to purchase or to sell using the two concepts of price over parity and cost-of-carry. Factors outside of price clearly influence such a decision. Nevertheless, price is a very important consideration in any financial transaction and will allow a trader to make increasingly intelligent decisions about how to put on a potentially profitable trade.

OTHER CONSIDERATIONS

The short stock problem for retail customers described at the beginning of this chapter must be addressed. Substantial margin requirements are a fact of life for retail customers who take a short stock position. However, the problem is avoidable as long as the trader sells stock as part of a synthetic package in a position in which he or she already owns stock. In essence, the stock sale could be accomplished by a reduction in long stock inventory rather than by selling stock short. Therefore, the margin issue is avoided as the trader creates synthetics using stock already present in the portfolio.

Synthetic Stock

Two other disadvantages exist when holding synthetic long stock instead of the real thing. The first is the fact that a trader holding synthetic long stock would not have voting rights and would not be entitled to the dividend paid to the owner of the actual common stock. However, if the trader were short synthetic stock, then he or she would not be responsible for providing the dividend to the actual stock owner, because short stock position holders are obligated in this regard.

Second, if trading American-style options, a risk is present of assignment on the short option position. In the case of the long synthetic stock position, the short put could be assigned prior to expiration, as the opposite party exercises the option early. Such an event would thereby force the trader to purchase the actual stock. Similarly, the short synthetic stock position holder also could be forced to sell the stock through assignment of the short call.

In contrast, one advantage unique to utilizing short synthetic stock is the avoidance of the uptick rule. A trader with short stock may have difficulties in selling the real thing because stock cannot be sold on a downtick unless the seller owns the stock first. A trader could easily create short stock by using synthetics to avoid this problem.

Synthetic Calls

Along with the possibility of unlimited losses, synthetic short call positions have dividend risk. Because the trader is short actual stock in combination with the short put, that trader is responsible for paying any dividend; this would reduce the position's overall maximum gain. As always with American-style options, there is the possibility of assignment. If your short put is assigned before expiration, you must then buy back the stock at the strike price, taking you out of your short synthetic call position.

The dividend issue affects the synthetic long call position differently. In this strategy, the trader is long stock. Therefore, the trader is entitled to any dividend that may occur. In calculating the position's break-even point, a more robust analysis would include receipt of the dividend, which would reduce the stock price necessary for the position to become profitable.

Synthetic Puts

In regard to the synthetic long put position, keep in mind that this strategy requires the selling of stock in combination with buying a call. Therefore, the position would subject a trader to the uptick rule. The responsibility of the dividend, furthermore, would also remain with the trader who holds a short stock position.

Unlike real short puts, the trader with the synthetic short put position is long the underlying stock and thus entitled to any dividends. As always with American-style options, the possibility of assignment exists in regard to the short call portion of the position. If the short call is assigned before expiration, the trader must then sell the stock at the strike price, taking him or her out of the short synthetic put position.

EXERCISE ONE: SYNTHETIC SPEED DRILL

This drill is designed to help increase the speed at which you recognize the synthetic equivalent of positions involving options. (Cover the answers column and see how well you can recognize the synthetic.)

There are four basic properties:

1. The synthetic of a single item in PUC (put underlying call) always contains the two missing items in the equivalent. Conversely, if there are two items in PUC, then the synthetic equivalent contains one.
2. The premium position will remain the same; that is, if the position has long/(short) premium, then the synthetic also must have long/(short) premium.
3. If the position has zero premium; that is, long an option and short an option, then the synthetic position has zero premium. Simply use the sign of C to determine the sign of U (i.e., $-C+P=-U$ *and* $+C-P=+U$).
4. To determine the sign of the underlying: When the call is with the underlying, on the same side of the (=), the sign of the underlying position will always be the opposite sign of the call (i.e., $+C-U=+P$ *and* $-C+U=-P$). The put and underlying are always the same sign; both long (+)(+) and short (–)(–), when on the same side of the (=) (i.e., $+P+U=+C$ *and* $-P-U=-C$).

Position	=	Synthetic Equivalent	Answers
1. +P	=	________________	+C–U
2. –U+C	=	________________	+P
3. +C	=	________________	+P+U
4. –U	=	________________	+P–C
5. –C+P	=	________________	–U
6. +C–U	=	________________	+P
7. +P+U	=	________________	+C
8. +C	=	________________	+U+P
9. +U–C	=	________________	–P
10. –P	=	________________	–C+U
11. –P+C	=	________________	+U
12. –C	=	________________	–U–P
13. +C–P	=	________________	+U
14. +U	=	________________	+C–P
15. –C+U	=	________________	–P
16. –C	=	________________	–P–U
17. +P–C	=	________________	–U
18. –U	=	________________	–C+P
19. –P	=	________________	+U–C
20. –P–U	=	________________	–C

CHAPTER THREE QUIZ

1. A synthetic long call is composed of two instruments. What are they? Indicate whether you are long or short.

2. True or false? A long (premium) option can be synthesized into a short (premium) option by trading an offsetting amount of underlying.

3. Identify each synthetic by completing the missing pieces:

	Actual	=	Synthetic
a.	Long underlying	=	Long call / ___________
b.	Long call	=	_______ underlying / ________
c.	Short call	=	________________ / short put

d. Long ______ = Short underlying / long call

e. Short put = Long underlying / _____ call

f. Short underlying = _____ call / _______ put

4. Identify synthetics that can be used as a hedge to the following actual positions:
   a. 10 long calls
   b. 19 short puts
   c. Short 4,200 shares
   d. 45 long calls
   e. 16 short calls
   f. 130 long puts

5. Name three reasons to use synthetics.

CHAPTER THREE QUIZ ANSWER KEY

1. Long put, long underlying

2. False

3. a. Long underlying = Long call / short put
   b. Long call = Long underlying / long put
   c. Short call = Short underlying / short put
   d. Long put = Short underlying / long call
   e. Short put = Long underlying / short call
   f. Short underlying = Short call / long put

4. a. HEDGE: Short 1,000 underlying and short 10 puts (synthetic short calls)
   b. HEDGE: Short 1,900 underlying and long 19 calls (synthetic long puts)
   c. HEDGE: Long 42 calls and short 42 puts (synthetic long underlying)
   d. HEDGE: Short 45 puts and short 4,500 underlying (synthetic short calls)
   e. HEDGE: Long 1,600 underlying and long 16 puts (synthetic long calls)
   f. HEDGE: long 13,000 underlying and short 130 calls (synthetic short puts)

5. 1. To take advantage of any mispricings in the market
   2. To lock in profits or to limit risk
   3. To hedge an existing position when the actual instrument is unavailable

CHAPTER 4

Directional Strategies

Vertical Spreads

CONCEPT REVIEW

Vertical spread: A spread in which one option is purchased and one option is sold. Both options are of the same type and must have the same expiration date but different exercise prices.

Credit spread: A spread in which the difference in the long and short option premiums results in a net credit. (greatest reward potential on spread)

Debit spread: A spread in which the difference in the long and short option premiums results in a net debit. (greatest risk of loss on spread)

Bull call spread: A spread that involves the purchase of a lower strike call and the sale of a higher strike call. It is a debit spread, having a limited reward and limited risk potential.

Bear put spread: A spread that involves selling the lower strike put and buying the higher strike put. It is a debit spread with limited reward and limited risk potential.

Bull put spread: A credit spread that involves selling the higher strike put and buying the lower strike put. It is a bullish position with both limited risk and limited profit potential.

Bear call spread: A credit spread that involves selling the lower strike call and buying a higher strike call. It is a bearish position with both limited risk and limited profit potential.

Market on close (MOC): Buy or sell at last price on the close.

One-to-one vertical spreads are some of the most commonly used options strategies. They have limited risk profiles while still maintaining a directional bias. They can be used as stand-alone strategies, or combined to form more complex strategies. For this reason, verticals are an actively traded and very liquid strategy. The extrinsic value component of the option does not necessarily move commensurate with the underlying's price changes. This gives the trader the opportunity to tailor the risk threshold to a greater degree.

Verticals are combinations of two options of the same type (call or put), at two different strike prices, with the same expiration date and the same underlying, with a ratio of 1:1.

For example, let's say an April call is bought at a strike price of 25, which gives the buyer the option to buy the underlying at $25. Simultaneously, a call also from April is sold at the 30 strike, thereby giving another market participant the option to buy the stock from the trader at $30. The trader would therefore hope to have the opportunity to buy the stock at 25 and sell it for some higher amount not exceeding 30. This would be the maximum payout for this spread. The essence of vertical spread trading is to capitalize on movements in the underlying while controlling financial risk to the trader. More broadly, vertical spreads are categorized first as either debit or credit spreads, and then second in terms of market bias as either bull or bear spreads.

DEBIT SPREADS

There are two different types of debit spreads: the bull call spread and the bear put spread. As the name *debit* suggests, both spreads require a cash outflow in order to initiate the position. In other words, the spread is entered into by purchasing one option at a higher price than that of the option that is sold. A bull call spread is used when the underlying is expected to go up in price, while the bear put spread is used in situations where the underlying is expected to go down in price. In order to fully explain the nature of the spreads, each will be discussed individually.

Bull Call Spread

The bull call spread consists of buying the lower strike call and selling the higher strike call with the same expiration. The difference between the two strikes is the maximum profit achievable. This is an important factor to remember in all vertical spreads: The maximum value of a vertical spread will always be the difference between the strikes less the debit paid or credit received from a spread to calculate your actual profit.

Obviously, the greater the difference between strikes, the greater the profit potential. For example, a Sep 20/25 call spread can expire with a maximum value of

5, and a Sep 110/125 call spread can expire with a maximum value of 15. Because of the nature of call pricing structure, the higher strike that is sold will be less expensive than the lower strike that is bought, because the call with the lower strike has a higher probability of finishing in-the-money, and therefore obviously gives the call holder the opportunity to buy the underlying at a lower price.

Following is the PQR April 150/155 call spread:

150 Call	=	$2.875 Debit ($287.50 per contract for the call purchased)
155 Call	=	$1.875 Credit ($187.50 per contract for the call sold)
Spread Cost	=	$1.00

Just as in the outright purchase of a call, $1.00 is the maximum loss you can experience on this spread. If the underlying closes below the lower strike call on expiration of the options, both calls expire worthless and the price paid for the spread, in this case $1.00, is lost.

In terms of upside potential, the maximum gain on any bull call spread will be the difference between the maximum value of the spread (i.e., the difference between strike prices) and the price paid for the spread. In the example given, the PQR Apr 150/155 call spread has a maximum price of $5.00 (155 – 150). Because we spent $1.00 to execute the spread, we have a profit potential of $4.00:

Maximum Value	=	$5.00
Spread Cost	=	$1.00
Profit Potential	=	$4.00

The break-even on a bull call spread can be determined by adding the price paid on the spread to the lower strike. The break-even at expiration is 150 + 1 or 151.

This break-even at 151 can be compared to the break-even of the outright buy of the 150 call at a price of 2.875. With the outright buy, the stock has to move above 152.875 in order for the call to be profitable.

Such controlled risk and reward is why verticals might be useful in a moderate market condition; it requires less movement to bring them up to a profitable position. In other words, we want the underlying stock to close above 151 at expiration in order to break even. At any price above 151, a profit will be realized.

At expiration, if the underlying stock closes above the upper call strike, both calls will expire in-the-money. If this is the case, the upper strike that you are short will be assigned to you, resulting in a short stock position. Not to worry though, because the long call at the lower strike will be exercised and balance out your position. The result of this is that you have bought the stock at 150 and sold it at 155, thus acquiring the maximum spread value of 5 (less the 1 point you paid for the spread). As explained earlier, this is the most you can make on the spread. Even if the stock goes up to 200, you still only make 4 points in profit.

The advantage of limited risk is offset by this limitation of profit. If the stock closes between the strike prices on expiration, a little maneuvering is required to flatten out the position. Let us say that the stock closes at 154. The 150 call you are long will be in-the-money, but the 155 call is out-of-the-money and expires worth-

Bull Call Spread

PQR Exercise	=	150/155	
April 150 Call Premium	=	–2.875	Long Call
April 155 Call Premium	=	1.875	Short Call
Spread Cost	=	–1	

Profit & Loss Scenario
PQR April 150/155 Call Spread

Exercise $ @150	Exercise $ @155	Stock Price	P&L Long Call @ 2.875	P&L Short Call @ 1.875	Net Spread
150	155	146	-2.875	1.875	-1
150	155	148	-2.875	1.875	-1
150	155	149	-2.875	1.875	-1
150	155	149.5	-2.875	1.875	-1
150	155	150	-2.875	1.875	-1
150	155	150.5	-2.375	1.875	-0.5
150	155	151	-1.875	1.875	0
150	155	151.5	-1.375	1.875	0.5
150	155	152	-0.875	1.875	1
150	155	153	0.125	1.875	2
150	155	154	1.125	1.875	3
150	155	154.5	1.625	1.875	3.5
150	155	155	2.125	1.875	4
150	155	155.5	2.625	1.375	4
150	155	156	3.125	0.875	4
150	155	156.5	3.625	0.375	4
150	155	157	4.125	-0.125	4
150	155	158	5.125	-1.125	4
150	155	159	6.125	-2.125	4

PQR April 150/155 Call Spread

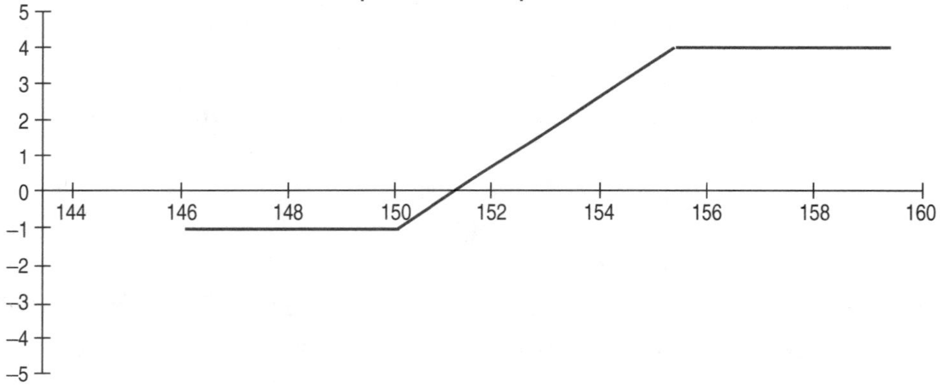

less. In this case, you will exercise your 150 call, resulting in a long position; but the 155 call is not assigned to you. You will be long the stock after expiration. To avoid this happening, you must sell the equivalent number of shares of stock on expiration day. If you were long 1 of the Apr 150/155 call spreads, you must sell 100 shares of stock on expiration day to flatten out your position. Most people make this adjustment on the close of expiration day as a market-on-close (MOC) order. You may wait until the open of the next trading day; however, you then face the risk of losing some or all of your profits if the stock opens lower than the previous day's close.

To summarize, profit for the bull call spread is realized when the underlying closes above the break-even price and the maximum profit potential is realized when the underlying closes above the upper strike price. In the example given, we are risking 1 in order to gain 4. This is how most vertical spreads are used. More often than not, you want to put on a spread where the maximum profit potential is greater than the amount of money at risk (cost of the spread). Because of the limited risk/limited reward nature of the vertical spread, you will want to match the size of the spread with the degree of expectation that the stock move will occur. A bull call spread is best used in a market about which you are moderately bullish.

EXERCISE ONE

Using the prices of MNO options, with the stock at 83, answer the following questions about the bull call spread.

1. What is the composition of the Sep 85/90 bull call spread?
2. What is the maximum profit of this position?
3. What is your potential for loss?
4. What is your break-even?
5. Graph the position.

Last	Bid	Theo	Ask	Strike	Bid	Theo	Ask	Last
83.00	82.94	**82.97**	83.00	**MNO**				
				Sep00				
20.00	33.00	**33.24**	33.50	**50.00**	0.06	**0.07**	0.19	1.00
16.75	28.00	**28.31**	28.50	**55.00**	0.13	**0.13**	0.25	0.25
19.25	23.13	**23.45**	23.63	**60.00**	0.19	**0.25**	0.31	0.38
19.38	18.50	**18.72**	18.88	**65.00**	0.44	**0.50**	0.56	0.50
13.00	14.00	**14.26**	14.38	**70.00**	0.81	**1.02**	1.00	1.00
8.75	10.00	**10.28**	10.38	**75.00**	1.81	**2.03**	2.00	1.94
6.25	6.63	**6.95**	7.00	**80.00**	3.38	**3.71**	3.63	3.50
3.75	4.13	**4.41**	4.38	**85.00**	5.88	**6.17**	6.25	6.25
2.25	2.44	**2.64**	2.50	**90.00**	9.25	**9.40**	9.63	9.25
1.13	1.25	**1.50**	1.44	**95.00**	13.13	**13.26**	13.50	13.75
0.88	0.63	**0.82**	0.81	**100.00**	17.38	**17.59**	17.75	23.00
0.50	0.25	**0.44**	0.38	**105.00**	22.00	**22.25**	22.50	0.00
0.50	0.13	**0.23**	0.25	**110.00**	26.88	**27.09**	27.38	0.00
0.25	0.06	**0.13**	0.19	**115.00**	31.75	**32.03**	32.25	0.00
0.13	0.00	**0.01**	0.13	**120.00**	36.75	**37.03**	37.25	49.25
0.13	0.00	**0.00**	0.13	**125.00**	41.75	**42.03**	42.25	0.00
0.00	0.00	**0.00**	0.13	**130.00**	46.75	**47.03**	47.25	0.00
				Oct00				
31.88	33.50	**33.73**	34.00	**50.00**	0.19	**0.29**	0.31	0.44
21.75	28.88	**29.05**	29.38	**55.00**	0.44	**0.56**	0.56	0.81
25.13	24.38	**24.57**	24.88	**60.00**	0.88	**1.04**	1.06	1.13
19.00	20.13	**20.37**	20.63	**65.00**	1.69	**1.82**	1.88	1.94
15.75	16.38	**16.54**	16.75	**70.00**	2.81	**2.96**	3.00	3.25
15.25	13.00	**13.16**	13.38	**75.00**	4.38	**4.53**	4.63	5.00
11.25	11.50	**11.65**	11.88	**77.50**	5.38	**5.53**	5.75	6.38
10.88	10.13	**10.26**	10.50	**80.00**	6.38	**6.63**	6.75	7.13
8.00	8.88	**8.99**	9.25	**82.50**	7.50	**7.84**	7.88	14.63
7.25	7.75	**7.85**	8.13	**85.00**	8.88	**9.21**	9.25	8.75
6.13	6.63	**6.82**	7.00	**87.50**	10.38	**10.64**	10.75	15.88
6.00	5.75	**5.90**	6.00	**90.00**	11.88	**12.24**	12.25	12.25
5.00	5.00	**5.09**	5.25	**92.50**	13.63	**13.92**	14.00	12.88
4.50	4.25	**4.37**	4.50	**95.00**	15.38	**15.70**	15.75	26.75
4.00	3.63	**3.74**	3.88	**97.50**	17.25	**17.57**	17.63	16.13
3.00	3.00	**3.19**	3.25	**100.00**	19.13	**19.52**	19.50	30.00
2.19	2.19	**2.30**	2.38	**105.00**	23.25	**23.65**	23.75	19.63
1.63	1.56	**1.64**	1.75	**110.00**	27.63	**28.01**	28.13	33.50
1.69	1.06	**1.16**	1.25	**115.00**	32.25	**32.58**	32.75	31.13
0.69	0.69	**0.82**	0.88	**120.00**	37.00	**37.29**	37.50	0.00
1.50	0.50	**0.57**	0.69	**125.00**	41.88	**42.13**	42.38	33.38
0.69	0.31	**0.40**	0.44	**130.00**	46.75	**47.04**	47.25	0.00

Bear Put Spread

The bear put spread is the other type of debit spread. The nature of this spread is very similar to that of the bull call spread except that it is used in markets about which you are moderately bearish, and it is made up of puts, not calls. In this spread, you buy the higher strike put and sell the lower strike put. As you can see, these are the exact opposite transactions used in the debit bull call spread. Once again, the nature of put pricing structure makes the purchase of the higher strike more expensive than the sale of the lower strike, because the higher strike put will be closer to being in-the-money. Because of this, the trader necessarily experiences a net cash outflow (debit) to initiate the position.

The process for examining the risk and reward for the bear put spread is similar to that of the bull call spread. The following example involves the VWX March 50/55 put vertical:

55 Put	=	$3.25	Debit ($325.00 per contract for the put purchased)
50 Put	=	<u>$1.4375</u>	Credit ($143.75 per contract for the put sold)
Spread Cost	=	$1.8125	

The spread cost is the maximum amount of money that can be lost on the spread. If the stock goes up during the time the spread is on, and closes above the upper limit strike price (55 in this example), both put options will expire worthless and the $1.8125 invested in the spread will be lost.

If, however, your hunch was correct and the stock declines, there is the potential to make a profit. The maximum value of the put spread is the difference between the strikes, just as in the call spread. In this example, the most the spread can be worth is 5 (55–50). This will only occur if the stock closes on expiration at or below the lower limit strike price of 50. If the stock closes below 50, the 50 put that you are short will be assigned to you, resulting in a long stock position at 50. Once again, no worries, because you will be exercising the 55 put you are long, resulting in your selling the stock at 55. Thus you have sold the stock at 55 and bought it at 50, giving you 5 credit and a net flat position. We then subtract the 1.8125 that was invested to put on the spread and come up with an overall profit of 3.1875.

Maximum Value	=	$5
Spread Cost	=	<u>$1.8125</u>
Profit Potential	=	$3.1875

The break-even point of the bear put spread is calculated by subtracting the cost of the spread from the upper limit strike price. In this example, the spread will begin to make a profit when the underlying stock trades below 53.1875 (55 – 1.8125). If the stock closes between the strikes at say 51, the 55 put is in-the-money and the 50 put is worthless. Because you are long the 55 put, you will no doubt want to exercise your right to sell the underlying stock at 55, because it is trading 4 points lower.

This short position will have to be closed out by the purchase of shares of stock before the market closes on expiration day. A buy MOC order is usually used in this case. You will then be long the actual stock and, upon exercising your put, sell the stock out to result in a net flat position. It is important to be aware of where the stock is going to close on expiration day. You must be prepared to make adjustments to your position in order to keep yourself flat if that is your preference.

To summarize, a profit in the bear put spread is realized once the underlying trades below the break-even point and the maximum profit potential is realized when the underlying moves below the lower limit strike in the spread. The cost was 1.8125, with a profit potential of 3.1875 if the stock closed below 50 on the day the options expire.

Bear Put Spread

VWX Exercise	=	50/55	
March 50 Put Premium	=	1.4375	Short Put
March 55 Put Premium	=	–3.25	Long Put
Spread Cost	=	–1.8125	

Profit & Loss Scenario

VWX March 50/55 Put Spread

Exercise $ @50	Exercise $ @55	Stock Price	P&L Long Put @ 3.25	P&L Short Put @ 1.4375	Net Spread
50	55	46	5.75	-2.56	3.19
50	55	48	3.75	-0.56	3.19
50	55	49	2.75	0.44	3.19
50	55	49.5	2.25	0.94	3.19
50	55	50	1.75	1.44	3.19
50	55	50.5	1.25	1.44	2.69
50	55	51	0.75	1.44	2.19
50	55	51.5	0.25	1.44	1.69
50	55	52	-0.25	1.44	1.19
50	55	53	-1.25	1.44	0.19
50	55	54	-2.25	1.44	-0.81
50	55	54.5	-2.75	1.44	-1.31
50	55	55	-3.25	1.44	-1.81
50	55	55.5	-3.25	1.44	-1.81
50	55	56	-3.25	1.44	-1.81
50	55	56.5	-3.25	1.44	-1.81
50	55	57	-3.25	1.44	-1.81
50	55	58	-3.25	1.44	-1.81
50	55	59	-3.25	1.44	-1.81

VWX March 50/55 Put Spread

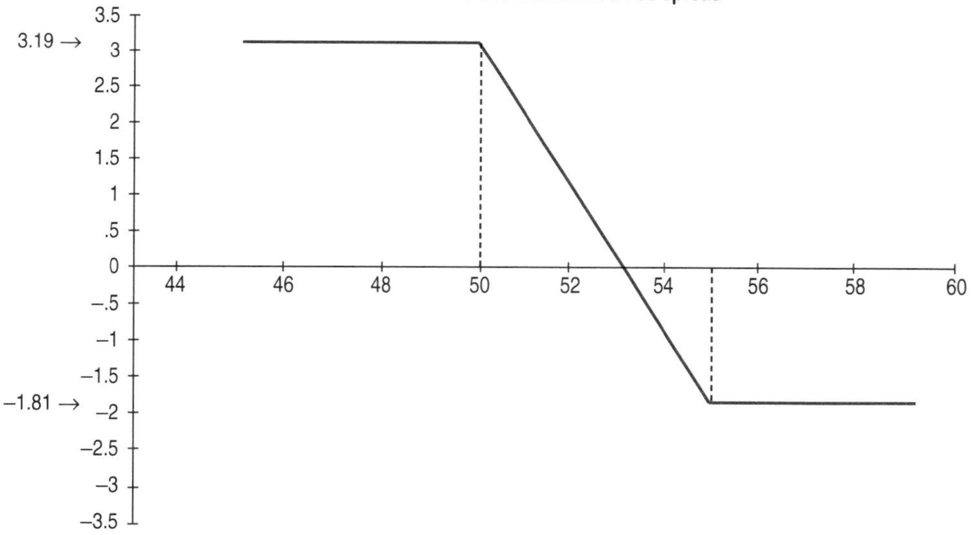

EXERCISE TWO

Last	Bid	Theo	Ask	Strike	Bid	Theo	Ask	Last
83.00	82.94	**82.97**	83.00	**MNO**				
				Sep00				
20.00	33.00	**33.24**	33.50	**50.00**	0.06	**0.07**	0.19	1.00
16.75	28.00	**28.31**	28.50	**55.00**	0.13	**0.13**	0.25	0.25
19.25	23.13	**23.45**	23.63	**60.00**	0.19	**0.25**	0.31	0.38
19.38	18.50	**18.72**	18.88	**65.00**	0.44	**0.50**	0.56	0.50
13.00	14.00	**14.26**	14.38	**70.00**	0.81	**1.02**	1.00	1.00
8.75	10.00	**10.28**	10.38	**75.00**	1.81	**2.03**	2.00	1.94
6.25	6.63	**6.95**	7.00	**80.00**	3.38	**3.71**	3.63	3.50
3.75	4.13	**4.41**	4.38	**85.00**	5.88	**6.17**	6.25	6.25
2.25	2.44	**2.64**	2.50	**90.00**	9.25	**9.40**	9.63	9.25
1.13	1.25	**1.50**	1.44	**95.00**	13.13	**13.26**	13.50	13.75
0.88	0.63	**0.82**	0.81	**100.00**	17.38	**17.59**	17.75	23.00
0.50	0.25	**0.44**	0.38	**105.00**	22.00	**22.25**	22.50	0.00
0.50	0.13	**0.23**	0.25	**110.00**	26.88	**27.09**	27.38	0.00
0.25	0.06	**0.13**	0.19	**115.00**	31.75	**32.03**	32.25	0.00
0.13	0.00	**0.01**	0.13	**120.00**	36.75	**37.03**	37.25	49.25
0.13	0.00	**0.00**	0.13	**125.00**	41.75	**42.03**	42.25	0.00
0.00	0.00	**0.00**	0.13	**130.00**	46.75	**47.03**	47.25	0.00
				Oct00				
31.88	33.50	**33.73**	34.00	**50.00**	0.19	**0.29**	0.31	0.44
21.75	28.88	**29.05**	29.38	**55.00**	0.44	**0.56**	0.56	0.81
25.13	24.38	**24.57**	24.88	**60.00**	0.88	**1.04**	1.06	1.13
19.00	20.13	**20.37**	20.63	**65.00**	1.69	**1.82**	1.88	1.94
15.75	16.38	**16.54**	16.75	**70.00**	2.81	**2.96**	3.00	3.25
15.25	13.00	**13.16**	13.38	**75.00**	4.38	**4.53**	4.63	5.00
11.25	11.50	**11.65**	11.88	**77.50**	5.38	**5.53**	5.75	6.38
10.88	10.13	**10.26**	10.50	**80.00**	6.38	**6.63**	6.75	7.13
8.00	8.88	**8.99**	9.25	**82.50**	7.50	**7.84**	7.88	14.63
7.25	7.75	**7.85**	8.13	**85.00**	8.88	**9.21**	9.25	8.75
6.13	6.63	**6.82**	7.00	**87.50**	10.38	**10.64**	10.75	15.88
6.00	5.75	**5.90**	6.00	**90.00**	11.88	**12.24**	12.25	12.25
5.00	5.00	**5.09**	5.25	**92.50**	13.63	**13.92**	14.00	12.88
4.50	4.25	**4.37**	4.50	**95.00**	15.38	**15.70**	15.75	26.75
4.00	3.63	**3.74**	3.88	**97.50**	17.25	**17.57**	17.63	16.13
3.00	3.00	**3.19**	3.25	**100.00**	19.13	**19.52**	19.50	30.00
2.19	2.19	**2.30**	2.38	**105.00**	23.25	**23.65**	23.75	19.63
1.63	1.56	**1.64**	1.75	**110.00**	27.63	**28.01**	28.13	33.50
1.69	1.06	**1.16**	1.25	**115.00**	32.25	**32.58**	32.75	31.13
0.69	0.69	**0.82**	0.88	**120.00**	37.00	**37.29**	37.50	0.00
1.50	0.50	**0.57**	0.69	**125.00**	41.88	**42.13**	42.38	33.38
0.69	0.31	**0.40**	0.44	**130.00**	46.75	**47.04**	47.25	0.00

Using the prices of MNO options with the stock at 83, answer the following questions about the bear put spread.

1. What is the composition of the Oct 75/80 bear put spread?
2. What is the maximum profit of this position?
3. What is your potential for loss?
4. What is your break-even?
5. Graph the position.

CREDIT SPREADS

As with debit spreads, there are two types of credit spreads: the bull put spread and the bear call spread. As the names suggest, a net cash inflow takes place when these spreads are initiated. These spreads are similar in nature to the outright selling of an option where the goal upon expiration is to have the options expire worthless, thus keeping all the cash that was gained when the position was put on.

Again, similar to the debit spreads, the primary advantage that the credit spread strategy has over a naked short position is that it offers a limited risk profile. Of course, the limited risk comes at a price. That is, you will not collect as much money if the stock moves in the desired direction as you would with a naked position. This is because you are taking some of the proceeds from the sale of the option and putting it toward the purchase of another, albeit less expensive, option in order to limit the risk. To fully explain, each type of spread will be discussed individually.

Bull Put Spread

The bull put spread consists of selling a higher strike put and buying the lower strike put. Because the price of puts increases as the strike price increases, the purchase of the lower strike put will be covered by the sale of the higher strike put. Another way of looking at it is that you are short the higher strike put, and the long put at the lower strike is insurance against the market going against you. It takes away the substantial risk characteristic that is associated with a short put position. Just as with any other vertical spread, the maximum value of the spread is the difference between the two strike prices. The example below shows the LMN April 50/55 put spread, a spread that is worth 5 (55 – 50).

55 Put	=	$5	Credit (put sold)
50 Put	=	$2.8125	Debit (put purchased)
Spread Credit	=	$2.1875	

The 2.1875 credit represents the maximum profit that can be made on the spread. Just as with a short put position, the ideal scenario is one in which the underlying moves above the higher strike, 55 in this example, and stays above it until expiration. If this occurs, both options expire worthless and you keep all 2.1875 initially received. The break-even point on the spread is the upper strike minus the credit gained on the spread. In this example, the stock must close at 52.8125 (55 – 2.1875) or higher for the spread to at least break even.

Starting below 52.8125, the spread begins to become more expensive, and because you are short it, this becomes a loss. As pointed out, however, this loss is limited. In this example, the maximum value of the spread is 5. If the stock closes below 50, the put you are long at 50 will be in-the-money and you will want to exercise it. This will make you short stock at 50 and will cover the long position you will have at 55, because the put you are short will be assigned to you. Thus, buying stock at 55 and selling it at 50 is a 5 loss to you. If we subtract the premium we gained when we first put on the spread, we have a net loss of 2.8125 (5 – 2.1875). This represents the most that we can lose on the spread.

Even if the stock drops down to 35, we still buy the stock at 55 and sell it at 50 because both puts in the position are in-the-money. If the stock closes between the strike prices on expiration, let's say 54, then you will have to make an adjustment to your stock position in order to stay flat the stock. In this example, the 50 put expires

Bull Put Spread

LMN Exercise	=	50/55	
April 55 Put Premium	=	5	Short Put
April 50 Put Premium	=	–2.8125	Long Put
Spread Credit	=	2.1875	

Profit & Loss Scenario
LMN April 50/55 Put Spread

Exercise $ @50	Exercise $ @55	Stock Price	P&L Long Put @ 2.8125	P&L Short Put @ 5	Net Spread
50	55	46	1.1875	-4.00	-2.81
50	55	48	-0.8125	-2.00	-2.81
50	55	49	-1.8125	-1.00	-2.81
50	55	49.5	-2.3125	-0.50	-2.81
50	55	50	-2.8125	0.00	-2.81
50	55	50.5	-2.8125	0.50	-2.31
50	55	51	-2.8125	1.00	-1.81
50	55	51.5	-2.8125	1.50	-1.31
50	55	52	-2.8125	2.00	-0.81
50	55	53	-2.8125	3.00	0.19
50	55	54	-2.8125	4.00	1.19
50	55	54.5	-2.8125	4.50	1.69
50	55	55	-2.8125	5.00	2.19
50	55	55.5	-2.8125	5.00	2.19
50	55	56	-2.8125	5.00	2.19
50	55	56.5	-2.8125	5.00	2.19
50	55	57	-2.8125	5.00	2.19
50	55	58	-2.8125	5.00	2.19
50	55	59	-2.8125	5.00	2.19

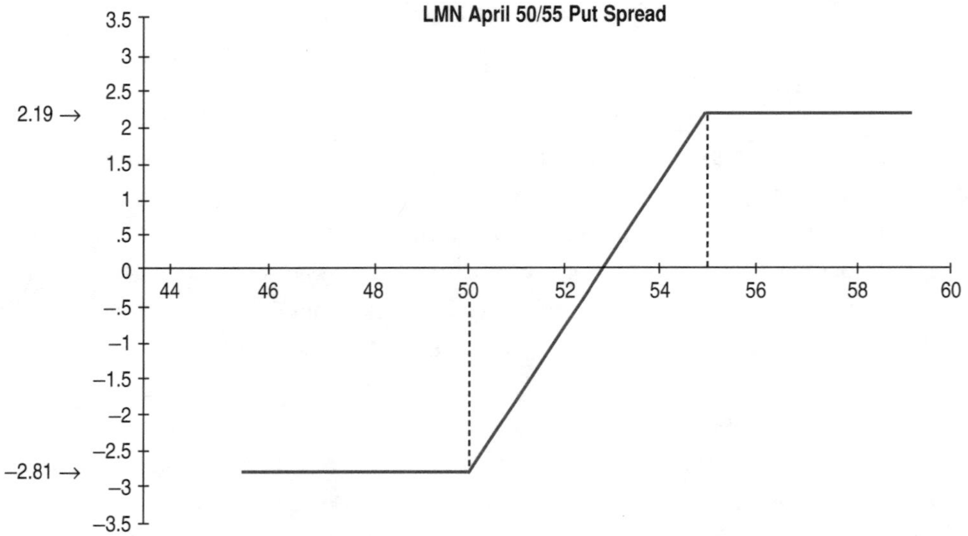

worthless, but the 55 put you are short is in-the-money and will, therefore, be exercised by the holder of the long 55 put position. As a result of the holder electing to sell the stock at 55, you will be long the stock at 55.

In order to balance your position, you will have to sell the proper amount of shares before the close of the market on expiration day. A sell MOC order will accomplish the job of flattening out the position. Thus, you have bought the stock at 55 and sold the stock at 54, resulting in a loss of 1. If we then subtract this from the money we collected when we put on the position, the result is a net profit of 1.1875 (2.1875 – 1).

To summarize, the bull put spread is similar to an outright short put position, except that the risk profile is now limited and the reward potential is reduced. With this spread, the goal is for the stock to close above the higher strike price upon expiration, resulting in the options expiring worthless and allowing for collection of the total cash flow generated at the initiation of the position.

EXERCISE THREE

Using the prices of MNO options with the stock at 83, answer the following questions about the bull put spread.

1. What is the composition of the Oct 85/90 bull put spread?
2. What is the maximum profit of this position?
3. What is your potential for loss?
4. What is your break-even?
5. Graph the position.

Last	Bid	Theo	Ask	Strike	Bid	Theo	Ask	Last
83.00	82.94	**82.97**	83.00	**MNO**				
				Sep00				
20.00	33.00	**33.24**	33.50	**50.00**	0.06	**0.07**	0.19	1.00
16.75	28.00	**28.31**	28.50	**55.00**	0.13	**0.13**	0.25	0.25
19.25	23.13	**23.45**	23.63	**60.00**	0.19	**0.25**	0.31	0.38
19.38	18.50	**18.72**	18.88	**65.00**	0.44	**0.50**	0.56	0.50
13.00	14.00	**14.26**	14.38	**70.00**	0.81	**1.02**	1.00	1.00
8.75	10.00	**10.28**	10.38	**75.00**	1.81	**2.03**	2.00	1.94
6.25	6.63	**6.95**	7.00	**80.00**	3.38	**3.71**	3.63	3.50
3.75	4.13	**4.41**	4.38	**85.00**	5.88	**6.17**	6.25	6.25
2.25	2.44	**2.64**	2.50	**90.00**	9.25	**9.40**	9.63	9.25
1.13	1.25	**1.50**	1.44	**95.00**	13.13	**13.26**	13.50	13.75
0.88	0.63	**0.82**	0.81	**100.00**	17.38	**17.59**	17.75	23.00
0.50	0.25	**0.44**	0.38	**105.00**	22.00	**22.25**	22.50	0.00
0.50	0.13	**0.23**	0.25	**110.00**	26.88	**27.09**	27.38	0.00
0.25	0.06	**0.13**	0.19	**115.00**	31.75	**32.03**	32.25	0.00
0.13	0.00	**0.01**	0.13	**120.00**	36.75	**37.03**	37.25	49.25
0.13	0.00	**0.00**	0.13	**125.00**	41.75	**42.03**	42.25	0.00
0.00	0.00	**0.00**	0.13	**130.00**	46.75	**47.03**	47.25	0.00
				Oct00				
31.88	33.50	**33.73**	34.00	**50.00**	0.19	**0.29**	0.31	0.44
21.75	28.88	**29.05**	29.38	**55.00**	0.44	**0.56**	0.56	0.81
25.13	24.38	**24.57**	24.88	**60.00**	0.88	**1.04**	1.06	1.13
19.00	20.13	**20.37**	20.63	**65.00**	1.69	**1.82**	1.88	1.94
15.75	16.38	**16.54**	16.75	**70.00**	2.81	**2.96**	3.00	3.25
15.25	13.00	**13.16**	13.38	**75.00**	4.38	**4.53**	4.63	5.00
11.25	11.50	**11.65**	11.88	**77.50**	5.38	**5.53**	5.75	6.38
10.88	10.13	**10.26**	10.50	**80.00**	6.38	**6.63**	6.75	7.13
8.00	8.88	**8.99**	9.25	**82.50**	7.50	**7.84**	7.88	14.63
7.25	7.75	**7.85**	8.13	**85.00**	8.88	**9.21**	9.25	8.75
6.13	6.63	**6.82**	7.00	**87.50**	10.38	**10.64**	10.75	15.88
6.00	5.75	**5.90**	6.00	**90.00**	11.88	**12.24**	12.25	12.25
5.00	5.00	**5.09**	5.25	**92.50**	13.63	**13.92**	14.00	12.88
4.50	4.25	**4.37**	4.50	**95.00**	15.38	**15.70**	15.75	26.75
4.00	3.63	**3.74**	3.88	**97.50**	17.25	**17.57**	17.63	16.13
3.00	3.00	**3.19**	3.25	**100.00**	19.13	**19.52**	19.50	30.00
2.19	2.19	**2.30**	2.38	**105.00**	23.25	**23.65**	23.75	19.63
1.63	1.56	**1.64**	1.75	**110.00**	27.63	**28.01**	28.13	33.50
1.69	1.06	**1.16**	1.25	**115.00**	32.25	**32.58**	32.75	31.13
0.69	0.69	**0.82**	0.88	**120.00**	37.00	**37.29**	37.50	0.00
1.50	0.50	**0.57**	0.69	**125.00**	41.88	**42.13**	42.38	33.38
0.69	0.31	**0.40**	0.44	**130.00**	46.75	**47.04**	47.25	0.00

Bear Call Spread

The bear call spread is composed of a short call at a lower strike and a long call at a higher strike. The nature of call pricing structure tells us that the higher strike call we are buying will cost less than the money collected from the sale of the lower strike call. It is for this reason that this spread involves a cash inflow to the trader. As was the case with the bull put spread, the ideal condition is for the spread to expire worthless, thus allowing you to keep the premium collected at the time of the sale of the spread. In order for this to happen, the underlying will have to close below the lower strike call option that you are short.

The example below shows that the OPQ 60/65 call spread is trading for 2.375 (9.625 – 7.25).

60 Call	=	\$9.625 Credit (call sold)
65 Call	=	\$7.25 Debit (call purchased)
Spread Credit	=	\$2.375

The bear call spread is similar to the outright sale of the call option except that you sacrifice some of the potential profit of an outright sale by limiting your potential loss. This limited loss is calculated by subtracting the premium collected on the spread from the maximum value the spread can be worth at expiration.

The spread has a maximum value of 5, therefore our maximum loss on the spread is 2.625 (5 – 2.375) or \$262.50. This maximum loss will occur if the stock closes above the higher strike price of 65. Let us say that the stock does in fact rally and closes at 68. Both of your calls would expire in-the-money. The call you are short would be exercised and you would have a short stock position at 60. You would exercise your long call, resulting in a long position at 65. These two positions, of course, net each other out and you would lose 5 in the process. The initial premium collected would then be subtracted from the loss to bring the net loss to 2.625 (5 – 2.375).

Bear Call Spread

OPQ Exercise	=	60/65	
Dec 60 Call Premium	=	9.625	Short Call
Dec 65 Call Premium	=	–7.25	Long Call
Spread Credit	=	2.375	

Profit & Loss Scenario
OPQ Dec 60/65 Call Spread

Exercise \$ @ 60	Exercise \$ @ 65	Stock Price	P&L Long Call @ 7.25	P&L Short Call @ 9.625	Net Spread
60	65	56	-7.25	9.63	2.38
60	65	58	-7.25	9.63	2.38
60	65	59	-7.25	9.63	2.38
60	65	59.5	-7.25	9.63	2.38
60	65	60	-7.25	9.63	2.38
60	65	60.5	-7.25	9.13	1.88
60	65	61	-7.25	8.63	1.38
60	65	61.5	-7.25	8.13	0.88
60	65	62	-7.25	7.63	0.38
60	65	63	-7.25	6.63	-0.63
60	65	64	-7.25	5.63	-1.63
60	65	64.5	-7.25	5.13	-2.13
60	65	65	-7.25	4.63	-2.63
60	65	65.5	-6.75	4.13	-2.63
60	65	66	-6.25	3.63	-2.63
60	65	66.5	-5.75	3.13	-2.63
60	65	67	-5.25	2.63	-2.63
60	65	68	-4.25	1.63	-2.63
60	65	69	-3.25	0.63	-2.63
60	65	70	-2.25	-0.38	-2.63
60	65	71	-1.25	-1.38	-2.63
60	65	72	-0.25	-2.38	-2.63
60	65	73	0.75	-3.375	-2.625

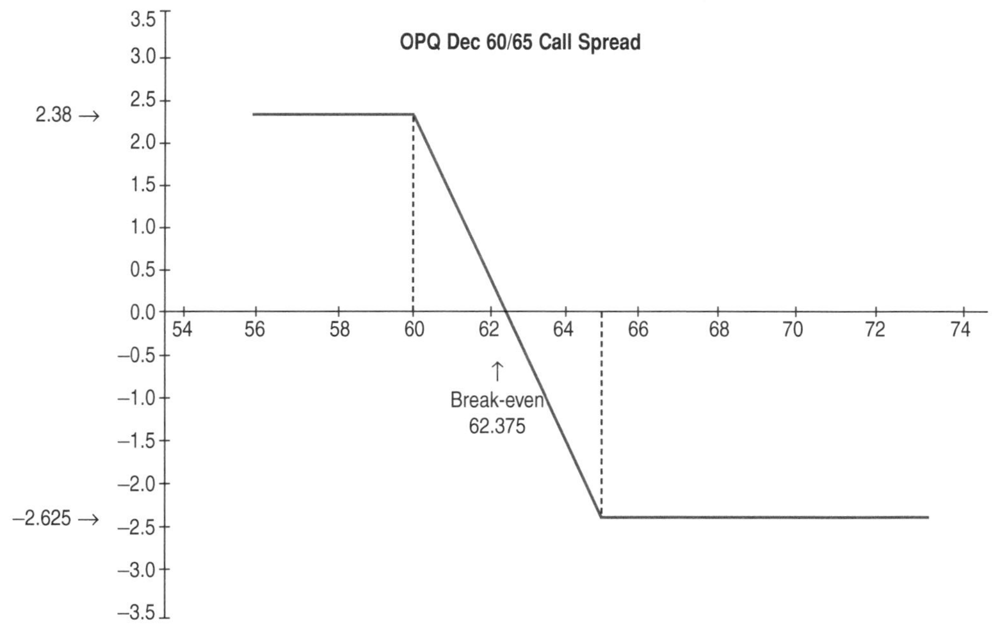

Let us instead suppose that the stock declines as opposed to rises. The break-even point of this spread is the lower strike price plus the premium collected for the spread. This example has a break-even price of 62.375 (60 + 2.375). At any price above 62.375, the 60 call that you are short will be worth more than the 2.375 of premium that you collected. If the stock closes below 62.375, you begin to make money all the way down to 60. At 60, the lower strike price in this case, the option will be worthless and you will get to keep all the premium collected from the sale of the spread.

If the stock closes between the strikes at expiration, for example 61, then you once again must make an adjustment to your stock position on expiration day to maintain a flat stock position. In this example, the 60 call you are short is 1.0 ITM. The 65 call you are long expires worthless. The 60 call will be exercised by the long position holder and you will be required to sell the stock at 60. To maintain a flat position, you must buy the stock before the day ends. You will use a buy MOC order to accomplish this. You have then bought the stock at 61 and sold it at 60. A $1 loss, which is then subtracted from the proceeds gained when you put on the position, leaves you with a net profit of 1.375 (2.375 – 1) or $137.50.

To summarize, profit for the bear call spread is realized when the underlying closes below the break-even price. The ideal situation for the holder of the bear call spread is for the underlying to close below the lower strike price at expiration, resulting in both calls expiring out-of-the-money and therefore worthless. Just as with the bull put spread, the maximum profit you can gain is the amount that was collected when the position was initiated.

EXERCISE FOUR

Last	Bid	Theo	Ask	Strike	Bid	Theo	Ask	Last
83.00	82.94	**82.97**	83.00	**MNO**				
				Sep00				
20.00	33.00	**33.24**	33.50	**50.00**	0.06	**0.07**	0.19	1.00
16.75	28.00	**28.31**	28.50	**55.00**	0.13	**0.13**	0.25	0.25
19.25	23.13	**23.45**	23.63	**60.00**	0.19	**0.25**	0.31	0.38
19.38	18.50	**18.72**	18.88	**65.00**	0.44	**0.50**	0.56	0.50
13.00	14.00	**14.26**	14.38	**70.00**	0.81	**1.02**	1.00	1.00
8.75	10.00	**10.28**	10.38	**75.00**	1.81	**2.03**	2.00	1.94
6.25	6.63	**6.95**	7.00	**80.00**	3.38	**3.71**	3.63	3.50
3.75	4.13	**4.41**	4.38	**85.00**	5.88	**6.17**	6.25	6.25
2.25	2.44	**2.64**	2.50	**90.00**	9.25	**9.40**	9.63	9.25
1.13	1.25	**1.50**	1.44	**95.00**	13.13	**13.26**	13.50	13.75
0.88	0.63	**0.82**	0.81	**100.00**	17.38	**17.59**	17.75	23.00
0.50	0.25	**0.44**	0.38	**105.00**	22.00	**22.25**	22.50	0.00
0.50	0.13	**0.23**	0.25	**110.00**	26.88	**27.09**	27.38	0.00
0.25	0.06	**0.13**	0.19	**115.00**	31.75	**32.03**	32.25	0.00
0.13	0.00	**0.01**	0.13	**120.00**	36.75	**37.03**	37.25	49.25
0.13	0.00	**0.00**	0.13	**125.00**	41.75	**42.03**	42.25	0.00
0.00	0.00	**0.00**	0.13	**130.00**	46.75	**47.03**	47.25	0.00
				Oct00				
31.88	33.50	**33.73**	34.00	**50.00**	0.19	**0.29**	0.31	0.44
21.75	28.88	**29.05**	29.38	**55.00**	0.44	**0.56**	0.56	0.81
25.13	24.38	**24.57**	24.88	**60.00**	0.88	**1.04**	1.06	1.13
19.00	20.13	**20.37**	20.63	**65.00**	1.69	**1.82**	1.88	1.94
15.75	16.38	**16.54**	16.75	**70.00**	2.81	**2.96**	3.00	3.25
15.25	13.00	**13.16**	13.38	**75.00**	4.38	**4.53**	4.63	5.00
11.25	11.50	**11.65**	11.88	**77.50**	5.38	**5.53**	5.75	6.38
10.88	10.13	**10.26**	10.50	**80.00**	6.38	**6.63**	6.75	7.13
8.00	8.88	**8.99**	9.25	**82.50**	7.50	**7.84**	7.88	14.63
7.25	7.75	**7.85**	8.13	**85.00**	8.88	**9.21**	9.25	8.75
6.13	6.63	**6.82**	7.00	**87.50**	10.38	**10.64**	10.75	15.88
6.00	5.75	**5.90**	6.00	**90.00**	11.88	**12.24**	12.25	12.25
5.00	5.00	**5.09**	5.25	**92.50**	13.63	**13.92**	14.00	12.88
4.50	4.25	**4.37**	4.50	**95.00**	15.38	**15.70**	15.75	26.75
4.00	3.63	**3.74**	3.88	**97.50**	17.25	**17.57**	17.63	16.13
3.00	3.00	**3.19**	3.25	**100.00**	19.13	**19.52**	19.50	30.00
2.19	2.19	**2.30**	2.38	**105.00**	23.25	**23.65**	23.75	19.63
1.63	1.56	**1.64**	1.75	**110.00**	27.63	**28.01**	28.13	33.50
1.69	1.06	**1.16**	1.25	**115.00**	32.25	**32.58**	32.75	31.13
0.69	0.69	**0.82**	0.88	**120.00**	37.00	**37.29**	37.50	0.00
1.50	0.50	**0.57**	0.69	**125.00**	41.88	**42.13**	42.38	33.38
0.69	0.31	**0.40**	0.44	**130.00**	46.75	**47.04**	47.25	0.00

Using the prices of MNO options with the stock at 83, answer the following questions about the bear call spread.

1. What is the composition of the Sep 70/75 bear call spread?
2. What is the maximum profit of this position?
3. What is your potential for loss?
4. What is your break-even?
5. Graph the position.

CHOOSING WHAT VERTICAL TO TRADE

Now that we know the basics of each type of vertical spread, let's take a moment to determine when it may be appropriate to use these spreads. As stated previously, the vertical spread is best used in a situation where a moderate market move is expected. Most often, you use a vertical spread where at least one of the strikes is at-the-money or slightly in-the-money. It doesn't make much sense to put on the Sep 50/55 bull call spread where the underlying is at 32. Sure the spread will be inexpensive because it is so far OTM, but why not just buy the 50 call outright. The proceeds from the sale of the 55 call will be very small, thus not lowering your break-even point on the trade significantly. The stock must move up 23 points to get to 55. This means the stock must move up more than 60 percent in order for the spread to be worth 5. This doesn't take advantage of the 20 point run up on the stock. If this is the type of move you were expecting, there are much better ways to take advantage of it. For example, the Sep 30/40 call spread or the Sep 35/45 call spread.

The key point to take away from this example is that, in the case of debit spreads, you want to have the option you buy close to the current underlying price, and you want the option you sell nearest to where you believe the underlying will go. The exact opposite is true for the credit spreads. The option you buy should be where the stock is going to go, and the option you sell is closest to where the underlying is at the time the spread is put on.

So the next question is when do you use the debit spread and when do you use the credit spread? This usually turns out to be a matter of personal preference. The amount of risk versus reward should be considered the most, in accordance with where you think the underlying is going to go. It is important to remember that one significant advantage of options as a financial instrument is the leverage that they can provide. Verticals create the opportunity for profit while controlling financial risks that could prevent investors from entering trades. Of course, options always carry risk.

Consequently, vertical spreads should be viewed as strategies that correspond to common sense when addressing risk and reward. Rarely do you ever want to put on a debit spread where the cost is more than 50 percent of the total value of the spread. Rare indeed is the strategy that makes sense in which the amount risked is greater than the amount of potential reward. In other words, you infrequently want to pay 6.5 for the Sep 50/60 call spread. This means that you can lose 6.5 but only gain 3.5 (10 – 6.5). You seldom want to risk more than you can make.

In the same vein, you rarely want to sell a credit spread for less than half the spread value. For example, selling the Sep 30/35 call spread for 1.625 is not considered a good strategy under most circumstances. The most you can make here is the 1.625 you collected to initiate the spread, but you are risking the loss of 3.375 (5 – 1.625). This, once again, is not effectively using the options market.

When considering the use of a vertical spread, look at all the possible combinations. The most important thing to keep in mind is where you think the stock will go and by when. Once these two factors are determined, you can then decide what spread to incorporate to give yourself the maximum profit potential while risking the least amount of money. If you think the market is going to go up, determine how far you think it will go and when. First look at the call spreads that you could buy, or the put spreads that you could sell. Determine which spread best suits the risk/reward profile you are comfortable with and trade it.

The risk of verticals is limited and clearly defined, as is the potential reward. While the spread is on, track it. Watch how the option prices fluctuate with the movement of the underlying. Price your spread every day, along with some of the other spreads you considered putting on. The experience you gain from watching these spreads will be valuable in the future when determining other options strategies to put on in other stocks.

SUMMARY

	Composition	Break-even	Max Reward	Max Risk
Debit Spreads				
Bull Call Spread	Buy lower strike, sell higher strike	Lower strike plus debit	Difference in strikes minus debit	Debit
Bear Put Spread	Buy higher strike, sell lower strike	Higher strike minus debit	Difference in strikes minus debit	Debit
Credit Spreads				
Bull Put Spread	Buy lower strike, sell higher strike	Higher strike minus credit	Credit	Difference in strikes minus credit
Bear Call Spread	Buy higher strike, sell lower strike	Lower strike plus credit	Credit	Difference in strikes minus credit

CHAPTER 4 EXERCISE ANSWER KEYS

EXERCISE ONE

MNO Sep 85/90 Bull Call Spread

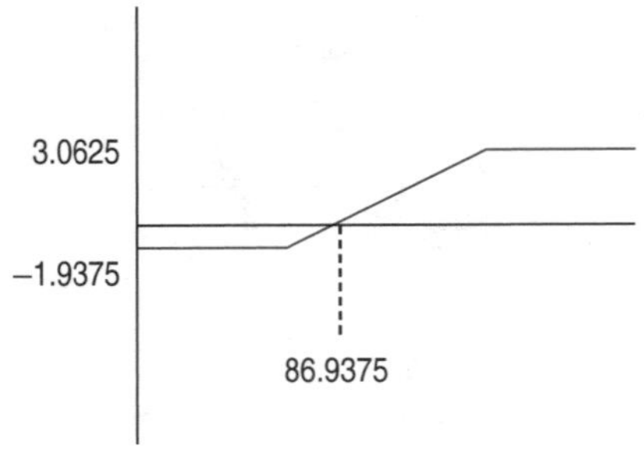

COMPOSITION: BUY SEP 85 call @ –$4.38
SELL SEP 90 call @ +$2.44
–$1.94

B/E: $86.9375 (price paid for spread [1.9375] + lower strike [85])

MAX LOSS: $1.9375 (price paid for spread)

MAX PROFIT: $3.0625 (difference between strikes [5] minus price paid for spread [1.9375])

EXERCISE TWO

MNO Oct 75/80 Bear Put Spread

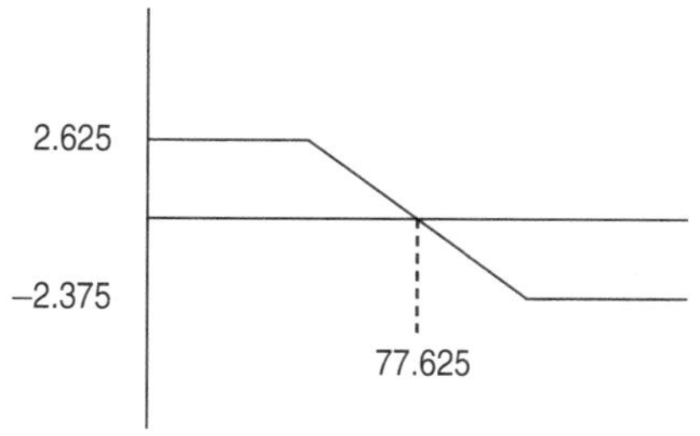

COMPOSITION: BUY OCT 80 put @ –$6.75
SELL OCT 75 put @ +$4.38
–$2.37

B/E: $77.625 (upper strike minus cost of spread)
MAX LOSS: $2.375 (amount paid for spread)
MAX PROFIT: $2.625 difference between strikes [5] minus the cost of spread [2.375])

EXERCISE THREE

MNO Oct 85/90 Bull Put Spread

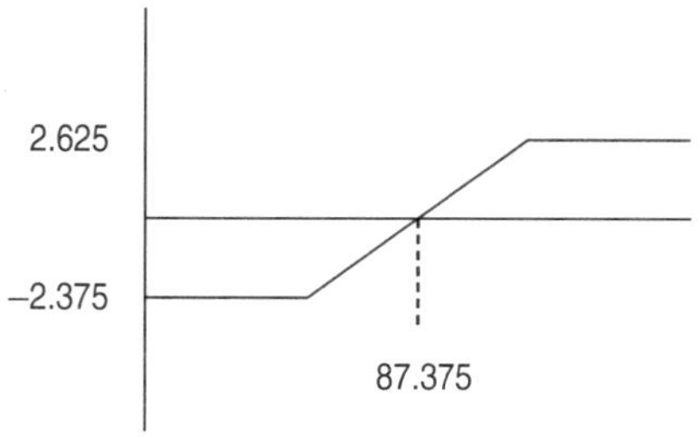

COMPOSITION: SELL OCT 90 put @ +$11.88
BUY OCT 85 put @ –$ 9.25
$ 2.63

B/E: $87.375 (upper strike [90] minus credit [2.625])
MAX LOSS: $2.375 (difference between strikes [5] minus credit 2.625)
MAX PROFIT: $2.625 (amount of credit you took in)

EXERCISE FOUR

MNO Sept 70/75 Bear Call Spread

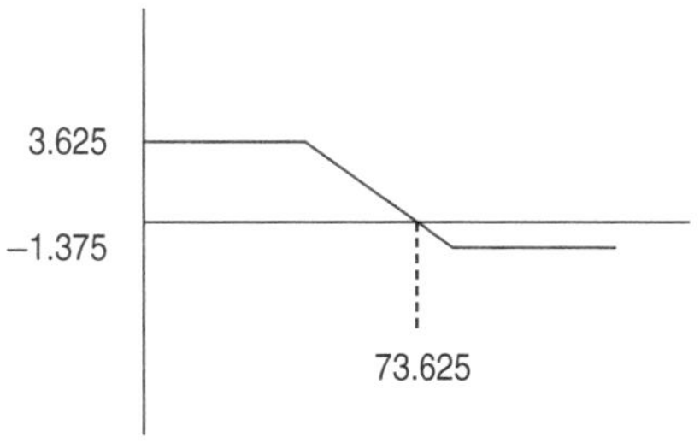

COMPOSITION:	SELL SEP 70 call @	$14.00
	BUY SEP 75 call @	–$10.38
		$ 3.62
B/E:	$73.625 (lower strike [70] plus credit 3.625)	
MAX LOSS:	$1.375 (difference between strikes [5] minus credit [3.625])	
MAX PROFIT:	$3.625	

CHAPTER FOUR QUIZ

If you sold a Dec 35 put for $0.75 and purchased a Dec 45 put for $3.375:

1. Did you buy or sell the spread?
2. At what price?
3. Is this spread bullish or bearish?
4. What is your maximum profit?
5. What is your break-even point?

Given the following market prices: March 520 call @ 8.625, March 540 call @ 2.50, construct a bearish call vertical spread and answer the following questions:

6. Did you buy or sell the spread?
7. At what price?
8. What is your maximum profit?
9. What is your maximum loss?
10. What is your break-even?

The underlying is trading at 117. The Sep 115 call is trading at 5.13 with a delta of 60. The Sep 120 call is trading at 2.63 with a delta of 39.

11. What is the delta of the Sep 115/120 vertical call spread?
12. Where should the Sep 115/120 put spread be trading?

13. What are the individual deltas for the 115 and 120 puts?

14. What is the delta of the Sep 115/120 put spread?

CHAPTER FOUR QUIZ ANSWER KEY

1. Buy
2. 3.375 – .75 = 2.625
3. Bearish
4. 7.375 (10 – 2.625)
5. 42.375
6. Sell
7. 8.625 – 2.5 = 6.125
8. 6.125 (what you sold it for)
9. 13.875 (20 – 6.125)
10. 526.125
11. 21
12. 2.50
13. 115 is –40
    120 is –61
14. 21

CHAPTER 5

Nondirection Dependent Strategies

Straddles and Strangles

CONCEPT REVIEW

Delta: Measures the sensitivity (rate of change) of the option's theoretical value relative to a 1-point move in the underlying asset.

Long straddle: Purchasing a call and a put having the same underlying, same expiration, and same strike prices.

Short straddle: Selling a call and a put having the same underlying, same expiration, and same strike price.

Long strangle: Purchasing an OTM call and an OTM put having the same underlying and same expiration.

Short strangle: Selling an OTM call and an OTM put having the same underlying and same expiration, but different strike prices.

"K": Abbreviation for strike price or exercise price.

Reminder: All prices should be considered having a multiplier of 100 because each option contract is actually worth 100 shares of stock

Straddles and strangles are nondirection dependent option strategies. They are capable of being profitable regardless of the direction the underlying moves; and depending on which side you're on (long or short), profitability may not depend on a move at all. If constructed in a theoretically sound manner, both straddles and strangles will have deltas that approach zero. If you think of delta as the "chance or probability of the option expiring in-the-money," it makes it easier to understand how an at-the-money straddle or equidistant strangle both have a delta close to zero, or a 50/50 chance of ending up in-the-money. Straddles and strangles are by no means, though, a neutral or flat strategy to "walk away from." Both can be expensive if not extremely risky—if neglected. We'll try to show how you can choose the right strategy for your investment needs.

Keep in mind that calls have positive deltas and puts have negative deltas. Therefore, the idea behind trading classic straddles and strangles is to keep your position delta neutral (selling or buying the same number of calls and puts).

Reminder:	long calls = long delta	long put = short delta
	short calls = short delta	short put = long delta

Stock always has a delta of 100.

Out-of-the-money options have lower deltas because they have less of a chance of expiring in-the-money.

At-the-money options have approximately a 50/50 chance of expiring in-the-money.

In-the-money options have the highest deltas as they have the greatest chance of expiring in-the-money (because they are already partially to that goal).

Long straddles and long strangles are similar in their risk/reward approach in that both have limited risk and unlimited reward potential. Short straddles and short strangles share the trader's desire for the underlying to remain stable because trading these from the short side is profitable when little or no movement occurs.

First we will look at long and short straddles and then at long and short strangles.

STRADDLES

When you think of straddles, think in terms of straddling a low fence, where one leg is on each side of the fence. Before you're off and running, you must decide which direction is best. With an options straddle strategy, you must make the same decision once the underlying begins to move.

A market in which the trader expects the underlying to move sharply in either direction may present a perfect situation in which to have a long straddle position. As will be explained in further detail, a long straddle involves purchasing a call and put with the same strike and same expiration. Adequate time prior to expiration is typically required—say one month—to allow time for the market to move considerably.

But a straddle with only days to go until expiration can also be quite profitable. It is just that these short-dated straddles carry much more risk, a higher requirement for being correct in your market assessment, and less time to react. This amount of time is commensurate with the investment you will have to risk, and thus the expected amount the stock will have to move for the position to be profitable.

Long Straddle

Composition: Long call at K_1
Long put at K_1

Max Profit: Unlimited to the upside; limited by price of stock to the downside

Max Loss: Debit incurred to buy straddle

Break-even Points: Downside: K_1 – Debit; upside: K_1 + Debit

Example: Long 1 DJX (Dow Jones Index) Dec 80 Call at $3.625 (delta = +50)
Long 1 DJX Dec 80 Put at $2.50 (delta = –50)
= Long DJX Dec 80 Straddle at 6.125

Delta: Long call = positive deltas (+50)
Long put = negative deltas (–50)
0 deltas (deltas cancel each other out, assuming the underlying is at the strike)
Note: The straddle will have a long or short net delta if constructed away from the strike.

As the graph illustrates, you would purchase the straddle for $6.125 ($3.625—the price of the Dec 80 call, + $2.50—the price of the Dec 80 put). Your two break-even points would be $86.125 and $73.875. Because your cash outlay for this position is $6.125, you know your risk is limited to this amount, thus the break-even points are found at the straddle strike plus and minus this outlay.

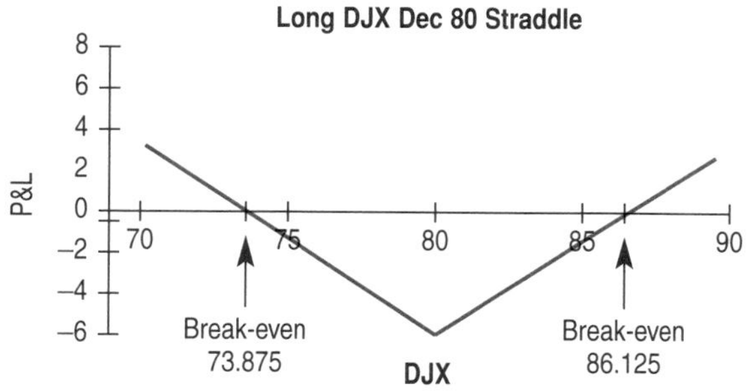

Let's look at the profit & loss (P&L) scenarios based on different underlying closing prices at expiration:

DJX at $89	
Long 1 DJX Dec 80 ITM call at $9.00	
Long 1 DJX Dec 80 put is worthless	
= Long DJX Dec 80 straddle at	$9.00
Less cost of the straddle	$6.125
Profit	$2.875

DJX at $69	
Long 1 DJX Dec 80 call is worthless	
Long 1 DJX Dec 80 ITM put at	$11.00
= Long DJX Dec 80 straddle at	$11.00
Less cost of the straddle	$ 6.125
Profit	$ 4.875

If your expectation of DJX price change is wrong and the underlying only moves to 81, then your actual loss is only $5.125, as you would be able to exercise your in-the-money Dec 80 call and take in $1.00. If the stock fell to 75, your loss would be only $1.125 as you could exercise your long Dec 80 in-the-money put and take in $5.00, netting you a loss of only $1.125 ($6.125 total cash outlay minus the $5.00 you received by exercising the put).

EXERCISE ONE

Let's walk through an example of how to buy a straddle using the QRx Market Window showing the option chain for OPQ stock. Currently there are 28 days left in the September cycle and you are long the September 75 straddle. Answer the following questions:

Bid	Theo	Ask	Strike	Bid	Theo	Ask
76.88	**76.91**	76.94	**OPQ**			
			Sep00			
36.88	**37.07**	37.88	**40.00**	0.06	**0.00**	0.19
34.50	**34.58**	35.50	**42.50**	0.06	**0.00**	0.25
32.13	**32.09**	33.13	**45.00**	0.13	**0.00**	0.31
29.75	**29.60**	30.75	**47.50**	0.25	**0.00**	0.44
27.38	**27.11**	28.38	**50.00**	0.31	**0.00**	0.50
22.88	**22.13**	23.88	**55.00**	0.81	**0.00**	1.00
18.75	**17.20**	19.50	**60.00**	1.38	**0.05**	1.63
14.75	**12.45**	15.50	**65.00**	2.38	**0.28**	2.75
11.25	**8.21**	12.00	**70.00**	3.75	**1.02**	4.13
8.50	**4.84**	8.88	**75.00**	5.75	**2.64**	6.25
5.88	**2.53**	6.38	**80.00**	8.25	**5.34**	8.75
4.00	**1.16**	4.50	**85.00**	11.38	**8.99**	11.88
2.56	**0.47**	3.00	**90.00**	14.75	**13.34**	15.50
1.69	**0.17**	1.94	**95.00**	18.75	**18.11**	19.50
0.88	**0.05**	1.13	**100.00**	23.13	**23.09**	24.00
0.44	**0.01**	0.69	**105.00**	27.75	**28.09**	28.63
0.25	**0.00**	0.44	**110.00**	32.75	**33.09**	33.63
			Dec00			
34.00	**32.82**	35.00	**45.00**	1.13	**0.13**	1.38
29.88	**28.14**	30.88	**50.00**	1.88	**0.37**	2.13
25.88	**23.71**	26.88	**55.00**	2.81	**0.86**	3.13
22.25	**19.64**	23.25	**60.00**	4.00	**1.70**	4.38
19.00	**15.93**	19.75	**65.00**	5.38	**2.93**	5.88
15.88	**12.75**	16.88	**70.00**	7.38	**4.68**	7.88
13.13	**10.04**	13.88	**75.00**	9.50	**6.92**	10.00
10.88	**7.77**	11.38	**80.00**	11.88	**9.63**	12.63
8.75	**5.93**	9.25	**85.00**	14.75	**12.77**	15.50
6.88	**4.48**	7.38	**90.00**	17.88	**16.32**	18.63
5.38	**3.34**	5.88	**95.00**	21.25	**20.21**	22.25
4.25	**2.48**	4.63	**100.00**	25.13	**24.40**	26.13

1. What would the P&L graph of this position at expiration look like?
2. What would it cost to purchase the Sep 75 straddle if you paid market price?
3. What would be the break-even points of your position?
4. What is your profit or loss if OPQ rallies to $95?
5. What is your profit or loss if OPQ stock moves to only $87?
6. What is your profit or loss if OPQ falls to $55?

Short Straddle

Trading a straddle from the short side requires a completely different mind-set. Whereas the long straddle can bring unlimited profits and has a defined risk characteristic, taking the opposite side of the trade will obviously bring the opposite risk/reward profile to your position. This will require more monitoring of the short position, as the risk will be greater than for the long straddle trader.

As you would imagine, everything that works for the long straddle works against the short straddle. The premium you collect is the maximum profit you can make. A close of the stock right on the strike at expiration will mean taking home the maximum profit. You would prefer little or no movement in the underlying during your holding; yet profits can be made with "round-trips" in the underlying that come back to where you started. (This only costs you gray hair.)

Here is the makeup of the short side of the straddle trade:

Composition: Short call at K_1
Short put at K_1

Max Profit: Credit received from sale of straddle

Max Loss: Unlimited to the upside, substantial on the downside to zero, minus the credit received

Break-even Points: K_1 – Credit; K_1 + Credit

Example: Short 1 NDX (Nasdaq 100) Oct 1140 call at $15 (–) +50 deltas = –50 deltas

Short 1 NDX Oct 1140 put at $15.50 (–) –50 deltas = +50 deltas = Short NDX Oct 1140 straddle at $30.50

Delta: short call = negative deltas (–50)

short put = positive deltas (+50)

0 deltas (deltas cancel each other out, assuming the underlying is at the strike)

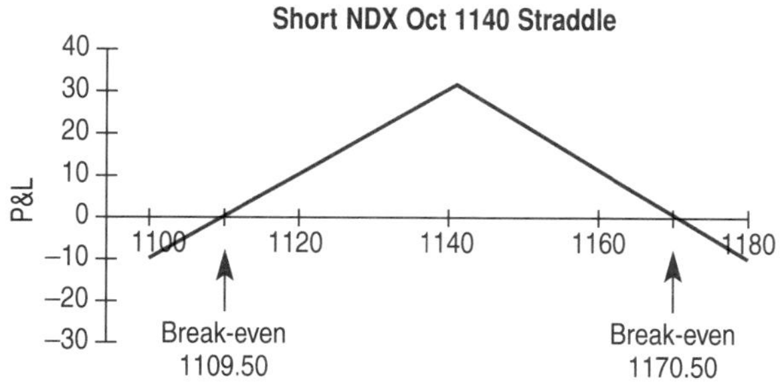

As the graph illustrates, by selling the NDX Oct 1140 straddle, you could realize a maximum profit of $30.50 (the price of the call—$15 + price of the put— $15.50), which is the amount for which you sold the straddle. Your two break-even points would be 1109.50 to the downside and 1170.50 on the upside (straddle strike of 1140 – $30.50 and straddle strike of 1140 + $30.50, respectively).

You would have unlimited risk to the upside above 1170.50 and unlimited risk to the downside below 1109.50. As it is the opposite of the long straddle (where you want the stock to make a big move in either direction), with the short straddle, you want the stock to sit still, staying as close to the 1140 strike as possible.

Consider your profit or loss if the index rallies to 1160 and 1190. If the index moves to 1160 at expiration, your net profit would be reduced to $10.50 ($30.50 – $20 = $10.50) because the call you are short would be exercised at 1160, resulting in a loss of $20.00. The put would simply expire worthless. If the index ends up at 1190 at expiration, you would experience a net loss of $19.50. Your upside break-even is 1170.50 (1140 + $30.50); therefore the difference at 1190 is $19.50.

Anywhere the index rallies over 1140, your short call goes in-the-money and you start giving up the premium you took in for the sale all the way up to 1170.50. At 1190, you not only have given up the entire premium you took in ($30.50), but also you would have an additional loss of $19.50 per straddle.

EXERCISE TWO

Let's step through an example of selling a straddle in a low-priced stock. Again we'll refer to the QRx Market Window that displays the prices, this time those of TUV stock. You are short the January 7.5 straddle. Answer the following questions:

Bid	Theo	Ask	Strike	Bid	Theo	Ask
5.81	**6.84**	5.88	**TUV**			
			Oct00			
1.19	**1.20**	1.44	**5.00**	0.19	**0.30**	0.38
0.25	**0.15**	0.31	**7.50**	1.75	**1.75**	1.94
0.00	**0.02**	0.13	**10.00**	4.00	**4.16**	4.25
			Jan01			
1.44	**1.50**	1.63	**5.00**	0.44	**0.52**	0.69
0.50	**0.51**	0.69	**7.50**	1.88	**2.00**	2.13
0.13	**0.18**	0.31	**10.00**	4.00	**4.20**	4.38
0.00	**0.01**	0.25	**12.50**	6.38	**6.66**	6.88
0.00	**0.00**	0.25	**15.00**	8.88	**9.16**	9.38

1. What would the P&L graph of this position look like?

2. How much would you receive for selling the TUV January 7.5 straddle, assuming market prices?

3. What would be the break-even points of your position?

4. What is your profit or loss if TUV stock rallies to $11 at expiration?

5. What is your profit or loss if TUV stock moves to $6 at expiration?

6. What is your profit or loss if TUV falls to $4 at expiration?

STRANGLE

When you hear the term *strangle,* you probably imagine a person's hands around someone's throat (certainly not a politically correct image). In this case, focus on the "around" portion of that thought. The distance between the two strike prices is the critical aspect of a strangle.

A long strangle is similar to a straddle in that it is not dependent on a certain directional move in the underlying. For the strategy to be profitable, an extreme move in the underlying either up or down is necessary. The composition of the strangle strategy is also similar to a straddle, in that it is composed of a put and a call, and you either buy or sell both options with the same expiration. The major difference between the strangle and the straddle is that with the strangle you are buying or selling options with different strike prices.

A long strangle is composed of the purchase of the same number of calls and puts that have the same expirations. A short strangle requires the sale of the same number of calls and puts that have the same expirations. The short strangle is used to attempt to take advantage of an underlying that is about to experience very low volatility. A short strangle is usually established by selling both an out-of-the-money put and an out-of-the-money call, with the stock approximately centered between the two strike prices. It is preferable in these strategies that when taking a position, it is timed with the expectation of a reverse in the volatility of the underlying.

The long strangle is best suited for a market that is about to experience very high volatility, as an extreme swing in the price of the underlying is necessary for the long strangle to be profitable. (The short strangle gives the trader a price range within which his or her position is comfortably profitable.)

The risk/reward aspects of the long strangle are similar to those of the long straddle in that it offers limited risk and unlimited return. The risk/reward aspects of the short strangle are similar to those of the short straddle in that it offers limited returns and unlimited risk. First, let's take a look at the long strangle.

Long Strangle

Composition: Long call at K_2 and long put at K_1

Max Profit: Unlimited to the upside, limited by the price of the stock to the downside.

Max Loss: Debit

Break-even Points: K_1 – Debit; K_2 + Debit

Example: Long 1 YZA Oct 110 put at $6.125
Long 1 YZA Oct 185 call at $6.50
= Long YZA Oct 110/185 strangle at $12.625

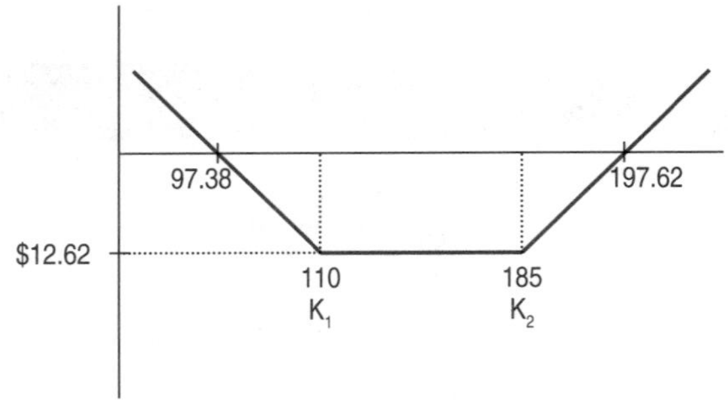

As the P&L graph of the YZA strangle illustrates, the price of the Oct 110 put is $6.125 and the price of the Oct 185 call is $6.50, therefore you would purchase the YZA Oct 110/185 strangle for a net debit of $12.625 (or $1,262.50 for a one-lot spread). As with all long option positions, you know your maximum risk is the amount you paid for the position.

The determination of the break-even points of the strangle is done in the same manner as with the straddle. For the put, you simply subtract the amount you paid for the entire position ($12.625) from the strike price of the put ($110) to determine that your break-even on the downside is $97.375. Your break-even for the upside is $197.625. Here you would add the $12.625 of premium to the call's $185 strike.

Let's say at expiration YZA ended up at $119. This would mean that your loss would be the entire $12.625 (or $1,262.50) of premium that you paid for the position. Because at $119 the long call would be out-of-the-money and the long put also would be out-of-the-money, both would be worthless. You were looking to take advantage of a severe move in YZA blowing through one of your break-even points, but instead it sat still right in between your two strikes.

Let's look at another scenario. What if the YZA price rallied and at expiration was at $209—exactly the move you were hoping to take advantage of? What would your profit be? $11.375 (or $1,137.50) would be your net profit.

Let's break down the example given above to see where the profit comes from. First, at $209, the long put would expire worthless. The Oct 185 call, however, would be ITM by 24 points. Therefore, your net profit would be $11.375 (or $1,137.50) ($24.00 – $12.625 cost of the position × 100).

EXERCISE THREE

By answering the following questions, you can see where your points of concern are in the example of buying a strangle. We'll again refer to the market window showing the prices of YZA. You are long the YZA Oct 90/210 strangle. Answer the following questions:

1. What would the P&L graph of this position look like?

2. What would it cost to purchase the YZA Oct 90/210 strangle?

3. What would be the break-even points of your position?

4. What is your profit or loss if YZA stock rallies to $225?

5. What is your profit or loss if YZA stock moves to only $212?

6. What is your profit or loss if YZA falls to $75?

Bid	Theo	Ask	Strike	Bid	Theo	Ask
139.00	**139.03**	139.06	**YZA**			
			Oct00			
65.88	**65.14**	66.50	**75.00**	1.06	**0.27**	1.25
61.25	**60.35**	61.88	**80.00**	1.25	**0.45**	1.44
56.75	**55.65**	57.38	**85.00**	1.63	**0.70**	1.81
52.50	**51.06**	53.13	**90.00**	2.19	**1.05**	2.44
48.38	**46.63**	49.00	**95.00**	3.00	**1.57**	3.38
44.38	**42.31**	45.00	**100.00**	3.75	**2.21**	4.13
39.88	**38.20**	40.63	**105.00**	4.50	**3.05**	4.88
36.38	**34.27**	37.13	**110.00**	5.75	**4.06**	6.13
32.75	**30.61**	33.50	**115.00**	7.13	**5.36**	7.50
29.63	**27.20**	30.38	**120.00**	8.88	**6.91**	9.13
26.50	**23.98**	27.25	**125.00**	10.75	**8.66**	11.25
23.75	**21.08**	24.50	**130.00**	12.75	**10.71**	13.25
21.00	**18.46**	21.75	**135.00**	15.13	**13.07**	15.63
18.75	**16.03**	19.25	**140.00**	17.75	**15.62**	18.25
16.75	**13.91**	17.25	**145.00**	20.50	**18.46**	21.25
14.75	**12.01**	15.25	**150.00**	23.38	**21.55**	24.13
13.25	**10.27**	13.88	**155.00**	27.00	**24.80**	27.63
11.75	**8.86**	12.00	**160.00**	30.38	**28.38**	31.00
10.13	**7.49**	10.75	**165.00**	33.88	**32.03**	34.50
9.13	**6.41**	9.25	**170.00**	37.75	**35.95**	38.38
8.00	**5.42**	8.38	**175.00**	41.63	**39.98**	42.25
6.88	**4.61**	7.25	**180.00**	45.50	**44.18**	46.13
6.13	**3.84**	6.50	**185.00**	49.75	**48.45**	50.38
5.38	**3.24**	5.75	**190.00**	54.00	**52.88**	54.63
4.63	**2.71**	5.00	**195.00**	58.25	**57.40**	58.88
4.13	**2.29**	4.50	**200.00**	62.88	**62.02**	63.50
3.38	**1.57**	3.75	**210.00**	71.88	**71.44**	72.88
2.44	**1.09**	2.81	**220.00**	81.13	**81.13**	82.13
1.88	**0.72**	2.13	**230.00**	90.75	**90.97**	91.75
1.44	**0.49**	1.69	**240.00**	100.50	**100.97**	101.50
1.06	**0.35**	1.31	**250.00**	110.50	**110.97**	111.50
0.81	**0.23**	1.06	**260.00**	120.50	**120.97**	121.50
0.63	**0.16**	0.88	**270.00**	130.50	**130.97**	131.50

Short Strangle

Just as the short straddle posed a problem for the trader if the stock suddenly made a move out of a price range, so too will the short strangle cause a sleepless night or two.

Composition: Short call at K_2 and Short put at K_1 (same expiration)

Max Profit: Credit received from sale of strangle

Max Loss: Unlimited on the upside; substantial on the downside

Break-even Points: K_1 – Credit; K_2 + Credit

Example: Short 1 SPX (S&P 500) Nov 950 put at $16.625
Short 1 SPX Nov 980 call at $20
= Short SPX Nov 950/980 strangle at $36.625

As the P&L graph of the SPX index options illustrates, the price of Nov 950 put is $16.625 and the price of the Nov 980 call is $20.00, therefore you would collect

Short SPX Nov 950/980 Straddle

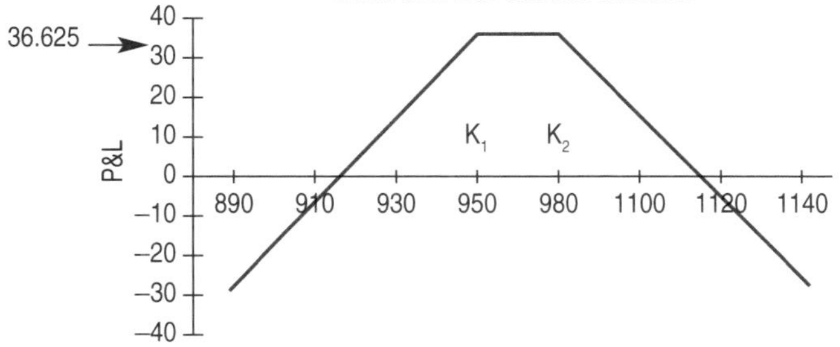

Bid	Ask	Strike	Bid	Ask
90.63	90.94	**UVW**		
52.25	54.50	**40.00**	1.75	2.25
51.25	53.50	**41.25**	1.94	2.44
50.25	52.50	**42.50**	2.00	2.94
49.13	51.38	**43.75**	2.19	3.13
48.25	50.50	**45.00**	2.44	3.38
47.13	49.38	**46.25**	2.56	3.50
46.13	48.38	**47.50**	2.81	3.75
45.13	47.38	**48.75**	3.00	4.00
44.25	46.50	**50.00**	3.38	3.75
42.50	44.75	**52.50**	4.00	5.00
40.63	42.88	**55.00**	4.50	5.50
38.88	41.13	**57.50**	5.13	6.63
37.25	39.50	**60.00**	5.88	7.38
35.63	37.88	**62.50**	6.63	8.13
34.00	36.25	**65.00**	7.50	9.00
32.38	34.63	**67.50**	8.38	9.88
31.00	33.25	**70.00**	9.38	10.63
29.63	31.88	**72.50**	10.13	12.13
28.25	30.50	**75.00**	11.00	13.00
26.88	29.13	**77.50**	12.13	14.13
25.75	28.00	**80.00**	13.38	15.38
24.63	26.88	**82.50**	14.75	16.75
23.50	25.75	**85.00**	16.13	18.13
22.25	24.50	**87.50**	17.38	19.38
21.25	23.50	**90.00**	18.75	20.75
20.13	22.38	**92.50**	20.13	22.38
19.50	21.50	**95.00**	21.63	23.88
18.50	20.50	**97.50**	23.13	25.38
17.63	19.63	**100.00**	24.75	27.00
16.75	18.75	**102.50**	26.38	28.63
15.75	17.75	**105.00**	27.88	30.13
15.13	17.13	**107.50**	29.63	31.88
14.50	16.50	**110.00**	31.50	33.75
13.88	15.88	**112.50**	33.63	35.88
13.13	15.13	**115.00**	35.38	37.63
12.38	14.38	**117.50**	37.25	39.50
11.75	13.75	**120.00**	39.13	41.38
11.25	13.25	**122.50**	41.00	43.25
10.75	12.75	**125.00**	43.00	45.25
10.00	11.50	**130.00**	47.00	49.25
9.13	10.63	**135.00**	51.13	53.38
8.25	9.75	**140.00**	55.13	57.38
7.50	9.00	**145.00**	59.38	61.63
6.88	8.38	**150.00**	63.75	66.00
6.25	7.75	**155.00**	68.13	70.38
5.50	7.00	**160.00**	72.50	74.75
5.13	6.63	**165.00**	77.00	79.25

$36.625 for the sale of the SPX Nov 950/980 strangle (or $3,662.50 for a one-lot spread). In this example, you know your maximum reward is the amount you received for selling the position. Opposite of the long strangle, the short strangle is a position that requires the underlying market to remain between the two short strike prices for maximum profit.

The determination of the break-even points of the position is done in the same manner as with the short straddle. For the put, you simply subtract the amount you received for the entire position ($36.625) from the strike price of the put (950) to determine that your break-even on the downside is $913.375. Your break-even for the upside is $1,016.625. Here you would add the $36.625 premium you collected to the call's 980 strike.

Let's step through the example of a short UVW Nov 70/110 strangle. There are 90 days until expiry. Note the QRx Market Window with the UVW option chain.

Because you are short the strangle, your maximum profit is the amount you collected when you sold the position. In this case, selling on the bids, you would take in a premium of $23.875 (price of the Nov 110 call is $14.50 and price of the Nov 70 put is $9.375). This is a reasonable amount to collect, it seems, as the stock would have to move more than 49 percent before there was risk of exposure to loss of the premium collected.

Your break-even for the upside is $133.875 ($110 + $23.875). Your break-even for the put is $46.125 ($70 – $23.875). As with the short straddle, you have unlimited risk exposure to the upside and extreme exposure to the downside. Anywhere the market rallies above $110, you begin giving back some of the premium you initially took in for the sale of the strangle.

At $133.875, your break-even, you have given back all of your premium and begin experiencing a loss on the next uptick. You would be assigned on your short call and would be required to buy the underlying at the market price to make delivery on it. Anywhere below $70, your short put goes ITM, and you begin giving up the premium that you initially took in for the sale of the put, all the way down to $46.125. Anywhere below this figure and you begin experiencing a loss.

If the stock ends up at $110 (a 21 percent move) at expiration, both options expire worthless and you get to keep the entire premium you collected when you sold the strangle. In fact, this would be true if the stock lands anywhere between $70 and $110 at expiration.

EXERCISE FOUR

Let's perform the same analysis as in Exercise Three with an example of selling a strangle. We'll refer to the market window for prices in EFG stock options. You are short the Oct 120/200 strangle. Answer the following questions:

Bid	Ask	Strike	Bid	Ask
160.13	160.38	**EFG**		
		Oct00		
82.50	83.50	**80.00**	1.25	1.50
78.00	79.00	**85.00**	1.63	1.88
73.63	74.63	**90.00**	2.13	2.50
69.50	70.50	**95.00**	3.00	3.38
65.25	66.25	**100.00**	3.63	4.00
61.38	62.38	**105.00**	4.75	5.13
57.63	58.63	**110.00**	5.75	6.25
54.00	55.00	**115.00**	7.13	7.63
50.13	51.13	**120.00**	9.13	9.25
46.63	47.63	**125.00**	10.00	10.50
43.38	44.38	**130.00**	11.63	12.38
40.63	41.63	**135.00**	13.50	14.25
37.75	38.75	**140.00**	15.63	16.38
34.88	35.88	**145.00**	17.75	18.50
32.50	33.50	**150.00**	20.13	21.13
30.13	31.13	**155.00**	22.63	23.63
27.88	28.88	**160.00**	25.25	26.25
25.88	26.88	**165.00**	28.25	29.25
24.00	25.00	**170.00**	31.25	32.25
21.63	22.63	**175.00**	34.00	35.00
20.00	20.75	**180.00**	37.13	38.13
18.25	19.00	**185.00**	40.50	41.50
16.25	17.00	**190.00**	43.38	44.38
14.75	15.50	**195.00**	46.88	47.88
13.63	14.38	**200.00**	50.75	51.75

1. What would the P&L graph of this position look like?

2. For how much could you sell the EFG Oct 120/200 strangle?

3. What would be the points of break-even of the position?

4. What is your profit or loss if EFG rallies to $195?

5. What is your profit or loss if EFG stock moves to $207 at expiration?

6. What is your profit or loss if at expiration EFG falls to $95?

ANSWERS TO EXERCISES

EXERCISE ONE:

1.

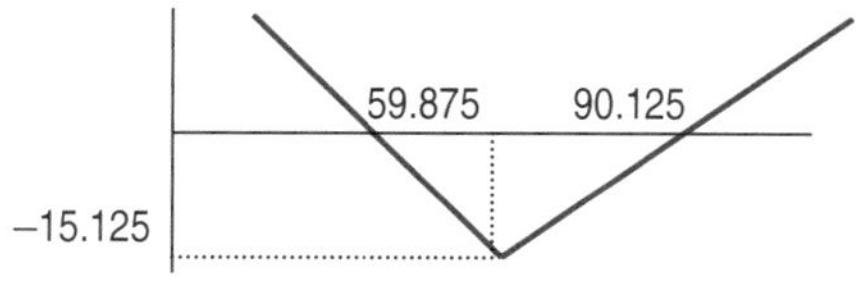

2. If the price of the 75 call is $8.875 and the price of the 75 put is $6.25, then your total cash outlay to purchase the 75 straddle is $15.125.

3. The break-even points would be $59.875 and $90.125. To determine the B/E for the call, simply add the price of the straddle to the 75 strike ($75 + $15.125 = $90.125). To determine the B/E for the put, simply subtract the price of the straddle from the 75 strike ($75 – $15.125 = $59.875).

4. If the stock rallies to $95, your profit will be $4.875. Your put is worthless, and the 75 call is ITM by $20. Therefore, you subtract the $15.125 (amount you paid for straddle) from the $20, thus netting you a profit of $4.875.

5. If the stock moves to $87, your position experiences a loss of $3.125. Although your long put is worthless at 87, you have at least reduced your loss by $12.00. To explain further, your long 75 put is OTM at 87, and thus has no value. However, your 75 call is ITM by $12.00. Therefore, your initial cash outlay of $15.125, less the $12.00 you would make by exercising the 75 call (or selling at parity the last trading day), gives you a total net loss of $3.125.

6. Your profit is $4.875. The 75 call expires worthless, however, the put is ITM by $20. Subtract the initial debit of $15.125 (amount you paid for the straddle) and you are left with a profit of $4.875.

EXERCISE TWO:

1.

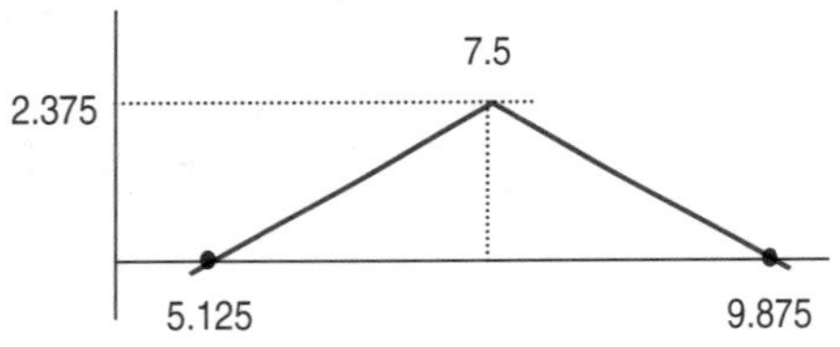

2. $2.375. The price of the call is $0.50 (selling on the bid) and the price of the put is $1.875 (selling on the bid).

3. Break-even on the upside would be $9.875 ($7.5 + $2.375). Break-even on the downside would be $5.125 ($7.5 – $2.375). Therefore, if the stock ends up anywhere between $5.125 and $9.875 at expiration, you would realize a profit.

4. You would experience a loss of $1.125. Because your short call would be ITM by $3.50, you would lose all of the premium that you originally took in when you sold the straddle ($2.375), plus the additional $1.125 that it would cost you to purchase that call and deliver the stock at $11.

5. If the stock moves to $6, you have a net profit of $0.875 ($2.375 – $1.50). At $6, your short 7.5 put is ITM by $1.50, therefore you give up $1.50 of your original $2.375 of premium you took in when you sold the straddle.

6. Your position would lose $1.125. Because the 7.5 put you sold will be ITM by $3.50, you give up all of the credit you collected when you sold the straddle and $1.125 additionally to cover the difference ($3.50 – $2.375).

EXERCISE THREE

1.

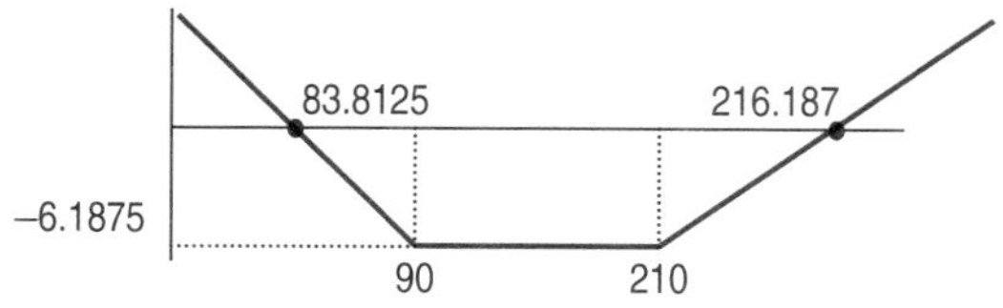

2. $6.1875 (or $618.75 per strangle)
   Cost of the 210 call = $3.75
   Cost of the 90 put = $2.4375
   $6.1875

3. Break-even on the upside is $216.1875 (210 strike plus the $6.1875 premium paid out for purchase of the position). Break-even on the downside is $83.8125 (90 strike minus the $6.1875 premium paid out for purchase of the position).

4. If the stocks rallies to $225 at expiration, your long call would be ITM by 15 points, thus netting you a profit of $8.8125 ($15 minus the $6.1875 premium).

5. If at expiration YZA ends up at $212, you would experience a loss of $4.1875. Your 90 put would be OTM (worthless) and your 210 call would be in-the-money by $2.

6. At $75, your call is far OTM, but your put is now ITM by $15. Therefore, your net profit would be $8.8125. (15 points ITM less the $6.1875 you paid for the position).

EXERCISE FOUR

1.

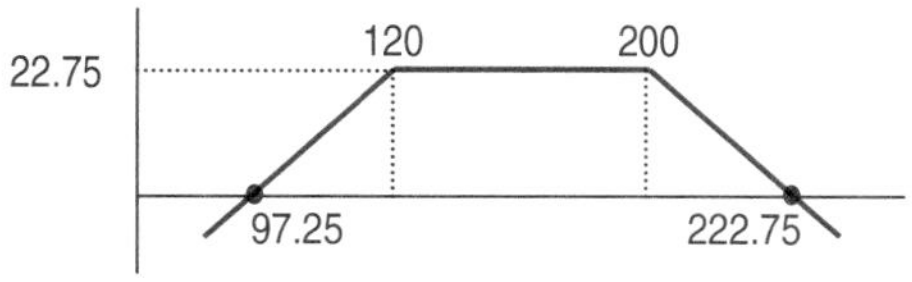

2. $22.75 ($2,275)
   Sell the 200 call for $13.625
   Sell the 120 put for $ 9.125
   $22.75

3. Upside break-even is $222.75 (200 + 22.75); downside break-even is $97.25 ($120 – $22.75).

4. At 195, your short put is OTM, as is your short call. Therefore, you retain the entire $22.75 ($2,275) premium you received for selling the strangle.

5. At 207, your short 120 put expires worthless, and the short 200 call finishes $7 ITM; therefore, you retain the $22.75 less the $7 for a profit of $15.75 ($1,575).

6. At $95 you will experience a loss of $2.25, or $225 per strangle sold, as your downside is covered only down to $97.25.

REVIEW QUIZ

1. Using the following strike prices: 120, 125, and 130, give an example of a long straddle and a long strangle.

2. Sell the straddle and buy the strangle using the following prices. Specify which calls you would buy or sell, and which puts you would buy or sell.

Call Price	Strike Price	Put Price
$8.25	$60	$ .1875
3.6875	65	.5625
1	70	2.75

3. Graph: long ITI Jan 60 straddle

4. What is your maximum profit from the long ITI Jan 60 straddle?

5. Graph: short ITI Mar 620/640 strangle

6. What are the break-even points?

7. A highly volatile market with the chance or probability to make a very large move, assuming there is more than 30 days until expiration, is a good candidate for a short strangle. True or false?

8. A strategy that requires buying the same number of at-the-money calls and puts, having the same expiration date, is a what?

9. To determine the upside break-even for the long straddle, you add the strike price to the net debit. True or false?

REVIEW QUIZ ANSWER KEY

1. Straddle: buy 125 call, buy 125 put, or buy 120 call and buy 120 put
   Strangle: buy 130 call, buy 120 put (OTM calls and puts)

2. Sell 65 call, sell 65 put
   Buy 70 call, buy 60 put

3. 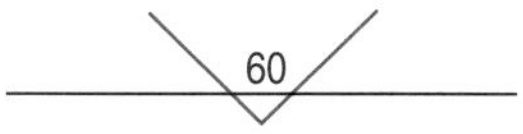

4. Unlimited to the upside, substantial to the downside

5. 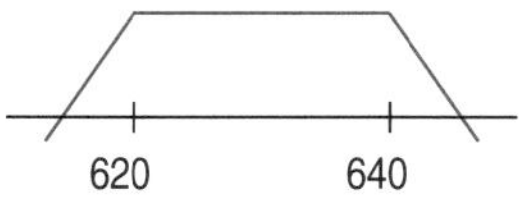

6. 620 less premium (downside)
   640 plus premium (upside)

7. False

8. Long straddle

9. True

CHAPTER 6

Strategies for Directionless Markets

Butterflies, Condors, Iron Butterflies

CONCEPT REVIEW

Support and resistance levels: If you consider the historical price of an underlying, the support level is the lowest price at which it tends to trade over a period of time before trading higher. The resistance level is the highest historical price at which the underlying tends to trade prior to falling.

Support and resistance are technical trading terms for price movement of traded products. Typically there is great importance placed on them in charting and technical analysis parlance. In the case of using a butterfly spread strategy, support and resistance refer more loosely to boundaries of an observed range of prices.

Directionless or sideways markets: A market that shows no definite direction (up or down) in price movement. This may mean some stability in prices or fluctuation within a certain range. The price of the underlying tends to trade within a range (high and low) over a period of time. The price may fluctuate, but doesn't penetrate either the support level or resistance level that has been identified.

Theta (time decay): The sensitivity of theoretical option prices with regard to small changes in time. Theta measures the rate of decay in the time value of options.

Intrinsic value: The amount by which an option is in-the-money. A call option is in-the-money if the price of the underlying is above the strike price; a put option is in-the-money if the underlying price is below the strike price.

Extrinsic value: The price or premium of an option, less its intrinsic value. The entire premium of an out-of-the-money option consists of extrinsic value.

Arbitrage: A trading technique that involves the simultaneous purchase and sale of identical assets with the intention of profiting by a difference in price. This can be accomplished by using different exchanges or by recognizing the synthetic relationship and carrying the synthetically similar assets until expiration (nonpure arbitrage).

Butterflies. What can one say about these magnificent creatures? They are truly beautiful. Perhaps William Wordsworth put it most aptly in his poem, "To a Butterfly":

> Stay near me—do not take thy flight! A little longer stay in sight! Much converse do I find in thee, Historian of my infancy! Float near me; do not yet depart! Dead times revive in thee: Thou bring'st, gay creature as thou art! A solemn image to my heart, My father's family!

What Wordsworth did not have in mind was how often option traders recant these words, or words very similar to these, when long a butterfly spread. For it is the nearness to "the money" at expiry, that brings the butterfly spread to its greatest splendor.

I, myself, can recall many an expiration where a butterfly friend would come to the rescue, its sweet wings carrying it to land near the strike of my favor to revive a near dead portfolio. I was so involved in butterflies during the '70s, '80s, and '90s, that I recognized their value in my sleep.

I began trading butterfly spreads in 1979. I became so enamored with their symmetry and flexibility that I became obsessed with them. In the beginning, I spent every chance I could working out pricing relationships that centered around various species of butterflies and their companions, condors. Eventually I migrated into looking at all pricing as it related to the "butterfly structure."

While trading in the pit, before electronic auto-quote reduced the majority of traders to hand-raising sharecroppers, making a market in a volatile stock required a few tricks. Large price and volatility swings led value sheets to become obsolete rather quickly (although I never used them to begin with) and electronic pricing had not yet arrived.

So, an acute understanding of the pricing characteristics of butterflies helped me weave a tapestry during the wild (and wide) markets of the '80s and thread the needle between the theoretical fabric of the likes of CRT, Timberhill, and Hull Trading in the '90s.

In the chapter that follows, I will share with you, on a fundamental basis, some of the flexibility, balance, and proportion that trading butterfly spreads may bring to your "book," at least as far as I have discovered over the years. Whether as a prime destination or a last resort, understanding butterfly spreads and their pricing habits can be as rewarding as any option strategy.

A directionless market is the most common market a trader will encounter. A market that trades within a certain range (support and resistance levels) over a certain period of time occurs more often than bull and bear markets. There are many stocks or underlyings that don't experience drastic moves, but rather trade between two numbers over a period of months or even years. Most sideways markets are recognized only in hindsight. For traditional investors, if identified in its early stages, they have an advantage for accumulating positions or rebalancing their portfolios.

But for the options trader that identifies such a potential market, there are strategies that have very advantageous risk/reward ratios; that is, large payouts for commensurately small amounts risked.

For example, let's say ITI stock has been consistently trading somewhere between \$93 and \$105 for the past three months. In this scenario, \$93 might be considered a "support level." If \$105 were the highest price observed over the three months before backing off and trading lower, it could be considered the "resistance level." This stock, which could be considered somewhat range-bound, would be a good candidate for profiting by utilizing an option strategy for directionless markets.

Besides recognizing these sideways, or consolidating, price movements in stocks currently held in your own portfolio, a good way to find a stock that fits this description is to look at price charts of different stocks. There are many Web sites that provide access to free charts. One such site is <www.thestreet.com>. It offers a complete selection of different types of user-friendly charting functions.

Several strategies that we will explore that may allow you to take advantage of a directionless market include butterflies, condors, and iron butterflies.

THE BUTTERFLY SPREAD

Directionless markets allow you the possibility of taking advantage of the noncommittal price movement of the underlying through the exploitation of the time premium of an option. The butterfly spread is the safest way to exploit this decay of premium, while being one of the most versatile of spreads an options trader has at his or her disposal. The butterfly gets its name from the shape these spreads portray when plotted on payout graphs. The distinct wings and body are apparent.

The long butterfly can be viewed in a number of different ways:

- It can be viewed in the traditional definition as an option spread strategy (in this case a call butterfly), spanning three consecutive strikes, that contains a long call at the lowest strike price, short two calls at the middle strike price, and one long call at the highest strike price.
- It can be viewed as two adjacent vertical spreads of the same class (one long and one short) with the short position sharing the same strike for both verticals.

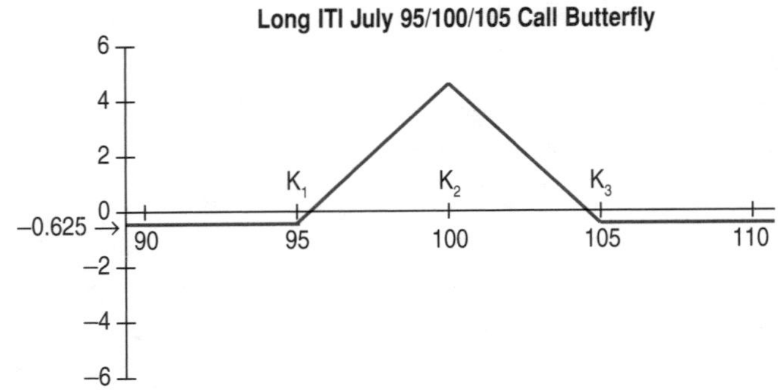

- It can be viewed as a short straddle at one strike bracketed by a long strangle at two different strikes, equidistant from the straddle strike (in the case of an iron butterfly).

The fact that the butterfly contains positions at three strikes gives this spread versatility. In an active trading account, the butterfly requires less management than most spreads, yet allows for the trading of multiple side-strategies from its basic structure. The fundamental reason to put on a butterfly is to target a price range that a stock will trade within at expiration. But these spreads may be wonderful trading vehicles.

Remember that options premiums are composed of both intrinsic and extrinsic value (discussed in Chapter 2). Intrinsic value is the value of the option that directly relates to the price of the underlying asset; it is the amount the option is in-the-money.

As an example, let's return to ITI stock, the market price of which is $97. Assume you bought the ITI 95 call option for $7. (This would mean the 95 call option has an intrinsic value of $2, because the call gives you the right to buy ITI at $95 and the option also has time value or extrinsic value of $5.)

With this amount of extrinsic value, you have to be concerned with theta or the time decay. (Remember, time works for the holder/owner of an option, because the more time you have until expiration of the contract, the more time you have for the underlying to move so that the option may end ITM. But the decay of the option costs the holder daily; the closer an option gets to its expiration, the more quickly it loses its time premium.)

If you are slightly bullish on ITI stock, but have witnessed the price trading in a range with $100 as a top, your purchase of the 95 call looks to be fairly risky. Turning it into a spread by selling a 100 call at $5 would reduce your risk to $2 (the debit of your spread), which is the difference between the strike of your long call at the current stock price and considerably less than the $7 you are risking in the straight call purchase.

But by selling twice as many of the 100 calls as the number of 95 calls you purchased, you will eliminate the debit altogether, and create a credit of $3 on the total transaction: ($7)+$5+$5=$3. This combination looks particularly better than the straight purchase of the 100 call or the 95/100 vertical spread. The problem with this spread is that there is considerable risk to the upside. How can you take advantage of such a combination without extreme risk in the event of a strong rally? One answer may be by establishing a long butterfly.

Long Butterfly (Call or Put)

To keep things simple, we are going to use call butterflies in our examples, keeping in mind that put and call butterflies have the same risk/reward profiles. Because in the example above, you would have a spread that is long a call and short two calls (a ratio spread that might be referred to as a "two-fer") with a resultant credit of $3, by purchasing a call that covers the upside exposure, say at the 105 strike, you will have established a long butterfly spread—the 95/100/105 call butterfly. Normally the spread is referred to with an expiry ahead of the strikes, with the underlying symbol placed before or after the expiry or strike complex (for example, ITI July 95/100/105 call butterfly, or July 95/100/105 ITI call butterfly).

To put on a long call butterfly position, you would purchase the lower strike call, sell two of the middle strike calls, and purchase the higher strike call, or "buy the wings and sell the body." You will always sell more of the middle strike (or body) than you will purchase of the outer strikes (wings). In a classic butterfly, that is on a 1:2:1 ratio, if your 105 call is purchased at $3.625, for instance, you will have established an inexpensive spread, with favorable risk/reward characteristics.

Example of a butterfly:

Composition:	Long 1 call at K_1 Short 2 calls at K_2 Long 1 call at K_3 Same expiration
Max Profit:	$(K_3 - K_1)/2$ – Debit
Max Loss:	Debit or amount you paid for the position
Break-even Points:	K_1 + Debit; K_3 – Debit
Example:	Long 1 ITI July 95 call at $7 Short 2 ITI July 100 calls at $5 Long 1 ITI July 105 call at $3.625 = Long ITI July 95/100/105 call butterfly at $0.625

Long ITI July 95/100/105 Call Butterfly Expiration Payout Graph

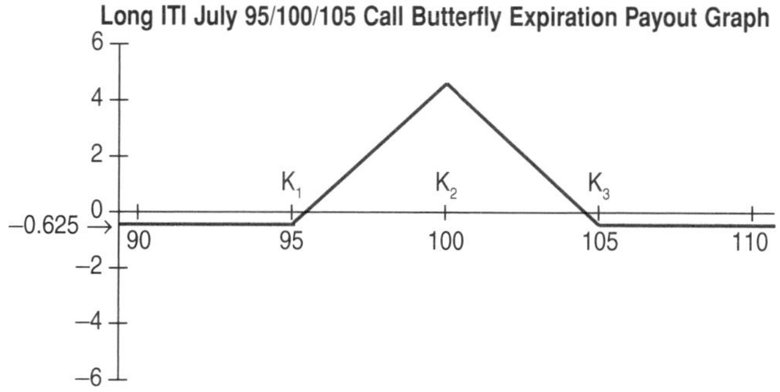

If the underlying falls from 97 to 96 at expiration, what would your profit or loss be? As you can now see from the expiration payout graph, the risk/reward profile resembles that of an object with wing-like representations. The larger part (or body) represents the most profit the spread can yield at expiration, in our example $437.50 for each one-lot spread that is established.

To break down the payouts on the graph, it may be useful to look at the components of the spread and their corresponding values at expiration:

Composition: Long 1 call at the 95 strike (K_1)
Short 2 calls at the 100 strike (K_2)
Long 1 call at 105 strike (K_3)

Max Profit: $(K_3 - K_1)/2$ – Debit (105–95)/2–.625 or $437.5

Max Loss: $62.50 (debit or amount you paid for the position)

Break-even Points: K_1 + debit; K_3 – debit ($95.625 and $104.375)

Consider the following:

The stock at $100: Long 1 ITI July 95 call is worth $5
Short 2 ITI July 100 calls are worthless
Long 1 ITI July 105 call is worthless

Net value of options = $5

Less the cost of the spread $0.625

= Long ITI July 95/100/105 call butterfly profit is $437.50

The stock at $103: Long 1 ITI July 95 call is worth $8
Short 2 ITI July 100 calls are worth $3 each (2 × $3 = $6) minus $6
Long 1 ITI July 105 call is worthless

Net value of options = $2

Less the cost of the spread $0.625

= Long ITI July 95/100/105 call butterfly profit is $137.50

The stock at $96: Long 1 ITI July 95 call is worth $1
Short 2 ITI July 100 calls are worthless
Long 1 ITI July 105 call is worthless

Net value of options = $1

Less the cost of the spread $0.625

= Long ITI July 95/100/105 call butterfly profit is $37.50

The stock at $90: Long 1 ITI July 95 call is worthless
Short 2 ITI July 100 calls are worthless
Long 1 ITI July 105 call is worthless

Net value of options = zero

Less the cost of the spread $0.625

= Long ITI July 95/100/105 call butterfly loss is $62.50

EXERCISE ONE: LONG BUTTERFLY (CALL)

DEF is trading at $64.9375 and you are slightly bullish. Construct a long October 65/70/75 call butterfly and calculate your profit or loss based on stock moves to these prices at expiration 71, 62, and 78. Remember, all trades must be done on the market prices shown (buy on the ask and sell on the bid).

Bid	Theo	Ask	Strike	Bid	Theo	Ask
64.88	**64.91**	64.94	**DEF**			
			Oct00			
34.75	**35.32**	35.75	**30.00**	0.00	**0.07**	0.19
29.88	**30.42**	30.88	**35.00**	0.00	**0.11**	0.19
25.00	**25.56**	26.00	**40.00**	0.06	**0.20**	0.25
20.38	**20.79**	21.38	**45.00**	0.31	**0.37**	0.50
18.25	**18.46**	18.75	**47.50**	0.50	**0.52**	0.69
16.00	**16.20**	16.50	**50.00**	0.69	**0.73**	0.88
13.88	**14.01**	14.38	**52.50**	1.00	**1.02**	1.19
11.75	**11.93**	12.25	**55.00**	1.38	**1.40**	1.56
9.88	**9.96**	10.25	**57.50**	1.88	**1.93**	2.06
8.00	**8.15**	8.38	**60.00**	2.50	**2.60**	2.75
6.38	**6.52**	6.75	**62.50**	3.38	**3.45**	3.50
4.88	**5.08**	5.25	**65.00**	4.25	**4.50**	4.63
3.63	**3.84**	4.00	**67.50**	5.50	**5.77**	5.88
2.63	**2.82**	2.88	**70.00**	7.00	**7.27**	7.38
1.81	**2.01**	2.00	**72.50**	8.63	**8.97**	9.00
1.19	**1.38**	1.31	**75.00**	10.50	**10.88**	11.00
0.75	**0.93**	0.94	**77.50**	12.63	**12.97**	13.13
0.50	**0.61**	0.63	**80.00**	14.88	**15.23**	15.38
0.25	**0.39**	0.44	**82.50**	17.38	**17.61**	17.88
0.13	**0.25**	0.31	**85.00**	19.88	**20.09**	20.38
0.13	**0.11**	0.19	**90.00**	24.63	**25.09**	25.63
0.00	**0.07**	0.19	**95.00**	29.63	**30.09**	30.63
0.00	**0.06**	0.13	**100.00**	34.63	**35.09**	35.63
0.00	**0.09**	0.19	**105.00**	39.63	**40.09**	40.63

Composition:

Max Profit:

Max Loss:

Break-even Points:

P&L with the stock at $71

P&L with the stock at $62

P&L with stock at $78

Graph:

Short Butterfly

The short butterfly position should be used when there is an opinion that the markets will *not* be directionless, unless there is a very short-term trading strategy to enter and exit it quickly. When you expect a breakout from a previously directionless market, or a move away from the current strike, a short position in a butterfly spread can net you some or all of the credit you would collect for selling it. But there are better risk/reward characteristics in other spreads when you have a directional bias to trade against.

Arbitraging Butterflies

Both long call butterflies and long put butterflies realize their maximum profit when the underlying is at the middle strike (body), if both types have the same expiration and strike prices. For example, if we look at the January 95/100/105 call butterfly and the January 95/100/105 put butterfly, with the underlying at 100, both will be worth $5. If at expiration, the underlying closes lower than the 95 wing or higher than the 105 wing, either one will be worthless. Their P&L graphs are identical.

Therefore, if both butterflies are trading at different prices, you can realize a profit by buying one and selling the other. This is not easily accomplished in the marketplace because professionals monitor such arbitrages closely. But it is this fundamental relationship that is the foundation of understanding the arbitrage strategies of butterfly spreads.

One such strategy is to close out a butterfly in the above manner. If it were a bearish position that initially led you to create a butterfly out of a put vertical spread, then closing out this position with the opposite call butterfly may be easier because of lower-priced individual options, more liquidity, or other factors.

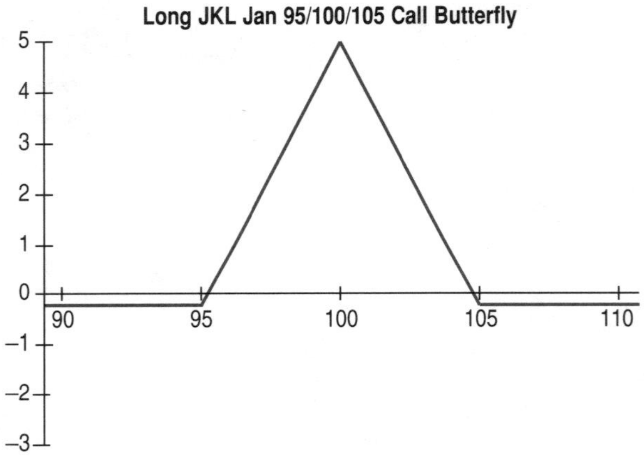

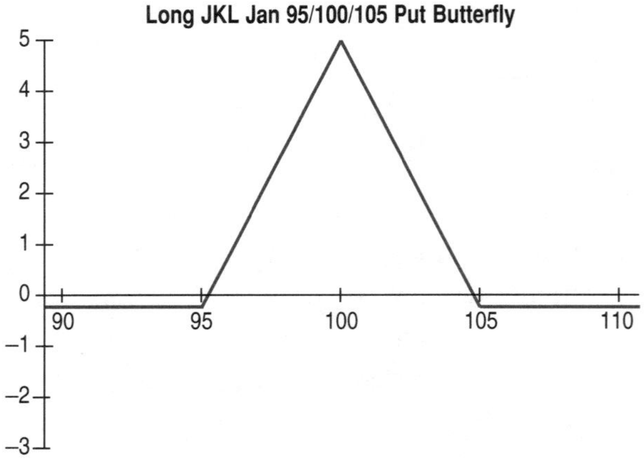

BEING BULLISH, BEARISH, OR NEUTRAL

You will want to consider your feelings about the market. Although butterflies are predominantly a delta neutral strategy, your selection of which options to buy and sell will be influenced by your feelings about whether the market is bullish or bearish.

If you are bullish about the market, you may wish to purchase a butterfly where the body is higher than the current market price of the underlying. For example: If the underlying market is at 98, you may wish to buy the 100/105/110 call butterfly spread. Because you will realize the most profit at 105, this would mean you have entered into a bullish call butterfly spread.

If you are bearish about the market, you may wish to purchase a butterfly where the body is lower than the current marketplace. For example: If the underlying market were at 98 you feel the market may fall a bit, you may wish to buy the 90/95/100 call butterfly spread. Conversely, you would want the underlying to end close to 95, where you would realize your greatest profit.

LONG CONDOR

The long condor is an interesting and semicomplicated nondirectional market strategy. It can be thought of as a modified butterfly spread (one where the body is disjointed, spanning two or more strikes) or it can be seen as a combination of a bull vertical and bear vertical (all calls or all puts) spread adjacent to or near each other.

The long condor is classically the sale of two options (of the same class) with consecutive exercise prices; with the purchase of two options, one with an immediately lower strike price and one with an immediately higher strike price to the two that are sold.

In a long condor, you end up with a position that is short two inner option strikes (that might look like the body of the condor) and long two outer strikes (that comprise the wings). Technically, a condor can't skip strikes in between. As we move further from this classic condor, and skip strikes between the body strikes, we can build a variation on this strategy called a pterodactyl . . . for its wide profit "wing span" and its various jointed points.

In both of these strategies, you are shorting the middle options to collect time premium as the underlying stock continues to trade in between your long strikes (the wings). The maximum risk on these strategies is the net debit that is created when putting them on as a spread. But each of these strategies also can be legged into as verticals, which allows for a potential flat cost or even a credit.

This strategy should make money with the passage of time as long as the price of the underlying stays in proximity to the spread. The strategy will make money if the underlying closes between the wings at a distance from either strike greater than the cost to put the spread on.

Long Call Condor

Composition: Long 1 call at K_1
Short 1 call at K_2
Short 1 call at K_3
Long 1 call at K_4
Same expiration

Max Profit: $K_3 - K_2$ – Debit or $(K_2 - K_1)$ – Debit

Max Loss: Debit

Break-even Points: K_1 + Debit; K_4 – Debit

Example: Long 1 HIJ Nov 55 call at $15.50
Short 1 HIJ Nov 60 call at $11.00
Short 1 HIJ Nov 65 call at $7.375
Long 1 HIJ Nov 70 call at $4.25
= Long HIJ Nov 55/60/65/70 call condor at $1.375

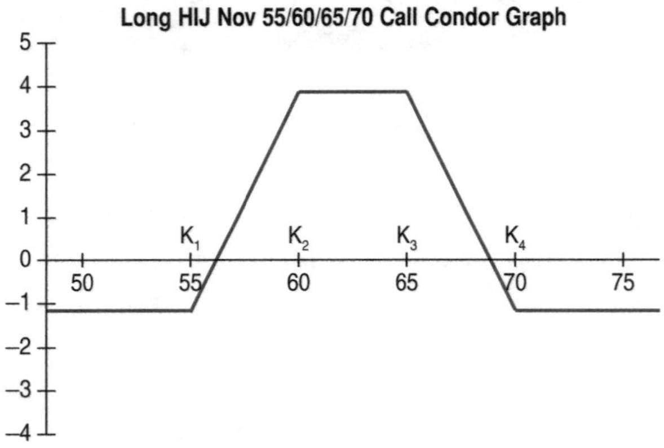

If the underlying falls from 65 to 55 at expiration, what would your profit or loss be? As you can now see from the expiration payout graph, the risk/reward profile also resembles that of an object with wing-like representations, albeit with a wide body. The larger part (or body) represents the profit the spread can yield at expiration, in our example $362.50 for each one-lot spread that is established.

To break down the payouts on the graph, it may be useful to look at the components of the spread and their corresponding values at expiration.

Consider the following:

The stock at $70: Long 1 HIJ Nov 70 call is worthless
Short 1 HIJ Nov 65 call is worth –$5

Short 1 HIJ Nov 60 call is worth –$10
Long 1 HIJ Nov 55 call is worth $15

Net value of options = zero

Less the cost of the spread $1.375

= Long HIJ Nov 55/60/65/70 call condor loss is $1.375 ($137.50 per spread)

The stock at $63: Long 1 HIJ Nov 70 call is worthless
Short 1 HIJ Nov 65 call is worthless
Short 1 HIJ Nov 60 call is worth –$3
Long 1 HIJ Nov 55 call is worth $8

Net value of options = $5

Less the cost of the spread $1.375

= Long HIJ Nov 55/60/65/70 call condor profit is $3.625 ($362.50 per spread)

The stock at $56: Long 1 HIJ Nov 70 call is worthless
Short 1 HIJ Nov 65 call is worthless
Short 1 HIJ Nov 60 call is worthless
Long 1 HIJ Nov 55 call is worth $1

Net value of options = $11

Less the cost of the spread $1.375

= Long HIJ Nov 55/60/65/70 call condor loss is $0.375 ($37.50 per spread)

The stock at $65: Long 1 HIJ Nov 70 call is worthless
Short 1 HIJ Nov 65 call is worthless
Short 1 HIJ Nov 60 call is worth –$5
Long 1 HIJ Nov 55 call is worth $10

Net value of options = $5

Less the cost of the spread $1.375

= Long HIJ Nov 55/60/65/70 call condor profit is $3.625 ($362.50 per spread)

The stock at $68: Long 1 HIJ Nov 70 call is worthless
Short 1 HIJ Nov 65 call is worth –$3
Short 1 HIJ Nov 60 call is worth –$8
Long 1 HIJ Nov 55 call is worth $13

Net value of options = $2

Less the cost of the spread $1.375

= Long HIJ Nov 55/60/65/70 call condor profit is $0.625 ($62.50 per spread)

EXERCISE TWO: LONG CONDOR

You wish to buy the DEF October 60/65/70/75 put condor spread. Based on the prices below, answer the following questions:

Bid	Theo	Ask	Strike	Bid	Theo	Ask
64.88	**64.91**	64.94	**DEF**			
			Oct00			
34.75	**35.32**	35.75	**30.00**	0.00	**0.07**	0.19
29.88	**30.42**	30.88	**35.00**	0.00	**0.11**	0.19
25.00	**25.56**	26.00	**40.00**	0.06	**0.20**	0.25
20.38	**20.79**	21.38	**45.00**	0.31	**0.37**	0.50
18.25	**18.46**	18.75	**47.50**	0.50	**0.52**	0.69
16.00	**16.20**	16.50	**50.00**	0.69	**0.73**	0.88
13.88	**14.01**	14.38	**52.50**	1.00	**1.02**	1.19
11.75	**11.93**	12.25	**55.00**	1.38	**1.40**	1.56
9.88	**9.96**	10.25	**57.50**	1.88	**1.93**	2.06
8.00	**8.15**	8.38	**60.00**	2.50	**2.60**	2.75
6.38	**6.52**	6.75	**62.50**	3.38	**3.45**	3.50
4.88	**5.08**	5.25	**65.00**	4.25	**4.50**	4.63
3.63	**3.84**	4.00	**67.50**	5.50	**5.77**	5.88
2.63	**2.82**	2.88	**70.00**	7.00	**7.27**	7.38
1.81	**2.01**	2.00	**72.50**	8.63	**8.97**	9.00
1.19	**1.38**	1.31	**75.00**	10.50	**10.88**	11.00
0.75	**0.93**	0.94	**77.50**	12.63	**12.97**	13.13
0.50	**0.61**	0.63	**80.00**	14.88	**15.23**	15.38
0.25	**0.39**	0.44	**82.50**	17.38	**17.61**	17.88
0.13	**0.25**	0.31	**85.00**	19.88	**20.09**	20.38
0.13	**0.11**	0.19	**90.00**	24.63	**25.09**	25.63
0.00	**0.07**	0.19	**95.00**	29.63	**30.09**	30.63
0.00	**0.06**	0.13	**100.00**	34.63	**35.09**	35.63
0.00	**0.09**	0.19	**105.00**	39.63	**40.09**	40.63

Composition:

Max Profit:

Max Loss:

Break-even Points:

P&L with the stock at $66:

P&L with the stock at $72:

Graph:

Short Condor

The same can be said for the short side of a condor spread as was mentioned for the short butterfly—it is to be used when movement away from the current price is anticipated. A short condor spread could be very risky in a directionless market.

Long Iron Butterfly

The long iron butterfly spread is the third strategy that can be used in a sideways market. It is a butterfly that combines two other option strategies: the straddle and the strangle. By selling a straddle and buying a strangle that brackets the straddle, you can create a profit profile identical to that of the long butterfly.

Some may prefer to view this combination as two vertical spreads: a bear call spread (short lower call and long higher call) and a bull put spread (long lower put and short higher put). If this is easier for you, it is understandable. We will cover both methods of constructing and breaking down this spread.

The long iron butterfly is similar to a butterfly, but employs both puts and calls. As you can see, the long iron butterfly is created by synthetically creating one of the vertical spreads.

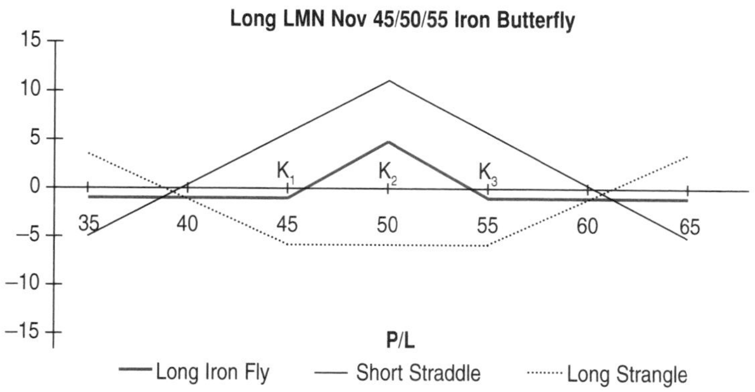

Composition: Long 1 put at the 45 strike (K_1) @ $3
Short 1 call at the 50 strike (K_2) @ $5.625
Short 1 put at the 50 strike (K_2) @ $5
Long 1 call at 55 strike (K_3) @ $3.25

Max Profit: $4.375 (Credit received)

Max Loss: (K_2–K_1) – Credit; ($50–$45) – $4.375 or $.625

Break-even Points: $45.625 and $54.375; ($K_2$ – Credit; K_2 + Credit)

Consider the following:

The stock at $58: Long 1 LMN Nov 45 put is worthless
Short 1 LMN Nov 50 put is worthless
Short 1 LMN Nov 50 call is worth –$8
Long 1 LMN Nov 55 call is worth $3

Net value of options = –$5

Less the credit received for the spread $4.375

= Long LMN Nov 45/50/55 iron butterfly loss is –$.625 ($62.50 per spread)

The stock at $51: Long 1 LMN Nov 45 put is worthless
Short 1 LMN Nov 50 put is worthless
Short 1 LMN Nov 50 call is worth –$1
Long 1 LMN Nov 55 call is worthless

Net value of options = –$1

Less the credit received for the spread $4.375

= Long LMN Nov 45/50/55 iron butterfly net gain of $3.375 ($337.50 per spread)

The stock at $47: Long 1 LMN Nov 45 put is worthless
Short 1 LMN Nov 50 put is worth –$3
Short 1 LMN Nov 50 call is worthless
Long 1 LMN Nov 55 call is worthless

Net value of options = –$3

Less the credit received for the spread $4.375

= Long LMN Nov 45/50/55 iron butterfly net gain of $1.375 ($137.50 per spread)

The stock at $45: Long 1 LMN Nov 45 put is worthless
Short 1 LMN Nov 50 put is worth –$5
Short 1 LMN Nov 50 call is worthless
Long 1 LMN Nov 55 call is worthless

Net value of options = –$5

Less the credit received for the spread $4.375

= Long LMN Nov 45/50/55 iron butterfly loss is $0.625 ($62.50 per spread)

EXERCISE THREE: LONG IRON BUTTERFLY

You wish to be long the October 60/65/70 iron butterfly spread. Based on the PQR prices, answer the following questions:

Composition:

Max Profit:

Max Loss:

Break-even Points:

Graph:

Bid	Theo	Ask	Strike	Bid	Theo	Ask
64.88	**64.91**	64.94	**PQR**			
			Oct00			
34.75	**35.32**	35.75	**30.00**	0.00	**0.07**	0.19
29.88	**30.42**	30.88	**35.00**	0.00	**0.11**	0.19
25.00	**25.56**	26.00	**40.00**	0.06	**0.20**	0.25
20.38	**20.79**	21.38	**45.00**	0.31	**0.37**	0.50
18.25	**18.46**	18.75	**47.50**	0.50	**0.52**	0.69
16.00	**16.20**	16.50	**50.00**	0.69	**0.73**	0.88
13.88	**14.01**	14.38	**52.50**	1.00	**1.02**	1.19
11.75	**11.93**	12.25	**55.00**	1.38	**1.40**	1.56
9.88	**9.96**	10.25	**57.50**	1.88	**1.93**	2.06
8.00	**8.15**	8.38	**60.00**	2.50	**2.60**	2.75
6.38	**6.52**	6.75	**62.50**	3.38	**3.45**	3.50
4.88	**5.08**	5.25	**65.00**	4.25	**4.50**	4.63
3.63	**3.84**	4.00	**67.50**	5.50	**5.77**	5.88
2.63	**2.82**	2.88	**70.00**	7.00	**7.27**	7.38
1.81	**2.01**	2.00	**72.50**	8.63	**8.97**	9.00
1.19	**1.38**	1.31	**75.00**	10.50	**10.88**	11.00
0.75	**0.93**	0.94	**77.50**	12.63	**12.97**	13.13
0.50	**0.61**	0.63	**80.00**	14.88	**15.23**	15.38
0.25	**0.39**	0.44	**82.50**	17.38	**17.61**	17.88
0.13	**0.25**	0.31	**85.00**	19.88	**20.09**	20.38
0.13	**0.11**	0.19	**90.00**	24.63	**25.09**	25.63
0.00	**0.07**	0.19	**95.00**	29.63	**30.09**	30.63
0.00	**0.06**	0.13	**100.00**	34.63	**35.09**	35.63
0.00	**0.09**	0.19	**105.00**	39.63	**40.09**	40.63

Short Iron Butterfly

As I mentioned in the paragraphs on short butterfly and condor, these strategies from the short side are to be used when movement away from the current price is anticipated. Thus, you are no longer looking for a directionless market. A short iron butterfly spread also could be very risky in a directionless market.

EXECUTION

In this book, I have tried to show you how to construct spreads. You may try to put these spreads on, one leg at a time, as components (two vertical spreads for butterflies for instance) or as the spread itself.

To find the best prices in spreads, the Web site <www.stcspreads.com> helps by linking options investors with other professionals competing for business in combination spreads.

The site offers users price indications for full spread execution. Depending on the execution service you use, you can directly trade one of the spreads shown in the spread window simply by clicking the side you prefer and filling in your quantity. However, the indicative prices are not firm quotes and may not be available when an order is sent for execution.

The posted values on either side of the strike range column (center) show the indicative prices that these professionals have posted for the type of spread you have selected.

The values in the far left and right columns calculate the amount that these indicative prices improve a theoretical value based on the exchanges' net posted prices for the individual legs of the spread.

Once you have a feel for the risk characteristics of these spreads, a tool that will help you find indicative prices and risk/reward profiles is the spread search. The spread search feature will enable you to sort through hundreds of spread opportunities.

You use the tool by defining the parameters by which your search will be constrained. First, you select the symbol, spread type, and expiration month(s) that are of interest. Next, you define your risk/reward in terms of money-to-money, risk/reward ratio, or percentage return on your investment.

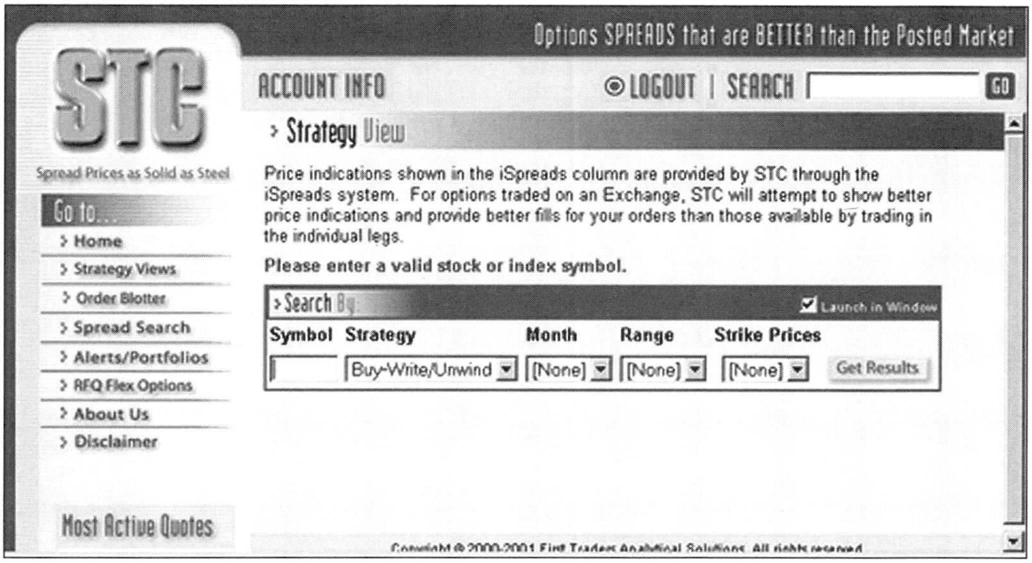

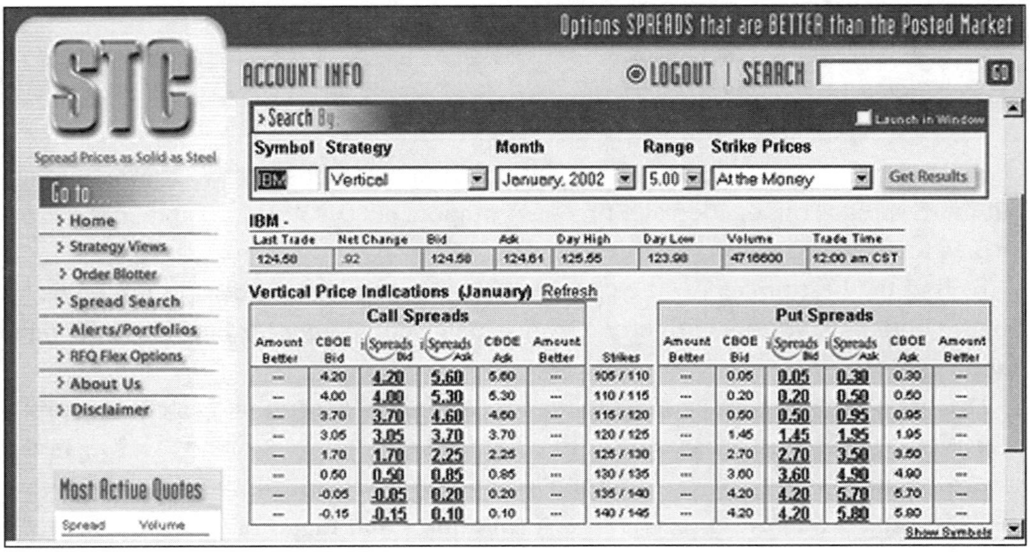

By defining the percentage move in the underlying price and the amount that you are investing, the search tool can return a specific set of strategies that meet your specific criteria.

The alert feature on this site allows you the opportunity to store away your favorite spread strategies and your target prices for each. When the spread reaches your target price, an alert is set for you on the site (if you are browsing the site) and an e-mail is sent to you alerting you to the fact that the specific price has been achieved.

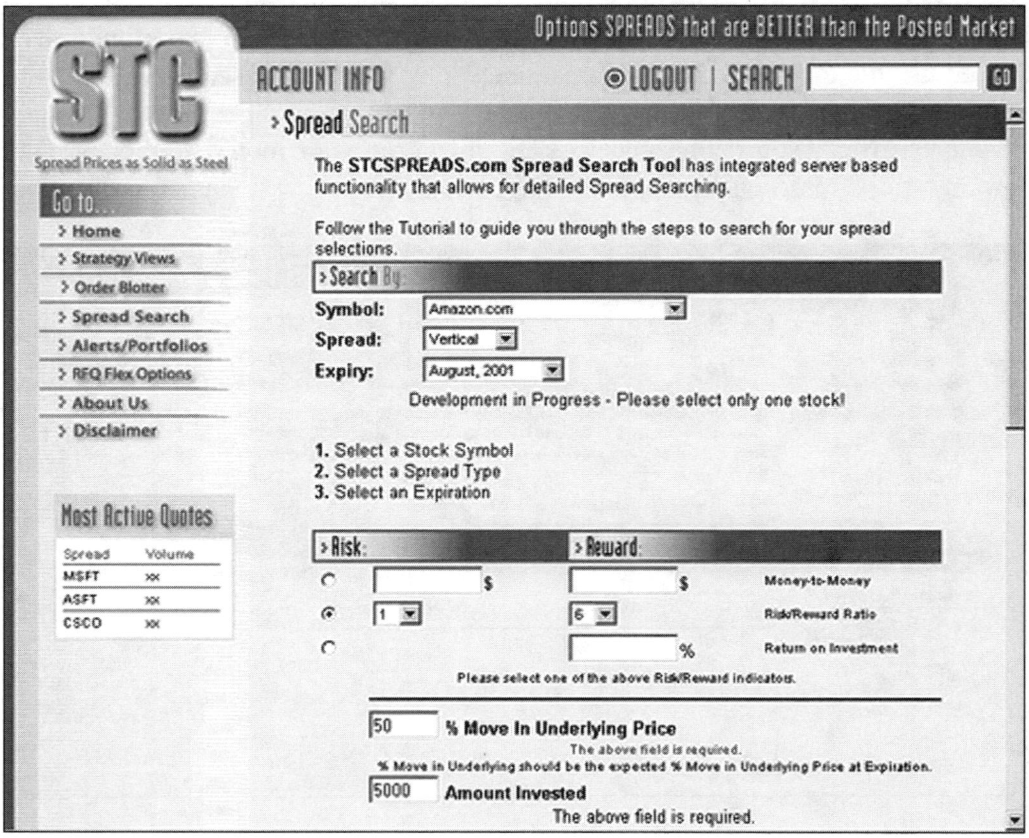

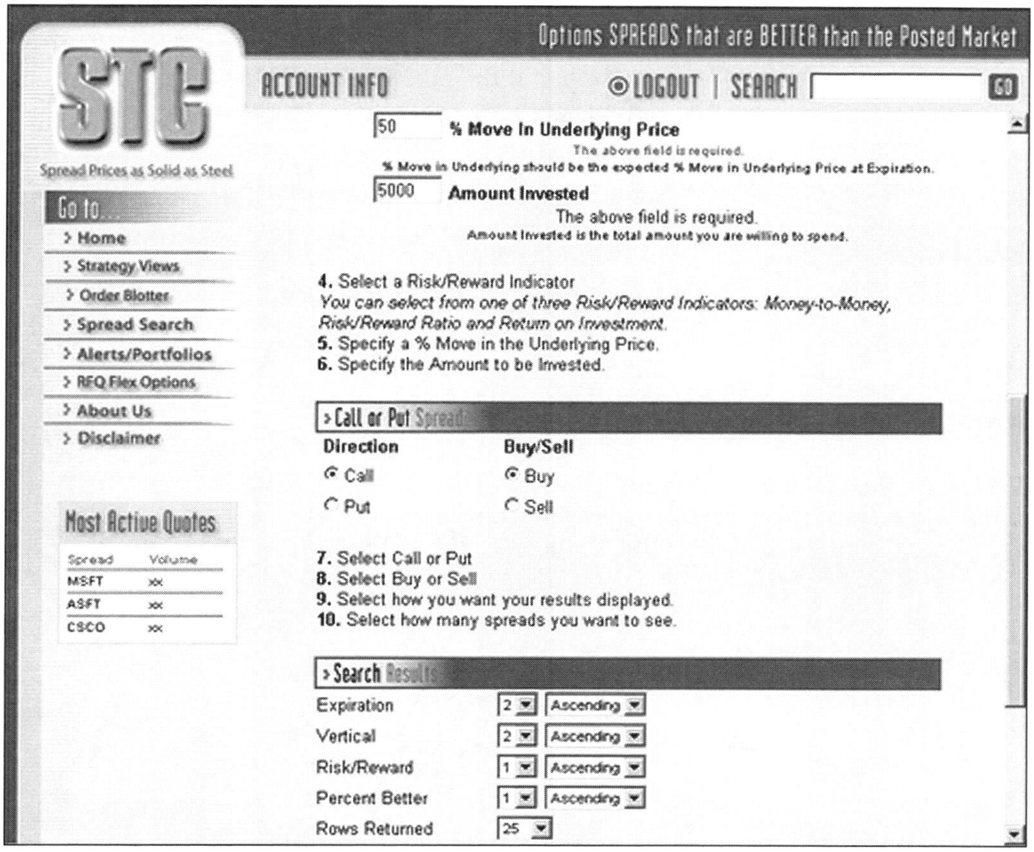

ANSWERS TO EXERCISES:

EXERCISE ONE: LONG BUTTERFLY (CALL)

Composition:	Long 1 call at the 65 strike at $5.25 Short 2 calls at the 70 strike at $2.625 Long 1 call at the 75 strike at $1.3125
Max Profit:	$3.6875
Max Loss:	$1.3125
Break-even Points:	$66.3125 and $73.6875
P&L with the stock at $71:	Profit of $2.6875
P&L with the stock at $62:	Loss of $1.3125
P&L with stock at $78:	Loss of $1.3125
Graph:	DEF Long Oct 65/70/75 Call Butterfly

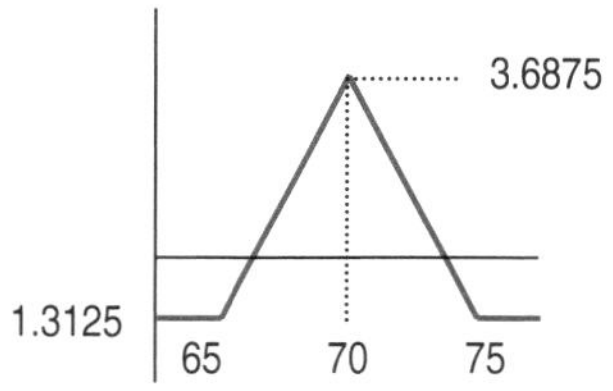

EXERCISE TWO: LONG CONDOR

Composition:	Long 1 put at the 60 strike at $2.75 Short 1 put at the 65 strike at $4.25 Short 1 put at the 70 strike at $7.00 Long 1 put at the 75 strike at $11.00
Max Profit:	$2.50
Max Loss:	$2.50
Break-even Points:	$62.50 and $72.50
P&L with the stock at $66:	$2.50
P&L with the stock at $72:	$.50
Graph:	DEF Long Oct 60/65/70/75 Put Condor Spread

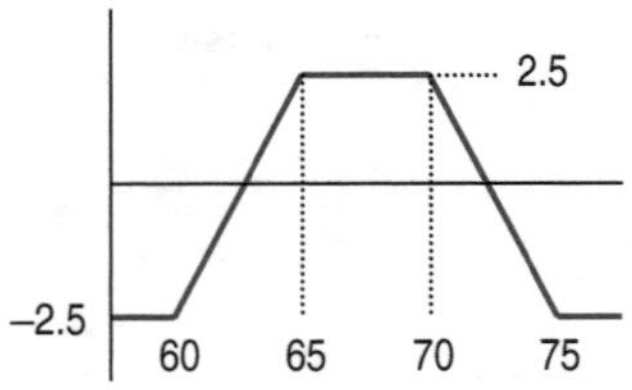

EXERCISE THREE: LONG IRON BUTTERFLY

Composition:	Long 1 put at the 60 strike at $2.75 Short 1 put at the 65 strike at $4.25 Short 1 call at the 65 strike at $4.88 Long 1 call at the 70 strike at $2.875
Max Profit:	$3.50
Max Loss:	$1.50
Break-even points:	$61.50 and $68.50
Graph:	

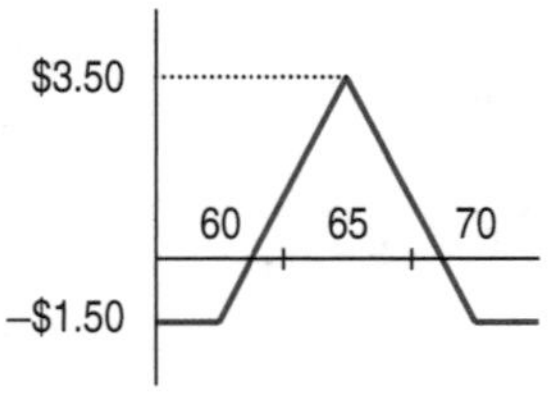

CHAPTER SIX QUIZ

1. The underlying is trading at 42. You are long the 30, 35, and 40 call butterfly one time for which you paid $0.50. The wings traded for $14 and $4.50 and the body traded for $9 each.
   a. Is the delta of the butterfly positive or negative?
   b. What are the break-even points at expiration?
   c. At which strike do you enjoy the best return at expiration? Is there a maximum risk/return on this butterfly?
   d. Are there any similarities in the characteristics of a long call butterfly (debit spread) and a long iron butterfly (credit spread)?

2. The June XYZ is trading at $61.21.
   The June XYZ 6000 call is at $1.28.
   The June XYZ 6050 call is at $0.75.
   The June XYZ 6100 call is at $0.37.
   Where is this June 6000/6050/6100 butterfly trading?

3. Calculate an iron butterfly based on the following prices:
   May 350 call @ $1.45
   May 350 put @ $6.45
   May 355 call @ $0.55
   May 345 put @ $3.50
   What is your maximum risk in this trade?

4. The long 50/55/60 call butterfly along with the long 55/60/65 call butterfly are known as:

5. A long 50/55/60 call butterfly would be long or short the 50 and 60 calls?

6. If you paid $1.75 for the 50/55/60 call butterfly;
   a. What is your maximum risk?
   b. What is your maximum gain?

7. If you bought a 40/45/50 put butterfly, at which price does the underlying have to close on expiration for you to earn maximum profit? For you to realize the maximum loss?

8. Given the following market prices, construct a long put butterfly:
   Oct 62.5 @ $3.30
   Oct 65 @ $4.5
   Oct 67.5 @ $5.90
   a. At what price did you buy this butterfly?

b. What are your break-even points?
c. What is your maximum profit?

9. If the underlying was trading at 63 when you placed the trade, are you bullish, bearish, or neutral?

10. This butterfly is a combination of which two vertical spreads (indicate long or short)?

11. If you purchased the 65/67.5/70 put butterfly after you went long the 62.5/65/67.5 put butterfly, what would be your resulting position?

12. This is a combination of which two vertical spreads?

CHAPTER SIX QUIZ ANSWER KEY

1. a. Delta is slightly negative; you want underlying down to break below 40.
   b. \$30.50 and \$39.50
   c. Best return is at the 35 strike.
      Max risk = \$0.50
      Maximum return = \$5 – (the \$0.50 point debit) = \$4.50
   d. The payout characteristics are identical.

2. \$0.15

3. The iron butterfly credit is \$3.85 with a risk of \$1.15.

4. Long a condor

5. Long

6. a. \$1.75, the amount that you paid for it
   b. \$3.25, or \$5 – \$1.75

7. Max profit = \$45
   Max loss = below \$40 or above \$50

8. a. + 3.30 – (4.50 × 2) + 5.90 = \$.20
   b. 62.50 + .20 = 62.70
      67.50 – .20 = 67.30
   c. \$2.50 – .20 = 2.30

9. Bullish; you want the underlying to close at the middle strike.

10. Short 62.5/65 put vertical; long the 65/67.5 put vertical

11. Long the 62.5/65/67.5/70 put condor

12. Short 62.5/65 put vertical; long the 67.5/70 put vertical

CHAPTER 7

Volatility Spreads

Ratio Spreads and Backspreads

CONCEPT REVIEW

At-the-money (ATM): An option is considered to be ATM when its exercise price is equal to the current market price of the underlying security.

Backspread: Usually a delta neutral spread that involves being long more options than you are short on the same underlying security; for example selling an ATM put or call option and buying a greater number of options at a higher strike.

Ratio spread: This involves buying an option at one strike and selling a greater number of OTM options at another strike, all having the same expiration date.

In-the-money (ITM): An option with intrinsic value. A call option is ITM when its exercise price is lower than the current market price of the underlying security, and a put option is ITM when its exercise price is higher than the current market price of the underlying security.

Out of the money (OTM): An option is OTM when its value is purely extrinsic. A call option is OTM when its exercise price is higher than the current market price of the underlying security, and a put option is OTM when its exercise price is lower than the current market price of the underlying security.

Delta: The sensitivity of an option's theoretical value to changes in the price of the underlying. Expressed as a percentage, it represents an equivalent amount of underlying. It also can be viewed as the probability of an option expiring ITM.

Implied volatility: A measure of the volatility of the underlying security, derived by applying current prices rather than historical prices. It measures the option's volatility rather than the underlying's.

Support and resistance levels: The lows (support) and highs (resistance) of an observed range of prices.

Range trading: A term that traders use to describe time periods wherein the underlying security establishes a certain set of values with fairly well-defined high and low prices and proceeds to trade within those bounds.

Trending: A market that tends to move in the same general direction over a time period.

Breakout: A market that has been trading within a defined range and then moves outside of (breaks out of) that range, whether to the upside (higher prices) or downside (lower prices).

Most market practitioners tend to think of daily price action in the markets in terms of two different types of trading days: (1) range trading days and (2) trending or breakout days. A general rule is that two out of three days tend to be range trading days and the third is (of course) a breakout or trending day. This is not to say that if Monday and Tuesday are range trading days that Wednesday will be a trend day—it describes the market's behavior over a period of time.

For the option trader, however, there is a strategy that might be able to take advantage of either one of these markets, depending on which way you are positioned. Ratio spreads and backspreads discussed in this chapter are popular speculative positions that normally need some risk management. These positions are very common in the trading pits and can be used to take advantage of not only underlying volatility or lack of it, but also the levels of implied volatility at which the options are trading.

THE RATIO SPREAD

A ratio spread differs from the other strategies that have been discussed in that it uses a disproportionate number of options to offset different strikes. A ratio spread involves buying an option at one strike and selling a greater number of OTM options of another strike. It can be thought of as being long a vertical (bull or bear) spread with extra units sold against the long position. A ratio spread, whether done with calls or puts, tends to take advantage of an underlying that is trading within a range of prices or is trending in a specific direction. It does this by exploiting time decay and/or differences in implied volatility. In general, the position is initiated as a fairly directional neutral position, although that is certainly not a hard-and-fast rule.

Here are a number of different ways to look at the ratio spread:

- It can be viewed in the traditional sense as an option spread that is done with two different strikes with the same expiration date, using solely calls or solely puts, and being net short more contracts than long.
- It can be viewed as a vertical call or put spread with the further OTM strike having proportionately more short contracts than the other strike has long contracts.
- It can be viewed as a long butterfly position with the furthest OTM "wing" missing in the case of a 1:2 ratio spread.

Like a butterfly spread, the ratio spread can be used to target a range that a stock is going to trade within until expiration. Unlike the limited risk/limited reward butterfly, however, the risks can be unlimited with the ratio spread, and the rewards and the range over which they can be collected can dramatically increase.

Let's look at some specific examples of a ratio spread.

The Ratio Call Spread

There are many different ways to initiate a ratio call spread. For example, in order to put on a ratio call spread, the trader will buy one ATM call and then sell proportionately more calls at a higher strike price (more OTM).

You can use just about any ratio, or any strike for that matter. It doesn't have to be 1:2. It could be 1:3, 2:3, or even 4:5. In the trading pits, there have been ratios as high as 1:8, but that's certainly not something advisable for anyone other than the professionals who are watching minute by minute (and even then it's risky!).

A ratio call spread is appropriate when the trader foresees either a small rally in the value of the underlying shares, a break in the market in the case of a ratio call spread initiated for a credit, or even a fairly stagnant underlying that stays within its recent trading range. The one thing that you definitely do not want to happen in the case of a ratio call spread is a sharp, substantial rally in the stock's price. You have unlimited risk on the upside because of the extra uncovered calls that you are short. You would like the underlying to expire right at the strike of the options that you are short in order to achieve the greatest profitability.

Let's look at an example. In the last few months, PQR stock has had a trading range between $55 and $85, with a narrowing of that range in the last month to within approximately $55 to $70. Let us say that you decide that the company has its share of problems and that the market as a whole is not looking the healthiest. In your opinion, the risk of breakout from this narrow range in the next couple of months is to the downside. In addition to your directional opinion, you feel that the implied volatilities on this stock are trading quite high. These variables are setting up for a nice ratio call spread to be initiated.

Let's assume PQR is trading for $62.50, right in the middle of its recent trading range. The October 65 calls are trading at $8. The October 75 calls are trading at $4.75. In order to do the ratio call spread and take advantage of both the high implied volatility (upwards of 100 percent) and the recent range, you buy one 65 call for $8 and sell two 75 calls for $4.75 each, for a net credit of $1.50. At this time this spread also happens to be unbiased directionally as it has a delta total close to neutral. With a .47 delta on the 65 call and a .25 delta on the 75 call that you sell, the net delta is –.03 ([1 × .47] + [–2 × .25] = –.03).

Your position looks something like this:

Composition: Long 1 call at K_1
Short 2 calls at K_2

Max Profit: $(K_2 – K_1)$ + Credit or – Debit (to establish ratio spread)

Max Loss: Unlimited on the upside. On the downside the debit to establish the ratio spread (if done for a debit)

Break-even Points: Downside: K_1 + Debit
Upside: K_2 + Maximum Profit Potential, or {[(# Long calls × Difference in Strike Prices) + Credit or – Debit] number of calls naked}

In this example:

Composition: Long 1 Oct 65 call
Short 2 Oct 75 calls

Max Profit: ($75 – $65) + $1.50 [$9.50 – $8.00 = $1.50] = $11.50

Max Loss: Unlimited on the upside

Break-even Points: $65 (downside) $75 + [1 × ($75 – $65) + $1.50 = $11.50 / 1] = $86.50 (upside)

PQR Oct 65/75 Ratio Call Spread, 1 × 2

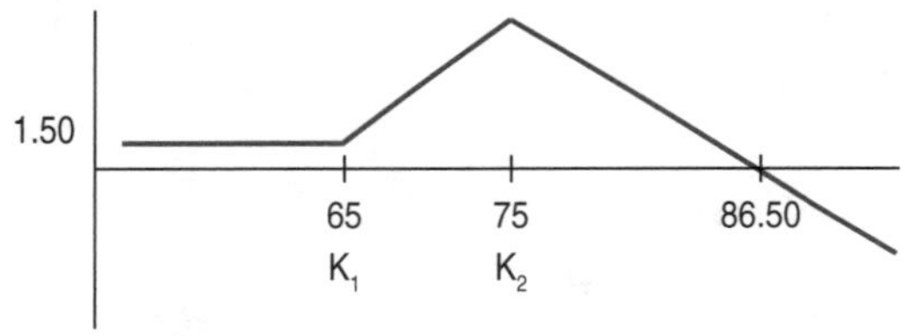

As you can see from the expiration payout graph, the risk/reward profile is similar to that of a butterfly, but with two exceptions. The downside will always yield a credit (if done for a credit), and the upside risk is unlimited.

These differences give you the possibility of unlimited loss if there is a substantial rally, as well as guaranteed profitability below the lowest strike because of the credit received per spread when the position was initiated. The good news in this case is that if PQR is trading anywhere between $0 and $86.50 at expiration, you will make money on this spread. Your greatest return of $11.50 (or $1,150.00) is achieved at the strike of your short options, or the 75 strike. Your break-even point on the upside is $86.50, which gives you some breathing room if the market trades outside of your expected range of $55 to $75.

On the downside, your worst-case scenario is if stock is trading beneath your 65 strike, which still leaves us with the $1.50 credit (or $150.00) that you received when you put on the spread.

It appears that you have put on a spread that might take advantage of your scenario, and that even with the unlimited risk possibility on the upside, you have a reasonable margin for error. Now let's take a look at a ratio put spread.

EXERCISE ONE: RATIO CALL SPREAD

Use the prices for MNO to determine the following for the Oct 82.50/87.50 ratio call spread:

Composition:

Max Profit:

Max Loss:

Break-even Points:

Plot a P&L graph:

Last	Bid	Theo	Ask	Strike	Bid	Theo	Ask	Last
83.00	82.94	**82.97**	83.00	**MNO**				
				Sep00				
20.00	33.00	**33.24**	33.50	**50.00**	0.06	**0.07**	0.19	1.00
16.75	28.00	**28.31**	28.50	**55.00**	0.13	**0.13**	0.25	0.25
19.25	23.13	**23.45**	23.63	**60.00**	0.19	**0.25**	0.31	0.38
19.38	18.50	**18.72**	18.88	**65.00**	0.44	**0.50**	0.56	0.50
13.00	14.00	**14.26**	14.38	**70.00**	0.81	**1.02**	1.00	1.00
8.75	10.00	**10.28**	10.38	**75.00**	1.81	**2.03**	2.00	1.94
6.25	6.63	**6.95**	7.00	**80.00**	3.38	**3.71**	3.63	3.50
3.75	4.13	**4.41**	4.38	**85.00**	5.88	**6.17**	6.25	6.25
2.25	2.44	**2.64**	2.50	**90.00**	9.25	**9.40**	9.63	9.25
1.13	1.25	**1.50**	1.44	**95.00**	13.13	**13.26**	13.50	13.75
0.88	0.63	**0.82**	0.81	**100.00**	17.38	**17.59**	17.75	23.00
0.50	0.25	**0.44**	0.38	**105.00**	22.00	**22.25**	22.50	0.00
0.50	0.13	**0.23**	0.25	**110.00**	26.88	**27.09**	27.38	0.00
0.25	0.06	**0.13**	0.19	**115.00**	31.75	**32.03**	32.25	0.00
0.13	0.00	**0.01**	0.13	**120.00**	36.75	**37.03**	37.25	49.25
0.13	0.00	**0.00**	0.13	**125.00**	41.75	**42.03**	42.25	0.00
0.00	0.00	**0.00**	0.13	**130.00**	46.75	**47.03**	47.25	0.00
				Oct00				
31.88	33.50	**33.73**	34.00	**50.00**	0.19	**0.29**	0.31	0.44
21.75	28.88	**29.05**	29.38	**55.00**	0.44	**0.56**	0.56	0.81
25.13	24.38	**24.57**	24.88	**60.00**	0.88	**1.04**	1.06	1.13
19.00	20.13	**20.37**	20.63	**65.00**	1.69	**1.82**	1.88	1.94
15.75	16.38	**16.54**	16.75	**70.00**	2.81	**2.96**	3.00	3.25
15.25	13.00	**13.16**	13.38	**75.00**	4.38	**4.53**	4.63	5.00
11.25	11.50	**11.65**	11.88	**77.50**	5.38	**5.53**	5.75	6.38
10.88	10.13	**10.26**	10.50	**80.00**	6.38	**6.63**	6.75	7.13
8.00	8.88	**8.99**	9.25	**82.50**	7.50	**7.84**	7.88	14.63
7.25	7.75	**7.85**	8.13	**85.00**	8.88	**9.21**	9.25	8.75
6.13	6.63	**6.82**	7.00	**87.50**	10.38	**10.64**	10.75	15.88
6.00	5.75	**5.90**	6.00	**90.00**	11.88	**12.24**	12.25	12.25
5.00	5.00	**5.09**	5.25	**92.50**	13.63	**13.92**	14.00	12.88
4.50	4.25	**4.37**	4.50	**95.00**	15.38	**15.70**	15.75	26.75
4.00	3.63	**3.74**	3.88	**97.50**	17.25	**17.57**	17.63	16.13
3.00	3.00	**3.19**	3.25	**100.00**	19.13	**19.52**	19.50	30.00
2.19	2.19	**2.30**	2.38	**105.00**	23.25	**23.65**	23.75	19.63
1.63	1.56	**1.64**	1.75	**110.00**	27.63	**28.01**	28.13	33.50
1.69	1.06	**1.16**	1.25	**115.00**	32.25	**32.58**	32.75	31.13
0.69	0.69	**0.82**	0.88	**120.00**	37.00	**37.29**	37.50	0.00
1.50	0.50	**0.57**	0.69	**125.00**	41.88	**42.13**	42.38	33.38
0.69	0.31	**0.40**	0.44	**130.00**	46.75	**47.04**	47.25	0.00

The Ratio Put Spread

The ratio put spread is similar to that of the ratio call spread in that you are short more contracts than you are long. In this case, however, the trader would buy a higher strike put and sell a greater number of OTM lower strike puts. Just like the ratio call spread, this strategy offers a great degree of risk and limited profit potential.

A ratio put spread may be used when the trader is anticipating a quiet market or one in which the potential for a rally outweighs that of a hard break. In the stock market, a put ratio spread really takes advantage of the implied volatility differences between strike prices and can be a wonderful tool. The maximum profit is realized when the stock closes at the lower strike or the strike of the short options at expiration, similar to that of the ratio call spread. The rewards might be lucrative, but the risks in a volatile market can be extreme if there is a big downdraft in the stock.

Let's take a look at another example. We'll use PQR again and its options. Let's suppose that the same scenario exists with the range of trading in the past few months between \$55 and \$85, and more recently the range being between \$55 and \$70, with the stock currently trading at \$62.50. Your view of the market and this stock, however, are quite different from the first scenario. You instead feel that PQR is a very strong stock going through a consolidation and forming a technical base from which to rally back up again. You think that the general market is also preparing to rally and that this stock in particular is oversold. In this case, you decide to initiate a ratio put spread using the October 55 and 60 puts.

You go into the market and buy one of the 60 puts for \$7 and sell two of the 55 puts for \$5 each. You've now got on the October 55/60 ratio put spread for a \$3 credit (or \$300). You took in a credit of \$10 for the two puts you sold and gave up \$7 for the put you bought, thus netting you \$3. There is a bit more risk in this spread as it is only a 5 point spread, without as much room for error, but you are fairly certain of your market call and the support below \$55 in the stock is fairly strong. In addition to that, you are taking in a nice credit for the spread.

Your position now looks like this:

Composition: Long 1 put at K_2
Short 2 puts at K_1

Max Profit: $(K_2 - K_1)$ + Credit or – Debit (to establish ratio spread)

Max Loss: Substantial on the downside; on the upside, the debit to establish the ratio spread (if done for a debit)

Break-even Points: Upside: K_2 – Debit
Downside: K_1 – Maximum Profit Potential or {[(# Long puts × Difference in Strike Prices) + Credit or – Debit] / number of puts naked}

In this Example:

Composition: Long 1 Oct 60 put
Short 2 Oct 55 puts

Max Profit: (\$60 – \$55) + \$3 = \$8

Max Loss: Substantial to the downside

Break-even Points: \$55 – [1 × (\$60 – \$55) + \$3 = \$8 / 1] = \$47

Oct 55/60 Ratio Put Spread, 1 × 2

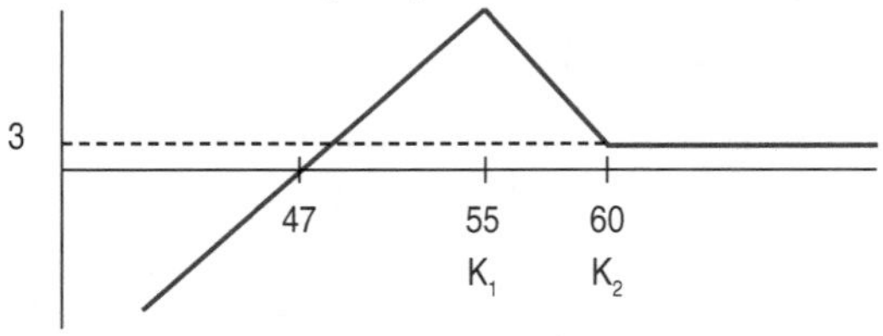

As you can see from the expiration payout graph, the risk/reward profile of the ratio put spread looks like the mirror image of that of the ratio call spread. You can see that losses can be substantial on the downside if the underlying falls to zero, although your "cushion"—because of the credit received when you initiated the spread—has you covered all the way down to your break-even of \$47 before you begin to lose money. The good news is that you make money anywhere between \$47 and \$60. The greatest return of \$8 (or \$800) is achieved at the strike of your short options (the 55 strike).

If the stock sits still, breaks back down to its support of $55, or rallies hard, you will make money with your spread. Worst-case scenario is if the stock breaks down and keeps going down. In that case there are actually a couple of fairly easy ways to close off your unlimited downside risk. The first would be the most logical: buy back the extra 55 put that you'd sold out and leave yourself simply long the 55/60 put bear spread. The other would be to leg into the equidistant lower strike put, in this case by buying the 50 put. By doing this you will have turned your ratio spread into a butterfly and limited your risk.

Now that you have a basic understanding and have seen how call and put ratio spreads function, we'll move on to a discussion of their counterparts—call and put backspreads.

EXERCISE TWO: RATIO PUT SPREAD

Use the prices of MNO to determine the following for the Oct 77.50/82.50 ratio put spread:

Composition:

Max Profit:

Max Loss:

Break-even Points:

Plot a P&L graph:

Last	Bid	Theo	Ask	Strike	Bid	Theo	Ask	Last
83.00	82.94	**82.97**	83.00	**MNO**				
				Sep00				
20.00	33.00	**33.24**	33.50	**50.00**	0.06	**0.07**	0.19	1.00
16.75	28.00	**28.31**	28.50	**55.00**	0.13	**0.13**	0.25	0.25
19.25	23.13	**23.45**	23.63	**60.00**	0.19	**0.25**	0.31	0.38
19.38	18.50	**18.72**	18.88	**65.00**	0.44	**0.50**	0.56	0.50
13.00	14.00	**14.26**	14.38	**70.00**	0.81	**1.02**	1.00	1.00
8.75	10.00	**10.28**	10.38	**75.00**	1.81	**2.03**	2.00	1.94
6.25	6.63	**6.95**	7.00	**80.00**	3.38	**3.71**	3.63	3.50
3.75	4.13	**4.41**	4.38	**85.00**	5.88	**6.17**	6.25	6.25
2.25	2.44	**2.64**	2.50	**90.00**	9.25	**9.40**	9.63	9.25
1.13	1.25	**1.50**	1.44	**95.00**	13.13	**13.26**	13.50	13.75
0.88	0.63	**0.82**	0.81	**100.00**	17.38	**17.59**	17.75	23.00
0.50	0.25	**0.44**	0.38	**105.00**	22.00	**22.25**	22.50	0.00
0.50	0.13	**0.23**	0.25	**110.00**	26.88	**27.09**	27.38	0.00
0.25	0.06	**0.13**	0.19	**115.00**	31.75	**32.03**	32.25	0.00
0.13	0.00	**0.01**	0.13	**120.00**	36.75	**37.03**	37.25	49.25
0.13	0.00	**0.00**	0.13	**125.00**	41.75	**42.03**	42.25	0.00
0.00	0.00	**0.00**	0.13	**130.00**	46.75	**47.03**	47.25	0.00
				Oct00				
31.88	33.50	**33.73**	34.00	**50.00**	0.19	**0.29**	0.31	0.44
21.75	28.88	**29.05**	29.38	**55.00**	0.44	**0.56**	0.56	0.81
25.13	24.38	**24.57**	24.88	**60.00**	0.88	**1.04**	1.06	1.13
19.00	20.13	**20.37**	20.63	**65.00**	1.69	**1.82**	1.88	1.94
15.75	16.38	**16.54**	16.75	**70.00**	2.81	**2.96**	3.00	3.25
15.25	13.00	**13.16**	13.38	**75.00**	4.38	**4.53**	4.63	5.00
11.25	11.50	**11.65**	11.88	**77.50**	5.38	**5.53**	5.75	6.38
10.88	10.13	**10.26**	10.50	**80.00**	6.38	**6.63**	6.75	7.13
8.00	8.88	**8.99**	9.25	**82.50**	7.50	**7.84**	7.88	14.63
7.25	7.75	**7.85**	8.13	**85.00**	8.88	**9.21**	9.25	8.75
6.13	6.63	**6.82**	7.00	**87.50**	10.38	**10.64**	10.75	15.88
6.00	5.75	**5.90**	6.00	**90.00**	11.88	**12.24**	12.25	12.25
5.00	5.00	**5.09**	5.25	**92.50**	13.63	**13.92**	14.00	12.88
4.50	4.25	**4.37**	4.50	**95.00**	15.38	**15.70**	15.75	26.75
4.00	3.63	**3.74**	3.88	**97.50**	17.25	**17.57**	17.63	16.13
3.00	3.00	**3.19**	3.25	**100.00**	19.13	**19.52**	19.50	30.00
2.19	2.19	**2.30**	2.38	**105.00**	23.25	**23.65**	23.75	19.63
1.63	1.56	**1.64**	1.75	**110.00**	27.63	**28.01**	28.13	33.50
1.69	1.06	**1.16**	1.25	**115.00**	32.25	**32.58**	32.75	31.13
0.69	0.69	**0.82**	0.88	**120.00**	37.00	**37.29**	37.50	0.00
1.50	0.50	**0.57**	0.69	**125.00**	41.88	**42.13**	42.38	33.38
0.69	0.31	**0.40**	0.44	**130.00**	46.75	**47.04**	47.25	0.00

BACKSPREADS

A backspread is simply the opposite side of a ratio spread trade. It is being net long more options than you are short. You would sell an option that is closer to the ATM and buy a greater amount of OTM options at another strike. It can be thought of as being short a vertical spread with extra units bought against the short position as a sort of a bonus. A backspread—whether done with calls or puts—tends to take advantage of an underlying that is getting ready to break out and make a quick, sharp move or is starting to trend in a specific direction. In any case you are looking for an increase in volatility. In general, the position is initiated as a fairly delta neutral position and should be done for a credit or even money (which at times may be difficult).

A backspread can be viewed and thought of in the same terms as a ratio spread: in the traditional sense of more longs than shorts or compared to vertical spreads or butterflies. A call backspread is the opposite side of the ratio call spread trade, or effectively being short the ratio call spread. The same applies to the put backspread. It is effectively the equivalent of being short the ratio put spread, although traders do not normally describe it as such; they instead speak of being either "ratioed off" or backspread.

We've seen with ratio spreads that problems can arise because of the unlimited risk component when there is a large move in the wrong direction; to the upside with a ratio call spread and to the downside with a ratio put spread. Imagine being on the other side of one of those trades, where you are the one with the unlimited profit potential if the market rallies hard or breaks hard—that is exactly what the backspread position can afford you. You need to carefully pick and choose the correct stock in which to execute one of these spreads, however, because time and lack of volatility are your enemies. Let's take a look at some specific examples of backspreads.

The Call Backspread

There are a few different ways to put on a call backspread, but we will look at a basic example wherein the trader sells a lower-strike (ATM) call and then buys proportionately more calls at a higher strike price (more OTM).

Just like ratio spreads, you can use just about any ratio or any strike. It does not have to be 1:2. In the case of backspreads, however, the general rule is that the ratio should be a multiple of 1:2 or 2:3, otherwise the payoff probabilities shrink dramatically. Call backspreads typically work the best in bull markets where the implied volatilities on the upside calls are not too great, relative to the other strikes.

Because backspreads are simply the flip side of the trade to ratio spreads, let's walk through a quick example using PQR options once again. You are trying to accomplish something different here; and you'll have to be choosing different strikes and maybe even change the expiration month in order to accommodate that.

Let's assume PQR is trading at $62.50 and you will choose the September expiration this time. Remember that you are now looking for a breakout to the upside in the stock. You can sell one of the September 65 calls for $4.50 and buy two of the 75 calls for $2.50 each and you will pay a debit of $0.50 for the spread. Once again you are left with a fairly delta neutral spread and your position now has a risk/reward profile that looks something like this at expiration:

Composition: Short 1 ATM call @ K_1
Long 2 OTM calls @ K_2

Max Profit: Unlimited to the upside; downside limited to debit to establish spread (if done for a debit)

Max Loss: $(K_2 - K_1)$ – Credit or + Debit (to establish backspread)

Break-even Point: K_2 + Maximum Loss, or {[$(K_2 - K_1)$ – Credit or + Debit] × # Extra Units Bought}

In this example:

Composition: Short 1 Sep 65 call
Long 2 Sep 75 calls

Max Profit: Unlimited above $85.50

Max Loss: ($75 – $65) + $0.50 = $10.50

Break-even Point: $85.50

September 65/75 Call Backspread, 1 × 2

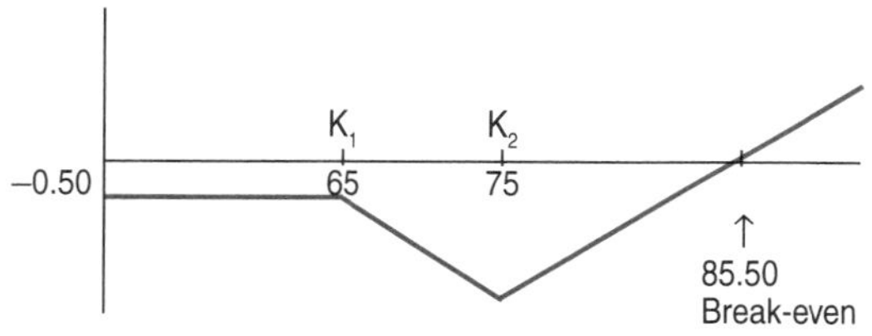

As you can see from the profile, it is like taking the call ratio spread and simply turning it upside down. Your profit is unlimited on the upside. On the downside (below the lower strike) you will lose the debit that was paid to put on the spread—which in this case is $0.50 (or $50). As is indicated by the graph, your biggest risk is of the underlying expiring right at the strike you are long, in this case the 75 strike. If that were to happen, you would lose the maximum value of the vertical spread plus or minus the cost of the backspread. In the example above we would calculate that as:

$(K_2 - K)$ +/– Debit/Credit *or* ($75 – $65) + $0.50 = $10.50 (or $1,050).

Your break-even in this case would be $85.50.

Of course your potential above $85.50 in the stock at expiration is unlimited as long as the stock keeps rallying. From the example, however, you can clearly see why there is a need for a sharp, substantial move in the underlying price in order to make this spread worth your while.

EXERCISE THREE: CALL BACKSPREAD

Last	Bid	Theo	Ask	Strike	Bid	Theo	Ask	Last
83.00	82.94	**82.97**	83.00	**MNO**				
				Sep00				
20.00	33.00	**33.24**	33.50	**50.00**	0.06	**0.07**	0.19	1.00
16.75	28.00	**28.31**	28.50	**55.00**	0.13	**0.13**	0.25	0.25
19.25	23.13	**23.45**	23.63	**60.00**	0.19	**0.25**	0.31	0.38
19.38	18.50	**18.72**	18.88	**65.00**	0.44	**0.50**	0.56	0.50
13.00	14.00	**14.26**	14.38	**70.00**	0.81	**1.02**	1.00	1.00
8.75	10.00	**10.28**	10.38	**75.00**	1.81	**2.03**	2.00	1.94
6.25	6.63	**6.95**	7.00	**80.00**	3.38	**3.71**	3.63	3.50
3.75	4.13	**4.41**	4.38	**85.00**	5.88	**6.17**	6.25	6.25
2.25	2.44	**2.64**	2.50	**90.00**	9.25	**9.40**	9.63	9.25
1.13	1.25	**1.50**	1.44	**95.00**	13.13	**13.26**	13.50	13.75
0.88	0.63	**0.82**	0.81	**100.00**	17.38	**17.59**	17.75	23.00
0.50	0.25	**0.44**	0.38	**105.00**	22.00	**22.25**	22.50	0.00
0.50	0.13	**0.23**	0.25	**110.00**	26.88	**27.09**	27.38	0.00
0.25	0.06	**0.13**	0.19	**115.00**	31.75	**32.03**	32.25	0.00
0.13	0.00	**0.01**	0.13	**120.00**	36.75	**37.03**	37.25	49.25
0.13	0.00	**0.00**	0.13	**125.00**	41.75	**42.03**	42.25	0.00
0.00	0.00	**0.00**	0.13	**130.00**	46.75	**47.03**	47.25	0.00
				Oct00				
31.88	33.50	**33.73**	34.00	**50.00**	0.19	**0.29**	0.31	0.44
21.75	28.88	**29.05**	29.38	**55.00**	0.44	**0.56**	0.56	0.81
25.13	24.38	**24.57**	24.88	**60.00**	0.88	**1.04**	1.06	1.13
19.00	20.13	**20.37**	20.63	**65.00**	1.69	**1.82**	1.88	1.94
15.75	16.38	**16.54**	16.75	**70.00**	2.81	**2.96**	3.00	3.25
15.25	13.00	**13.16**	13.38	**75.00**	4.38	**4.53**	4.63	5.00
11.25	11.50	**11.65**	11.88	**77.50**	5.38	**5.53**	5.75	6.38
10.88	10.13	**10.26**	10.50	**80.00**	6.38	**6.63**	6.75	7.13
8.00	8.88	**8.99**	9.25	**82.50**	7.50	**7.84**	7.88	14.63
7.25	7.75	**7.85**	8.13	**85.00**	8.88	**9.21**	9.25	8.75
6.13	6.63	**6.82**	7.00	**87.50**	10.38	**10.64**	10.75	15.88
6.00	5.75	**5.90**	6.00	**90.00**	11.88	**12.24**	12.25	12.25
5.00	5.00	**5.09**	5.25	**92.50**	13.63	**13.92**	14.00	12.88
4.50	4.25	**4.37**	4.50	**95.00**	15.38	**15.70**	15.75	26.75
4.00	3.63	**3.74**	3.88	**97.50**	17.25	**17.57**	17.63	16.13
3.00	3.00	**3.19**	3.25	**100.00**	19.13	**19.52**	19.50	30.00
2.19	2.19	**2.30**	2.38	**105.00**	23.25	**23.65**	23.75	19.63
1.63	1.56	**1.64**	1.75	**110.00**	27.63	**28.01**	28.13	33.50
1.69	1.06	**1.16**	1.25	**115.00**	32.25	**32.58**	32.75	31.13
0.69	0.69	**0.82**	0.88	**120.00**	37.00	**37.29**	37.50	0.00
1.50	0.50	**0.57**	0.69	**125.00**	41.88	**42.13**	42.38	33.38
0.69	0.31	**0.40**	0.44	**130.00**	46.75	**47.04**	47.25	0.00

Use the prices of MNO to determine the following for the Oct 82.50/97.50 call backspread:

Composition:

Max Profit:

Max Loss:

Break-even Points:

Plot a P&L graph:

The Put Backspread

Here again, there are many different paths to take when you are looking to initiate a put backspread. We will look at the basic example where we'll be selling a higher strike put (ATM) and buying proportionately more puts at a lower strike price (OTM). Put backspreads are the mirror image of call backspreads, and the opposite side of the trade to a ratio put spread. With a put backspread you are looking for the market to drop, and the more the better. Implied volatilities come into play here once again, and can make things easy or tough for you depending on the volatility skew at that time.

Again using PQR, we'll go through a quick example. You are going to attempt to once again put this trade on for as close to even money as possible, although in the stock market this is harder to do because of the nature of implied volatilities in these downside puts. You will have to look over a few months and various strikes in order to find a spread with a reasonable risk/reward profile for what you are trying to accomplish.

Looking at the option valuations once again with the stock still at $62.50, you will settle on the September expiration for your backspread. This time, however, you will be using the 50 and 55 strikes. The 55 put can be sold once for $3.50 and the 50 put can be bought twice for $2.00 each, so you can initiate the backspread for a $0.50 debit. Our position now has a composition that looks something like this at expiration.

Composition: Long 2 puts at K_1
Short 1 put at K_2

Max Profit: Limited as the underlying price falls below the break-even point to zero on the downside; the upside is limited to the credit received (if done for a credit.)

Max Loss: $(K_2 - K_1)$ – Credit or + Debit (to establish backspread)

Break-even Point: K_2 – Max Loss, or $K_1 - \{[(K_2 - K_1)$ +/– Debit/Credit$] \times$ # Extra Units Bought$\}$

In this example:

Composition: Long 2 Oct 50 puts
Short 1 Oct 55 put

Max Profit: Limited as the underlying price falls below the break-even point to zero on the downside; the upside is limited to the credit received (if done for a credit.)

Max Loss: ($55 – $50) + $0.50 = $5.50 (or $550).

Break-even Point: $44.50 on the downside.

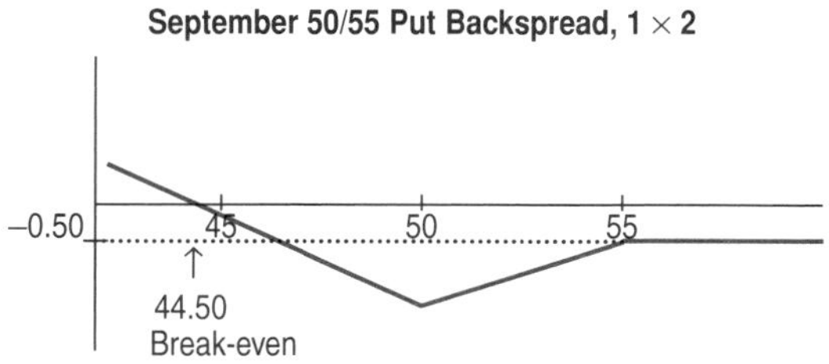

As mentioned before, the put backspread is simply the mirror image of the call backspread, or like taking the ratio put spread and turning it upside down. Your maximum profit is limited as the underlying price falls below the break-even point to zero on the downside and on the upside (above the higher strike) you simply lose what you paid to put on the position or you get to keep the credit received if the spread was done for a credit. In this case you established the position for a debit of $0.50; you lose $50 at 55.50 or above.

Your greatest risk is if the underlying expires at the strike in which you are holding the long options—in this case, the 50 strike. If that were to happen you would lose the maximum value of the backspread plus the debit or minus the credit of the backspread. In our current example, that would be $550 ([$55 – $50] + $0.50 = $5.50 × 100).

Your potential gain down below $44.50 at expiration is substantial on the downside to the stock falling to zero. As you can see, there is definitely a need for a sharp, substantial down move in the underlying stock price in order to make this spread really profitable.

EXERCISE FOUR: PUT BACKSPREAD

Last	Bid	Theo	Ask	Strike	Bid	Theo	Ask	Last
83.00	82.94	**82.97**	83.00	**MNO**				
				Sep00				
20.00	33.00	**33.24**	33.50	**50.00**	0.06	**0.07**	0.19	1.00
16.75	28.00	**28.31**	28.50	**55.00**	0.13	**0.13**	0.25	0.25
19.25	23.13	**23.45**	23.63	**60.00**	0.19	**0.25**	0.31	0.38
19.38	18.50	**18.72**	18.88	**65.00**	0.44	**0.50**	0.56	0.50
13.00	14.00	**14.26**	14.38	**70.00**	0.81	**1.02**	1.00	1.00
8.75	10.00	**10.28**	10.38	**75.00**	1.81	**2.03**	2.00	1.94
6.25	6.63	**6.95**	7.00	**80.00**	3.38	**3.71**	3.63	3.50
3.75	4.13	**4.41**	4.38	**85.00**	5.88	**6.17**	6.25	6.25
2.25	2.44	**2.64**	2.50	**90.00**	9.25	**9.40**	9.63	9.25
1.13	1.25	**1.50**	1.44	**95.00**	13.13	**13.26**	13.50	13.75
0.88	0.63	**0.82**	0.81	**100.00**	17.38	**17.59**	17.75	23.00
0.50	0.25	**0.44**	0.38	**105.00**	22.00	**22.25**	22.50	0.00
0.50	0.13	**0.23**	0.25	**110.00**	26.88	**27.09**	27.38	0.00
0.25	0.06	**0.13**	0.19	**115.00**	31.75	**32.03**	32.25	0.00
0.13	0.00	**0.01**	0.13	**120.00**	36.75	**37.03**	37.25	49.25
0.13	0.00	**0.00**	0.13	**125.00**	41.75	**42.03**	42.25	0.00
0.00	0.00	**0.00**	0.13	**130.00**	46.75	**47.03**	47.25	0.00
				Oct00				
31.88	33.50	**33.73**	34.00	**50.00**	0.19	**0.29**	0.31	0.44
21.75	28.88	**29.05**	29.38	**55.00**	0.44	**0.56**	0.56	0.81
25.13	24.38	**24.57**	24.88	**60.00**	0.88	**1.04**	1.06	1.13
19.00	20.13	**20.37**	20.63	**65.00**	1.69	**1.82**	1.88	1.94
15.75	16.38	**16.54**	16.75	**70.00**	2.81	**2.96**	3.00	3.25
15.25	13.00	**13.16**	13.38	**75.00**	4.38	**4.53**	4.63	5.00
11.25	11.50	**11.65**	11.88	**77.50**	5.38	**5.53**	5.75	6.38
10.88	10.13	**10.26**	10.50	**80.00**	6.38	**6.63**	6.75	7.13
8.00	8.88	**8.99**	9.25	**82.50**	7.50	**7.84**	7.88	14.63
7.25	7.75	**7.85**	8.13	**85.00**	8.88	**9.21**	9.25	8.75
6.13	6.63	**6.82**	7.00	**87.50**	10.38	**10.64**	10.75	15.88
6.00	5.75	**5.90**	6.00	**90.00**	11.88	**12.24**	12.25	12.25
5.00	5.00	**5.09**	5.25	**92.50**	13.63	**13.92**	14.00	12.88
4.50	4.25	**4.37**	4.50	**95.00**	15.38	**15.70**	15.75	26.75
4.00	3.63	**3.74**	3.88	**97.50**	17.25	**17.57**	17.63	16.13
3.00	3.00	**3.19**	3.25	**100.00**	19.13	**19.52**	19.50	30.00
2.19	2.19	**2.30**	2.38	**105.00**	23.25	**23.65**	23.75	19.63
1.63	1.56	**1.64**	1.75	**110.00**	27.63	**28.01**	28.13	33.50
1.69	1.06	**1.16**	1.25	**115.00**	32.25	**32.58**	32.75	31.13
0.69	0.69	**0.82**	0.88	**120.00**	37.00	**37.29**	37.50	0.00
1.50	0.50	**0.57**	0.69	**125.00**	41.88	**42.13**	42.38	33.38
0.69	0.31	**0.40**	0.44	**130.00**	46.75	**47.04**	47.25	0.00

Use the prices of MNO to determine the following for the Oct 70/82.50 put backspread:

Composition:

Max Profit:

Max Loss:

Break-even Points:

Plot a P&L graph:

ANSWERS TO EXERCISES

EXERCISE ONE: Ratio Call Spread

Composition:	Long one Oct MNO 82.50 call @ $9.25	= $ (9.25) debit
	Sell two Oct MNO 87.50 calls @ $6.63	= $13.26 credit
		$ 4.01 credit

Max Profit: $5 + $4.01 = $9.01 (× 100) = $901

Max Loss: Unlimited above $91.51 on the upside

Break-even Points: $96.50, or $4.01 + (1 × $5) = $9.01 + $87.50 = $96.51 (on the upside)
Below $82.50 you keep the $4.01 credit (on the downside)

Plot a P&L graph:

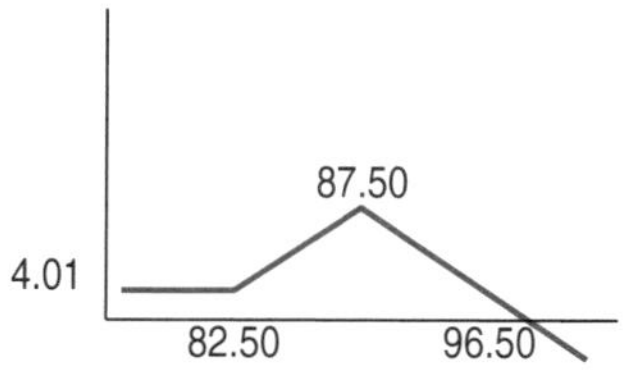

EXERCISE TWO: Ratio Put Spread

Composition:	Long one Oct MNO 82.50 put @ $7.88	= $ (7.88) debit
	Short two Oct MNO 77.50 puts @ $5.38	= $10.76 credit
		$ 2.88 credit

Max Profit: $5 + $2.88 = $7.88 (× 100) = $788.00

Max Loss: Substantial on the downside.

Break-even Points: $69.62 (on downside) and above $82.50 on upside keep $2.88 credit

Plot a P&L graph:

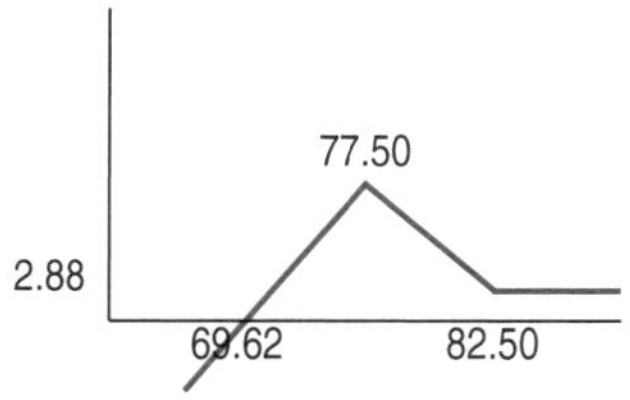

EXERCISE THREE: Call Backspread

Composition:	Sell one MNO Oct 82.50 call @ $8.88	= $ 8.88 credit
	Buy two MNO Oct 97.50 calls @ $3.88	= $(7.76) debit
		$ 1.12 credit

Max Profit: Unlimited on upside

Max Loss: At the 97.50 strike, it loses $1,388 ($15 – $1.12 = $13.88 × 100)

Break-even Points: $83.62 ($82.50 + $1.12) (on the downside) and $111.38 ($97.50 + $15 – $1.12) (on the upside)

Plot a P&L graph:

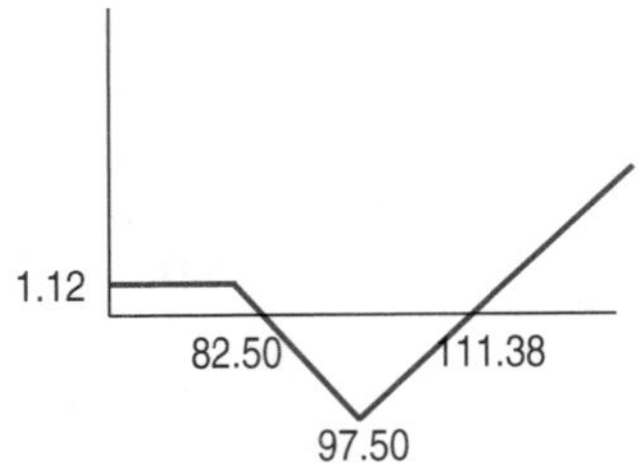

EXERCISE FOUR: Put Backspread

Composition:	Sell one MNO Oct 82.50 put @ $7.50	= $ 7.50 credit
	Buy two MNO Oct 70 puts @ $3.00	= $(6.00) debit
		$ 1.50 credit

Max Profit: Limited as the underlying price falls below break-even point to zero on the downside

Max Loss: $1,100 [at 70 strike, you lose difference of spread ($12.50 – $1.50 credit = $11 × 100)]

Break-even Points: $81 (on upside) ($82.50 – $1.50 credit)
$59 (on downside) (70 strike – $11 (difference of spread) – $1.50 credit)

Plot a P&L graph:

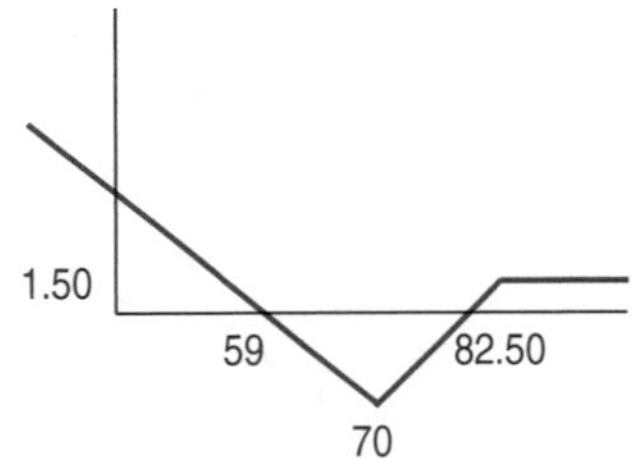

CHAPTER 7 QUIZ

1. True or false? With a call backspread you sell the lower strike and buy more of the higher strike.

2. True or false? With put backspreads, you sell the higher strike and buy more of the lower strike.

3. Is your outlook bullish or bearish if you construct a call backspread for a .25 credit? At what point do you have risk?

4. How does time affect a backspread?

5. How would volatility affect this position?

6. How do you determine the maximum profit of a ratio put spread?

7. True or false? A put backspread is the opposite side of the trade of a ratio put spread.

8. True or false? A ratio call spread tends to take advantage of an underlying that is trading within a range of prices or is trending in a specific direction.

CHAPTER 7 QUIZ ANSWER KEY

1. True

2. True

3. Bullish. If the underlying moves significantly up (past the upper strike), a profit will result. If it moves below the lower strike, you keep the .25 point credit.

4. Time works for a backspread if the underlying remains at the strike of the short options and the spread was put on for a credit (positive theta).

5. Normally, volatility works for this position (positive vega). A backspread should be put on in a low volatility for a credit, in anticipation of a large upward move in the underlying or an increase in implied volatility.

6. $(K_2 - K_1)$ + Credit or – Debit

7. True

8. True

CHAPTER 8

The 21st Century Trader

Current Technology and Its Evolution

This chapter presents the trading landscape: past, present, and future. Today, options trading may be accessible to everyone willing to educate themselves in the discipline and use of technology. This chapter presents the electronic "trading tool kit" within the context of the current state of the art. Before our discussion, though, a brief chronology of how we arrived at this point is appropriate. Finally, we will discuss the uncertain direction technology will take option traders in the future. The possibilities, like our imaginations, are boundless. CBOE rules are based on SEC regulations. Federal securities laws prohibit the mention of specific securities. Therefore, we had to use fictitious stock symbols in all examples.

THE PAST

If the American trading environment were fashioned together to form a building, the cornerstone would be our open outcry system of buying and selling. The Securities and Exchange Commission (SEC) oversees the U.S. securities markets and exchanges, where all buyers and sellers meet to transact business. It is at the various exchanges that list options contracts that the execution of each option trade has taken place over the past decades. After the trader or broker makes a trade, the process of matching that order, called execution, begins. Other aspects of order execution, such as *clearing,* are required, but matching your order with that of another's is fundamental—for every seller there must be a buyer, and vice versa. The execution of an options order involves a sequence of steps that is dependent on the number of contracts called for, contingencies on the order, and the capabilities of your broker.

The fundamentals of trading in person remain the same, but today they are expedited with the assistance of technology. First, an order must be communicated by calling a broker or using an electronic means. It is necessary to specify whether to buy or sell (open or close), the quantity desired, the underlying stock, the contract expiration month, the strike price, contingencies (market order, limit order, good-til-canceled), and an account number. Next, the broker communicates the order to the floor of an exchange. Alternatively, an electronic system routes the order to the exchange floor—either way, an order will be presented *in person* or electronically to a floor broker. It is the job of the floor broker to represent the trade within the trading pit, so-called because of the descending steps into a round area on the exchange floor allowing the participants to clearly see and hear one another. The floor broker may ask for a general quote from the pit (other participants) or may buy/sell directly. Or the broker could decide to "bid the market." This means asking for a specific lower price when purchasing contracts or asking for a specific higher price when selling contracts. Once a commitment is made between the broker and the market maker within the pit, an order becomes a trade and the reporting of the trade begins its journey back to its originator. An order is part of what is known as the order flow. The order flow is referred to as "paper" in floor speak. Where paper is routed depends on a number of variables, such as, which exchange trades the underlying stocks, or the relationship between a brokerage house and a particular exchange.

How an option order was executed in the past involved a familiar set of tools. Contracts were found via the newspaper or an industry publication. Checking the ticker tape provided an idea of where that underlying stock had been trading and where it was trading currently. Next, the order was placed by phoning a broker who used effective, yet now obsolete, tools such as a phone or teletype to communicate the customer's order to the exchange floor. Later, the communication was made back to the broker from the exchange that the buy or sell had been completed. These steps used the nondigital tools available to all market participants. The use of the phone as a primary means of communication is diminishing, yet will continue to be popular for institutional brokers who facilitate large orders for their client base.

The Options Exchanges

There are four physical options exchanges in the United States:

1. Chicago Board Options Exchange
2. American Stock Exchange
3. Pacific Stock Exchange
4. Philadelphia Stock Exchange

These four exchanges house the specialists (market makers or contra parties) that make markets for a particular stock option series. In Chicago, market makers provide liquidity for each of the options offered. An order for JKL August 50 put contracts is routed to the CBOE specialist who fills that stock's order. Let us assume that an order is written for the JKL 50s and the order price falls between available bid and ask prices. The specialist, when presented with that order, will supply the matching transaction. Remember, for every buyer there must be a matching seller. Therefore, when you sell, the specialist buys; when you buy, the specialist sells. How does the specialist make money? By buying lower and selling higher than the orders they receive. When a customer buys then the contra party is selling; likewise, when a customer is selling, the contra party is buying. That order is known as the *contra order.* All of the four physical exchanges function similarly.

We might add the International Security Exchange (ISE) into the mix. The ISE is a bona fide exchange. It is registered with the SEC and has incorporated rules providing for its equitable operation. Not to be confused with an Electronic Communications Network (ECN), where bids and offers are presented to market specialists, the ISE allows the trader to match up with other retail customers. An interesting aspect of the ISE is the rule that customer orders are executed before professional orders.

How Trades Were Managed

The management of trades in times past was only as good as a trader's filing system. Trade confirmations were at one time paper statements, so it was necessary for the trader to physically organize and track these trades. The trader often transcribed the appropriate information to other computation sheets to find out what his or her position was at any given time. After an order is executed, it is more appropriately termed a *trade,* or sometimes a *fill*—meaning a filled order. When a trader listed these trades by expiration date, by underlying stock, by type (call or put), etc., we say that the trader has tracked his or her position. This tracking process was the first step toward risk management. Current tracking methods and risk management will be discussed shortly in the context of the trader's electronic workstation.

How Traders Assessed Their Risk

Prior to the advent of electronic risk and order management systems, traders were required to monitor the risk exposure of their positions manually. Traders went through lots of paper and pencils tallying up positions to get a clearer view of risk.

It was a natural evolution to add automation to the options trading industry. The recordkeeping and computational aspects were burdensome. It is hard to imagine now that the options industry once operated without computer automation.

THE PRESENT

Today we find ourselves in a semi-technical trading environment. Many of the electronic puzzle pieces are coming together. Some mundane tasks that brokers, floor traders, and retail consumers must perform are being automated. We still lack a fully integrated solution for any of the defined roles: brokers have some tools available to them, but a completely integrated solution has yet to emerge. Floor traders have many tools provided to them by the exchanges, but their needs are not fully met, and the technology is changing more rapidly than the exchanges can adapt. Consumer-oriented software is hard to use, too specialized, and largely separate from the systems that the brokerages use. Software that is adept for relaying quotes is typically not sufficient for managing risk and vice versa. Many of the interfaces that are necessary for these software systems to operate optimally have yet to be standardized, let alone be offered on a widespread basis. Alas, we find ourselves spending too much time trying to discern the thoughts of the software developer rather than concentrating on the discipline of trading options. The future is bright, though, and there is no better time than the present to familiarize yourself with the electronic age of trading options.

Electronic Prices and Analytics

Providing real-time prices (and values derived from these prices) to the user has some inherently unique challenges. The most difficult aspect is dealing with the sheer volume of data. A particular underlying stock could have hundreds of options series associated with it. Additionally, for each change in the bid or offer price, a host of new calculations is necessary to provide vital information to the trader. These derived values are loosely termed *analytics,* and are necessary for analyzing particular conditions. An important class of analytical values discussed earlier in this book is called the *greeks.* Another example is implied volatility. When computing the volatility of a contract by using all of the other parameters in the equation, such as price, days to expiration, dividends, interest rate, etc., then the resulting value would be the volatility of the contract as implied by the market. Several examples are discussed later.

Real-time prices. The importance and timeliness of the trader's prices cannot be overemphasized. Traders must receive them from a reliable source, and the electronic connection with that source must be of sufficient bandwidth to provide the streaming prices flawlessly. This is an enormous task when one realizes that the trader's computer is performing numerous calculations on these prices as they come in, many of them simultaneously, and on a periodic basis relating current incoming prices to the trader's position.

Below are representative screens depicting the typical view for spot prices. Notice that the quantity column shows the trader's current position for the underlying symbols. This trader is short 100 shares of stock B; short 7,600 shares of stock C; short 2,700 shares of stock D; and long 1,100 shares of stock E.

The first task is allowing the user to subscribe to the contracts of interest. In most cases, the user would like to see all of the contracts (call and put) associated with an underlying stock. In fact, the user may be interested in watching many stock option

	Qty	Symbol	Last	NET
1	0	A	84.50	7.25
2	-100	B	68.69	-1.56
3	-7600	C	25.25	-0.31
4	-2700	D	64.63	1.06
5	1100	E	32.88	-0.23

BidSZ	Bid	Ask
35	84.50	84.63
1	68.69	68.69
400	25.19	25.25
10	64.63	64.63
1	32.88	32.94

AskSZ	LastSZ	Volume
71	3100	1,434,200
10	7000	2,581,400
400	700	5,808,100
1	100	13,886,000
15	100	1,385,500

(Courtesy *First Traders Analytical Solutions, LLC*)

chains concurrently. Note the *Bid* and *Ask* columns. (Call prices are found on the left side and put prices on the right separated by the strike column.) As the trading day progresses, the option prices change vigorously, especially at the active opening of the market. The Bid and Ask columns will flash new prices continually—green letters for ticks up and red letters for ticks down. The challenge of all software developers is to produce a pricing engine that funnels the incoming prices from the quote vendor and paints a number in the appropriate cell on the machine. All these steps must occur in a fraction of a second. If the trader has ten market views open, then the system is working ten times as hard! It is quickly apparent that network bandwidth (i.e., computing power) is always at a premium within the trading business.

Note in the view to the right that some of the months are "hidden." This allows the trader to view only the month(s) of interest while not filling too much of their display. By double clicking the "Sep00" text in the strike column the contracts for that month will be expanded back into view.

QRxMarket1.mkt - Market

File Edit Format Settings View Help

Bid	Theo	Ask	Strike	Bid	Theo	Ask
64.88	64.91	64.94				
			Sep00			
			Oct00			
34.75	35.32	35.75	30.00	0.00	0.07	0.19
29.88	30.42	30.88	35.00	0.00	0.11	0.19
25.00	25.56	26.00	40.00	0.06	0.20	0.25
20.38	20.79	21.38	45.00	0.31	0.37	0.50
18.25	18.46	18.75	47.50	0.50	0.52	0.69
16.00	16.20	16.50	50.00	0.69	0.73	0.88
13.88	14.01	14.38	52.50	1.00	1.02	1.19
11.75	11.93	12.25	55.00	1.38	1.40	1.56
9.88	9.96	10.25	57.50	1.88	1.93	2.06
8.00	8.15	8.38	60.00	2.50	2.60	2.75
6.38	6.52	6.75	62.50	3.38	3.45	3.50
4.88	5.08	5.25	65.00	4.25	4.50	4.63
3.63	3.84	4.00	67.50	5.50	5.77	5.88
2.63	2.82	2.88	70.00	7.00	7.27	7.38
1.81	2.01	2.00	72.50	8.63	8.97	9.00
1.19	1.38	1.31	75.00	10.50	10.88	11.00
0.75	0.93	0.94	77.50	12.63	12.97	13.13
0.50	0.61	0.63	80.00	14.88	15.23	15.38
0.25	0.39	0.44	82.50	17.38	17.61	17.88
0.13	0.25	0.31	85.00	19.88	20.09	20.38
0.13	0.11	0.19	90.00	24.63	25.09	25.63
0.00	0.07	0.19	95.00	29.63	30.09	30.63
0.00	0.06	0.13	100.00	34.63	35.09	35.63
0.00	0.09	0.19	105.00	39.63	40.09	40.63
			Jan01			
			Apr01			
			Jan02			
			Jan03			

Ready

(Courtesy *First Traders Analytical Solutions, LLC*)

Real-time analytics. Analytics are those calculations that are performed either on a real-time tick-by-tick basis or in the background on a periodic basis. Typically, analytics are calculations performed on updated prices and are displayed in a window alongside those prices. Examples of these are greeks

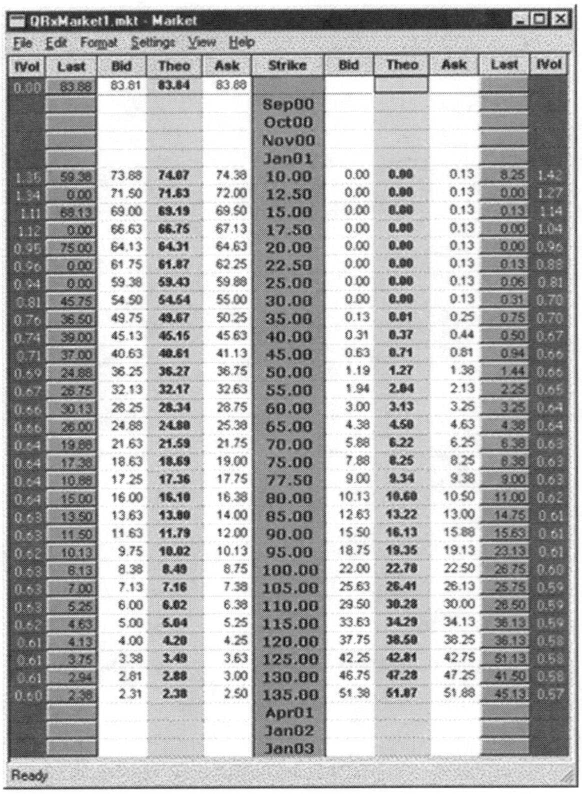

QRxMarket1.mkt - Market

File Edit Format Settings View Help

IVol	Last	Bid	Theo	Ask	Strike	Bid	Theo	Ask	Last	IVol
0.00	83.88	83.81	83.84	83.88						
					Sep00					
					Oct00					
					Nov00					
					Jan01					
1.35	59.38	73.88	74.07	74.38	10.00	0.00	0.00	0.13	8.25	1.42
1.34	0.00	71.50	71.63	72.00	12.50	0.00	0.00	0.13	0.00	1.27
1.11	68.13	69.00	69.19	69.50	15.00	0.00	0.00	0.13	0.13	1.14
1.12	0.00	66.63	66.75	67.13	17.50	0.00	0.00	0.13	0.00	1.04
0.95	75.00	64.13	64.31	64.63	20.00	0.00	0.00	0.13	0.00	0.96
0.96	0.00	61.75	61.87	62.25	22.50	0.00	0.00	0.13	0.13	0.88
0.94	0.00	59.38	59.43	59.88	25.00	0.00	0.00	0.13	0.06	0.81
0.81	45.75	54.50	54.54	55.00	30.00	0.00	0.00	0.13	0.31	0.70
0.76	36.50	49.75	49.67	50.25	35.00	0.13	0.01	0.25	0.75	0.70
0.74	39.00	45.13	45.15	45.63	40.00	0.31	0.37	0.44	0.50	0.67
0.71	37.00	40.63	40.61	41.13	45.00	0.63	0.71	0.81	0.94	0.66
0.69	24.88	36.25	36.27	36.75	50.00	1.19	1.27	1.38	1.44	0.66
0.67	26.75	32.13	32.17	32.63	55.00	1.94	2.04	2.13	2.25	0.65
0.66	30.13	28.25	28.34	28.75	60.00	3.00	3.13	3.25	3.25	0.64
0.66	26.00	24.88	24.80	25.38	65.00	4.38	4.50	4.63	4.38	0.64
0.64	19.88	21.63	21.59	21.75	70.00	5.88	6.22	6.25	6.38	0.63
0.64	17.38	18.63	18.69	19.00	75.00	7.88	8.25	8.25	8.38	0.63
0.64	10.88	17.25	17.36	17.75	77.50	9.00	9.34	9.38	9.00	0.63
0.64	15.00	16.00	16.10	16.38	80.00	10.13	10.60	10.50	11.00	0.62
0.63	13.50	13.63	13.80	14.00	85.00	12.63	13.22	13.00	14.75	0.61
0.63	11.50	11.63	11.79	12.00	90.00	15.50	16.13	15.88	15.63	0.61
0.62	10.13	9.75	10.02	10.13	95.00	18.75	19.35	19.13	23.13	0.61
0.63	8.13	8.38	8.49	8.75	100.00	22.00	22.78	22.50	26.75	0.60
0.63	7.00	7.13	7.16	7.38	105.00	25.63	26.41	26.13	25.75	0.59
0.63	5.25	6.00	6.02	6.38	110.00	29.50	30.28	30.00	26.50	0.59
0.62	4.63	5.00	5.04	5.25	115.00	33.63	34.29	34.13	36.13	0.59
0.61	4.13	4.00	4.20	4.25	120.00	37.75	38.50	38.25	36.13	0.58
0.61	3.75	3.38	3.49	3.63	125.00	42.25	42.81	42.75	51.13	0.58
0.61	2.94	2.81	2.88	3.00	130.00	46.75	47.28	47.25	41.50	0.58
0.60	2.38	2.31	2.38	2.50	135.00	51.38	51.87	51.88	45.13	0.57
					Apr01					
					Jan02					
					Jan03					

Ready

(Courtesy *First Traders Analytical Solutions, LLC*)

and theoretical value calculations. Above is a representative screen showing the implied values for volatility associated with a particular contract. The market view shows the market prices and any associated calculation that the trader chooses. The *First Traders* system allows for different calculations to be plugged in and represented in a column format. It is typical for traders or trading groups to employ proprietary calculations or models that provide a trading edge in the marketplace.

Real-Time Alerts

Alerts are alarms presented to the trader in response to a given condition. There are two general attributes of an alert. The first is the condition. It may be a particular price versus a target theoretical value. For example, the trader may be observing a particular contract when a condition occurs where the theoretical pricing of the contract is higher than the actual price in the market. The trader may wish to be alerted in such a case. It may be possible for the trader to buy low in hopes of selling the contract at a higher price in the future. This is a typical alert condition for most trading systems.

Another alert condition occurs when a position accumulates that is outside parameters set by the firm or the trader, and therefore far too risky to maintain. This will be discussed later in the chapter within the subject of risk management.

The second general attribute of an alert is the delivery mechanism. Once they have been defined, it is necessary to determine how they will be coded. There are

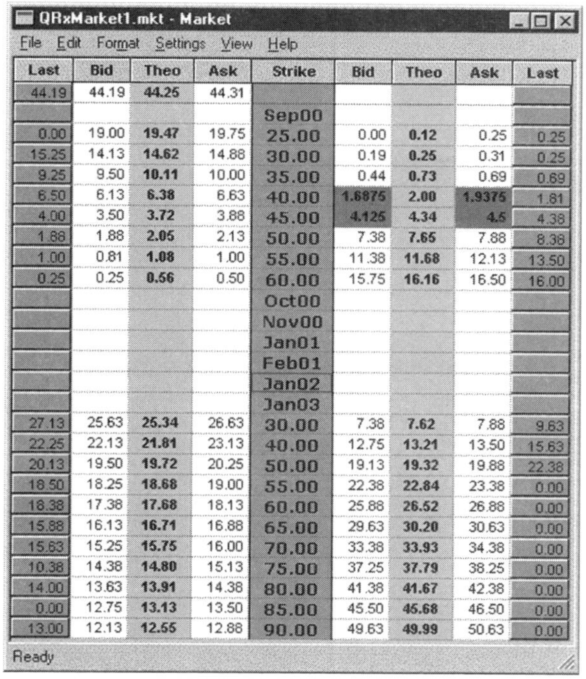

QRxMarket1.mkt - Market

File Edit Format Settings View Help

Last	Bid	Theo	Ask	Strike	Bid	Theo	Ask	Last
44.19	44.19	44.25	44.31					
				Sep00				
0.00	19.00	19.47	19.75	25.00	0.00	0.12	0.25	0.25
15.25	14.13	14.62	14.88	30.00	0.19	0.25	0.31	0.25
9.25	9.50	10.11	10.00	35.00	0.44	0.73	0.69	0.69
6.50	6.13	6.38	6.63	40.00	1.6875	2.00	1.9375	1.81
4.00	3.50	3.72	3.88	45.00	4.125	4.34	4.5	4.38
1.88	1.88	2.05	2.13	50.00	7.38	7.65	7.88	8.38
1.00	0.81	1.08	1.00	55.00	11.38	11.68	12.13	13.50
0.25	0.25	0.56	0.50	60.00	15.75	16.16	16.50	16.00
				Oct00				
				Nov00				
				Jan01				
				Feb01				
				Jan02				
				Jan03				
27.13	25.63	25.34	26.63	30.00	7.38	7.62	7.88	9.63
22.25	22.13	21.81	23.13	40.00	12.75	13.21	13.50	15.63
20.13	19.50	19.72	20.25	50.00	19.13	19.32	19.88	22.38
18.50	18.25	18.68	19.00	55.00	22.38	22.84	23.38	0.00
18.38	17.38	17.68	18.13	60.00	25.88	26.52	26.88	0.00
15.88	16.13	16.71	16.88	65.00	29.63	30.20	30.63	0.00
15.63	15.25	15.75	16.00	70.00	33.38	33.93	34.38	0.00
10.38	14.38	14.80	15.13	75.00	37.25	37.79	38.25	0.00
14.00	13.63	13.91	14.38	80.00	41.38	41.67	42.38	0.00
0.00	12.75	13.13	13.50	85.00	45.50	45.68	46.50	0.00
13.00	12.13	12.55	12.88	90.00	49.63	49.99	50.63	0.00

Ready

(Courtesy *First Traders Analytical Solutions, LLC*)

any number of possibilities, and the most common ones are audible or visual codes. The trader can be notified audibly by using distinct sounds representing various conditions. Visual codes are equally useful. A flashing price, color, bold text, and other means can be used to attract the trader's attention. Pagers, e-mail messages, or similar electronic notification are also practical.

Electronic Execution

The electronic execution begins when the trader enters a trade online or via a software system that is electronically linked to a broker. Your brokerage company converts the input into a valid electronic order, where it is in turn transferred to the routing function. At this point, the routing decisions are made. The order is routed on quantity requested, best available price, system availability, etc., or any permutation thereof. The following sections explain each of these functions.

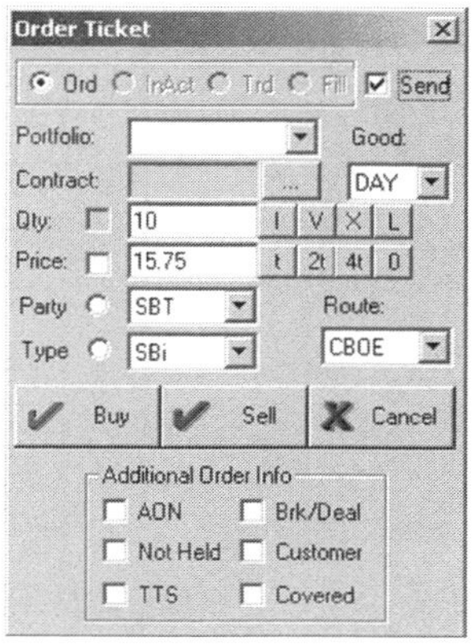

(Courtesy *First Traders Analytical Solutions, LLC*)

Order entry. At right is a typical order ticket used to electronically send an order to an exchange. Though most retail customers do not have this level of sophistication, the function is similar to the order entry screen found on the Web sites of most online brokerages. All of the order specifications are accounted for: the contract, quantity, price, exchange, and order contingencies.

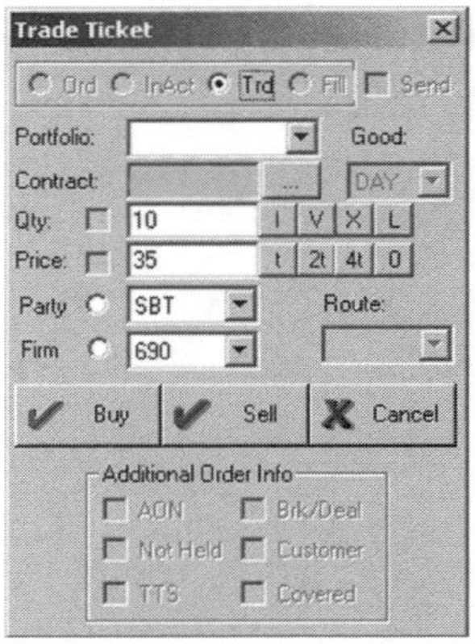

(Courtesy *First Traders Analytical Solutions, LLC*)

To the left is a ticket similar to the order ticket, but its function is quite different. A trade entry ticket is used for manual trades, which are necessary, for example, with phone orders. Frequently, complex orders need to be phoned to a floor broker, in which case the resulting phone fill for the order will need to be keyed in by hand. Once the trade exists within the system, it can be analyzed, reported, and added to the trader's position.

Routing. A popular subject of late is that of routing. Specifically, "intelligent routing" has entered the trading scene and has significantly changed the way the industry handles orders. Imagine receiving an order from an online customer and routing the order so that it receives the best possible price. The intelligent router has all of the connectivity and logic necessary to scan all market participants in order to sell at the highest possible, or buy at the lowest possible, prices. With computers able to compare prices within thousandths of a second, and virtually communicate instantly to/from the exchanges, new levels of efficiency are being realized. The customers win as they obtain the best possible pricing, and the brokerage houses win as they attract new customers to more efficient trading platforms. The algorithms driving the order routers are becoming subtler and more flexible, so that routing decisions can be changed throughout the trading day. Brokers are moving their paper depending on the responses of the pit traders at a certain location. If the brokerage house feels it is treated well at the Pacific Coast Exchange, for example, but even better at the CBOE for a particular series of contracts, then the order flow will be routed accordingly.

Transaction blotter. The transaction, or order blotter, is the facility used to determine the status of orders asserted. Once orders are made, they can go through a number of stages prior to being executed or rejected. At a minimum, the trader desires to view all orders, or only the open orders, filled orders, and manual trades that have been made.

As shown on the order blotter here, each transaction has a corresponding order number identifying that transaction. Other useful information is the underlying and contract, the strike price, quantity, buy/sell indication, and open quantity. The depiction at left shows all of the orders without regard to how they were entered or the current state of the order.

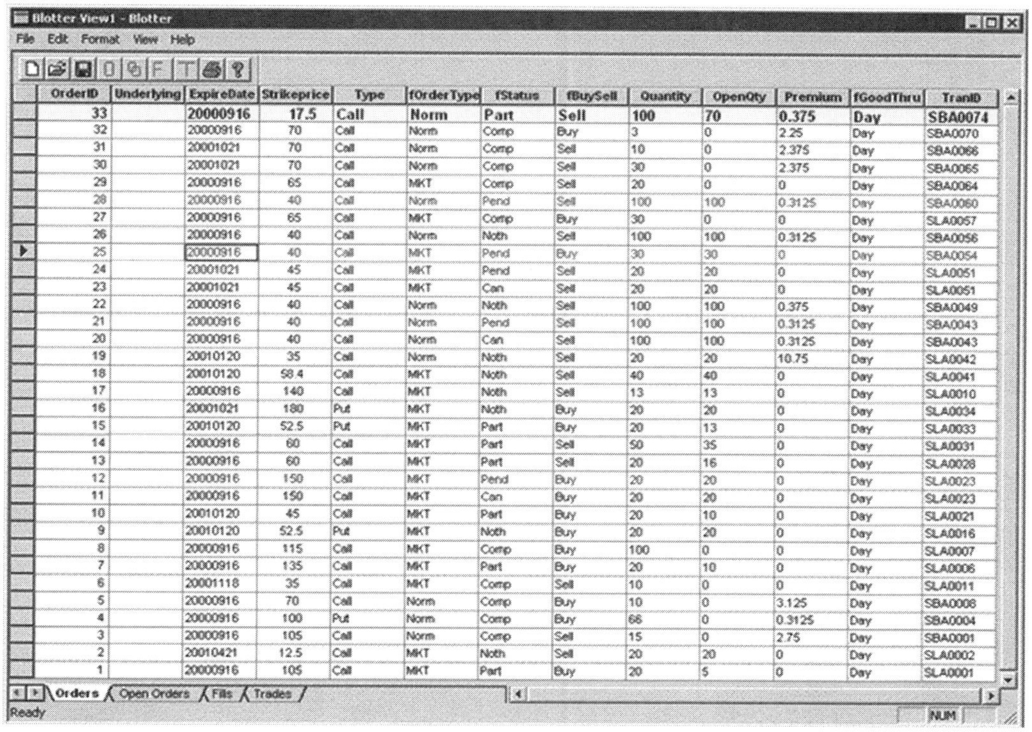

OrderID	Underlying	ExpireDate	Strikeprice	Type	fOrderType	fStatus	fBuySell	Quantity	OpenQty	Premium	fGoodThru	TranID
33		20000916	17.5	Call	Norm	Part	Sell	100	70	0.375	Day	SBA0074
32		20000916	70	Call	Norm	Comp	Buy	3	0	2.25	Day	SBA0070
31		20001021	70	Call	Norm	Comp	Sell	10	0	2.375	Day	SBA0066
30		20001021	70	Call	Norm	Comp	Sell	30	0	2.375	Day	SBA0065
29		20000916	65	Call	MKT	Comp	Sell	20	0	0	Day	SBA0064
28		20000916	40	Call	Norm	Pend	Sell	100	100	0.3125	Day	SBA0060
27		20000916	65	Call	MKT	Comp	Buy	30	0	0	Day	SLA0057
26		20000916	40	Call	Norm	Noth	Sell	100	100	0.3125	Day	SBA0056
25		20000916	40	Call	MKT	Pend	Buy	30	30	0	Day	SBA0054
24		20001021	45	Call	MKT	Pend	Sell	20	20	0	Day	SLA0051
23		20001021	45	Call	MKT	Can	Sell	20	20	0	Day	SLA0051
22		20000916	40	Call	Norm	Noth	Sell	100	100	0.375	Day	SBA0049
21		20000916	40	Call	Norm	Pend	Sell	100	100	0.3125	Day	SBA0043
20		20000916	40	Call	Norm	Can	Sell	100	100	0.3125	Day	SBA0043
19		20010120	35	Call	Norm	Noth	Sell	20	20	10.75	Day	SLA0042
18		20010120	58.4	Call	MKT	Noth	Sell	40	40	0	Day	SLA0041
17		20000916	140	Call	MKT	Noth	Sell	13	13	0	Day	SLA0010
16		20001021	180	Put	MKT	Noth	Buy	20	20	0	Day	SLA0034
15		20010120	52.5	Put	MKT	Part	Buy	20	13	0	Day	SLA0033
14		20000916	60	Call	MKT	Part	Sell	50	35	0	Day	SLA0031
13		20000916	60	Call	MKT	Part	Sell	20	16	0	Day	SLA0028
12		20000916	150	Call	MKT	Pend	Buy	20	20	0	Day	SLA0023
11		20000916	150	Call	MKT	Can	Buy	20	20	0	Day	SLA0023
10		20010120	45	Call	MKT	Part	Buy	20	10	0	Day	SLA0021
9		20010120	52.5	Put	MKT	Noth	Buy	20	20	0	Day	SLA0016
8		20000916	115	Call	MKT	Comp	Buy	100	0	0	Day	SLA0007
7		20000916	135	Call	MKT	Part	Buy	20	10	0	Day	SLA0006
6		20001118	35	Call	MKT	Comp	Sell	10	0	0	Day	SLA0011
5		20000916	70	Call	Norm	Comp	Buy	10	0	3.125	Day	SBA0008
4		20000916	100	Put	Norm	Comp	Buy	66	0	0.3125	Day	SBA0004
3		20000916	105	Call	Norm	Comp	Sell	15	0	2.75	Day	SBA0001
2		20010421	12.5	Call	MKT	Noth	Sell	20	20	0	Day	SLA0002
1		20000916	105	Call	MKT	Part	Buy	20	5	0	Day	SLA0001

(Courtesy *First Traders Analytical Solutions, LLC*)

This blotter shows a view of the open orders tab. It is selected by the user to present only the orders that are open—all other orders are filtered out. Notice that the status indicated is that of "pend." This means that the order is still pending—it has been neither filled nor rejected.

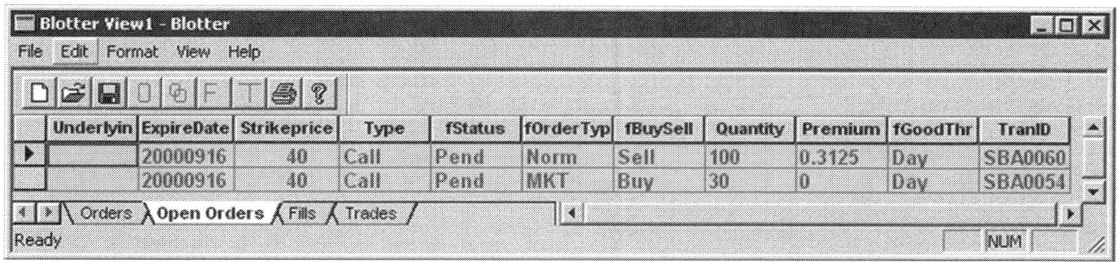

Underlyin	ExpireDate	Strikeprice	Type	fStatus	fOrderTyp	fBuySell	Quantity	Premium	fGoodThr	TranID
	20000916	40	Call	Pend	Norm	Sell	100	0.3125	Day	SBA0060
	20000916	40	Call	Pend	MKT	Buy	30	0	Day	SBA0054

(Courtesy *First Traders Analytical Solutions, LLC*)

The fills tab is selected by the user to present the orders that are filled only—all other orders are filtered out. Note the columns showing quantity, premium, contra firm, and contra broker. These fields would be helpful to the trader when evaluating details of the fill.

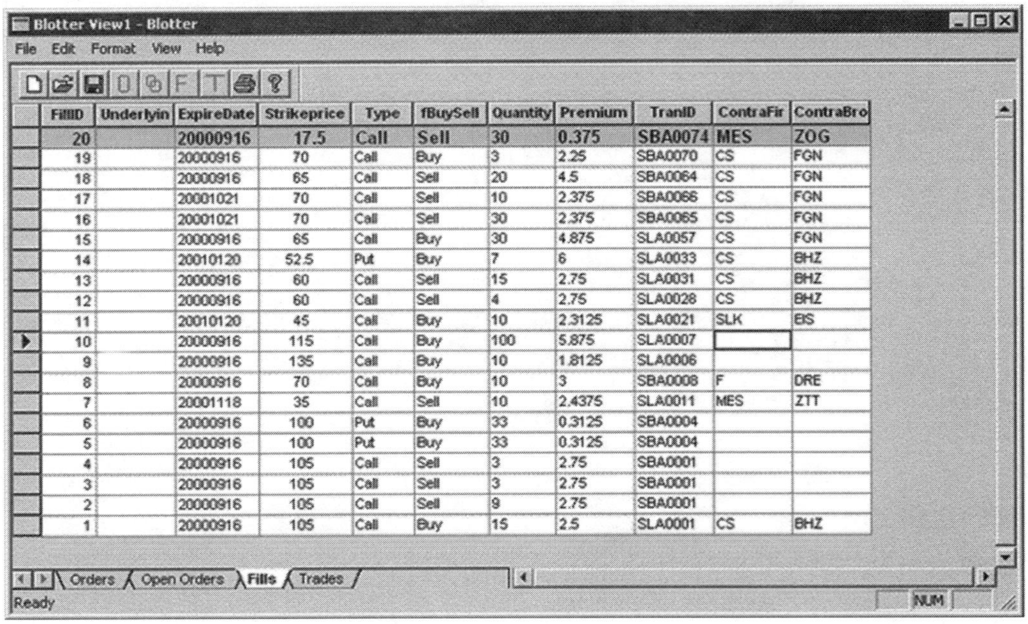

FillID	Underlyin	ExpireDate	Strikeprice	Type	fBuySell	Quantity	Premium	TranID	ContraFir	ContraBro
20		20000916	17.5	Call	Sell	30	0.375	SBA0074	MES	ZOG
19		20000916	70	Call	Buy	3	2.25	SBA0070	CS	FGN
18		20000916	65	Call	Sell	20	4.5	SBA0064	CS	FGN
17		20001021	70	Call	Sell	10	2.375	SBA0066	CS	FGN
16		20001021	70	Call	Sell	30	2.375	SBA0065	CS	FGN
15		20000916	65	Call	Buy	30	4.875	SLA0057	CS	FGN
14		20010120	52.5	Put	Buy	7	6	SLA0033	CS	BHZ
13		20000916	60	Call	Sell	15	2.75	SLA0031	CS	BHZ
12		20000916	60	Call	Sell	4	2.75	SLA0028	CS	BHZ
11		20010120	45	Call	Buy	10	2.3125	SLA0021	SLK	BIS
10		20000916	115	Call	Buy	100	5.875	SLA0007		
9		20000916	135	Call	Buy	10	1.8125	SLA0006		
8		20000916	70	Call	Buy	10	3	SBA0008	F	DRE
7		20001118	35	Call	Sell	10	2.4375	SLA0011	MES	ZTT
6		20000916	100	Put	Buy	33	0.3125	SBA0004		
5		20000916	100	Put	Buy	33	0.3125	SBA0004		
4		20000916	105	Call	Sell	3	2.75	SBA0001		
3		20000916	105	Call	Sell	3	2.75	SBA0001		
2		20000916	105	Call	Sell	9	2.75	SBA0001		
1		20000916	105	Call	Buy	15	2.5	SLA0001	CS	BHZ

(Courtesy *First Traders Analytical Solutions, LLC*)

The trades tab is selected by the user to view the trades that were manually entered into the system. A manual report is nothing more than a manually entered fill report. Any fill that is reported to the trader outside of the electronic system must be keyed by hand into the system. This would include phone confirmations or paper fill reports from other brokers. Additionally, adjustments can be made to an order after clearing has completed the next day. Periodic adjustments are made to trade entries due to human or system errors.

Blotter View1 - Blotter

File Edit Format View Help

Underlyin	ExpireDat	Strikepric	Type	fBuySell	Quantity	Premium	fStatus
	20000916	17.5	Call	Sell	30	0.375	Fill
	0		Spot	Buy	1100	58.5	Man
	20000916	70	Call	Buy	3	2.25	Fill
	20000916	65	Call	Sell	20	4.75	Man
	20000916	65	Call	Sell	20	4.5	Fill
	20001021	70	Call	Sell	10	2.375	Fill
	20001021	70	Call	Sell	30	2.375	Fill
	20000916	145	Call	Sell	15	0.4375	Man
	0		Spot	Sell	1800	67.6875	Man
	20000916	65	Call	Buy	30	4.875	Fill
	20000916	40	Call	Sell	100	0.3125	Man
	0		Spot	Buy	300	58.875	Man
	0		Spot	Buy	1600	35.5625	Man
	0		Spot	Sell	2000	125	Man
	0		Spot	Sell	1000	59.3125	Man
	20010120	52.5	Put	Buy	7	6	Fill
	0		Spot	Sell	100	125.5	Man
	0		Spot	Buy	1000	59	Man
	0		Spot	Buy	500	58.875	Man
	20000916	60	Call	Sell	15	2.75	Fill
	0		Spot	Buy	500	58.875	Man
	20000916	60	Call	Sell	4	2.75	Fill
	0		Spot	Sell	2000	124.75	Man
	0		Spot	Sell	400	40	Man

Orders | Open Orders | Fills | **Trades**

Ready NUM

(Courtesy *First Traders Analytical Solutions, LLC*)

Electronic Risk and Portfolio Management

The display of portfolios is vitally important. The individual trader needs to fully understand the potential risk at any given time. The risk of large swings in the underlying stocks is obvious, but in trading options there are numerous other risks. Time is either working for you or against you and volatility in the market is constantly changing. The electronic environment must provide a quick visual display of a trader's discrete positions and an aggregate display.

Portfolio View3 - Portfolio

File Edit Format Settings View Help

	Symbol	Expires	Strike	ConType
1		0	0	Spot
2	**Expiry**	**UL**		
3		20000722	75	Call
4		20000722	80	Call
5	**Expiry**	**20000722**		
6		**Totals**		

Ready

(Courtesy *First Traders Analytical Solutions, LLC*)

Portfolio management. This view displays the portfolio of each trader or an aggregate one comprised of positions from all traders within a group. The risk manager may choose to aggregate the portfolio view by underlying asset or through the use of some other filter.

The view below shows the volume (quantity in current position) and simple profit and loss-related columns. The volume (or quantity) represents the current position. (A negative value defines a short position.) The amount invested putting on the position is shown, as is the current market value. The resulting profit and loss is easily referenced. All of the values can be updated on a tick-by-tick basis, but such frequent updates are rarely needed. An update every few seconds is sufficient, freeing the processor to calculate analytical values and meet other real-time requirements.

Volume	Invested	Mkt Value	Result	Price
-100	-44775	-6868.75	37906.25	68.6875
---	**-44775**	**-6868.75**	**14756.25**	
15	10312.5	656.25	-9656.25	0.4375
-20	-1750	-250	1500	0.125
---	**8562.5**	**406.25**	**-8156.25**	
---	**-36212.5**	**-6462.5**	**6600**	**68.69**

(Courtesy *First Traders Analytical Solutions, LLC*)

Examples of other columns that are available include the amount of edge (net profit realized on a trade) captured on a particular day, and the total edge captured for a given position. The market value of the trader's position for the current day is useful, as is the theoretical value. Similarly, the market value and the theoretical value of the portfolio, excluding the current day, are also useful. There is really no end to the column definitions that one can devise.

Risk assessment. Every option trader knows that there are many factors at work determining the value of an option. These factors (or parameters) are continually being evaluated to determine what risk exposure exists. Though delta risk is often the first metric scrutinized, the delta of a position (portfolio) is only one of many useful indicators. The models used to create risk values are as varied as the number of trading groups in existence. As an individual trader, the development and integration of custom models into your software package of choice is largely out of reach. However, it is conceivable that in the near future add-on software packages will be available to facilitate custom trading systems for the individual trader.

Delta	Gamma	Theta	Vega	Rho
-100	0	0	0	0
-100	**0**	**0**	**0**	**0**
124	55	-46	25	2
-24	-14	13	-7	-0
100	**41**	**-33**	**17**	**2**
0	**41**	**-33**	**17**	**2**

(Courtesy *First Traders Analytical Solutions, LLC*)

Risk Alerts

Earlier in this chapter a reference was made to risk management. When a trader accumulates a position that is too risky, at a minimum the trader needs to be notified. Usually the trader's risk manager is also electronically notified. This alert can be asserted just prior to a trade order being sent. However, keep in mind that the trader's position is affected by time, volatility, changes in interest rate, and other factors. Therefore, it is typical for a position to generate an alert due to nothing more than changes in the market.

Trading Software Utilities

There are numerous software utilities available to enhance the traders' profitability. Brief surveys of such packages follow. Each trader develops a system or strategic approach that they become comfortable with over time. Though not every software offering is appropriate for all traders, all of the utilities discussed are worthy of evaluation.

CORE. The purpose of CORE is to allow market makers to rearrange their inventory, resulting in a position that is easier to understand and therefore easier to manage. Inventory is rearranged by removing risk-free and limited risk spreads from the position (such as conversions, reversals, boxes, jelly rolls, time spreads, and butterflies). By using this technique, market makers can view their entire position as out-of-the-money (OTM) options. This is desirable because OTM options are typically more liquid, which allows viewing net units by strike across calls and puts. CORE also allows market makers to consolidate several months into one by removing risk-free jellyrolls and limited risk time spreads from their position. Viewing net units by strike across several months results in quick identification of net long or short positions that are not offset by a close strike or a close expiration. CORE also is useful when nearing expiration because it allows the market maker to remove limited risk butterfly spreads from view. This becomes important as the butterfly nears expiration because it can generate extremely large deltas and gammas that possibly should not be hedged as doing so would turn the limited risk butterfly into an unlimited risk hedged butterfly.

The stock view shows all of the stocks for the selected contract list and their associated positions, both raw and residual. The top line shows the aggregate raw and residual stock positions.

The position view displays the option positions for the selected expiration, symbol, and contract list. The top line shows the aggregate butterfly and residual option positions, including calls and puts, for the given expiration.

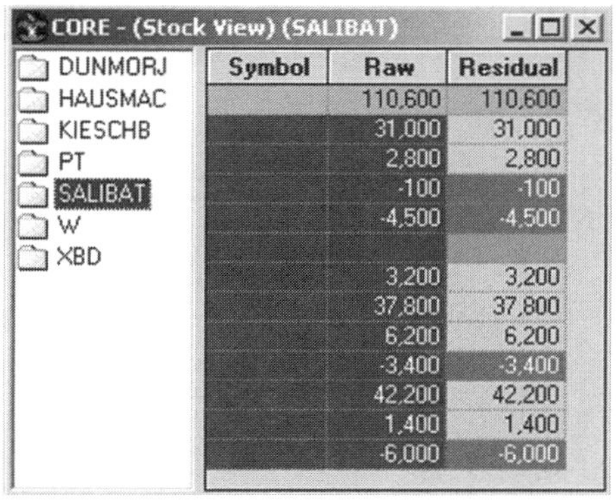

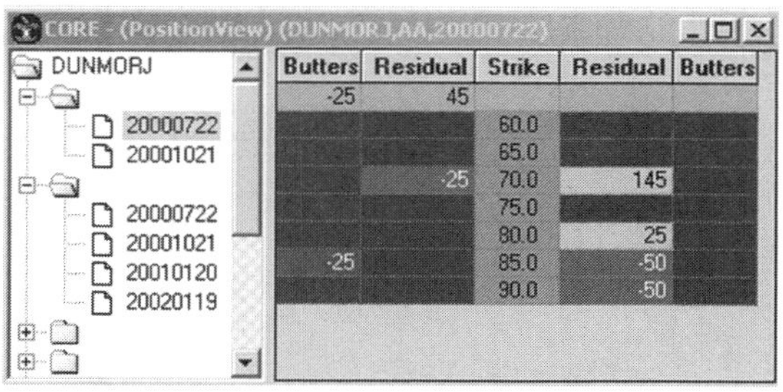

(Courtesy *First Traders Analytical Solutions, LLC*)

From the tree view to the left of the position view the user can modify and create contract lists, import positions, and contracts by right clicking on a given contract list.

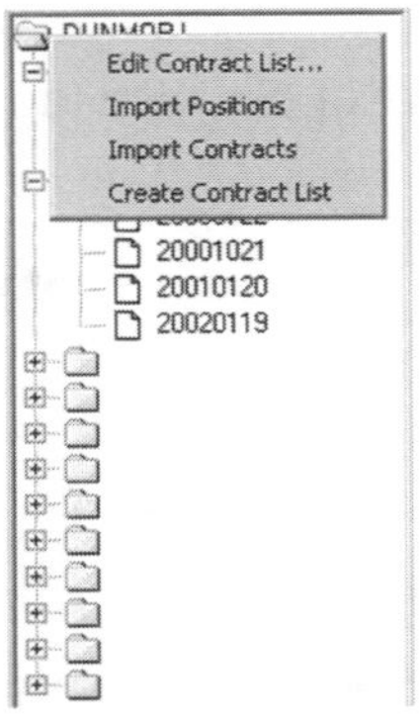

(Courtesy *First Traders Analytical Solutions, LLC*)

Context sensitive menus allow the user to break down their position in the position view. By right clicking on the strike button, the user can force conversions or reversals to turn calls into puts, or puts into calls. Calls and puts also can be dragged back and forth, creating conversions and reversals.

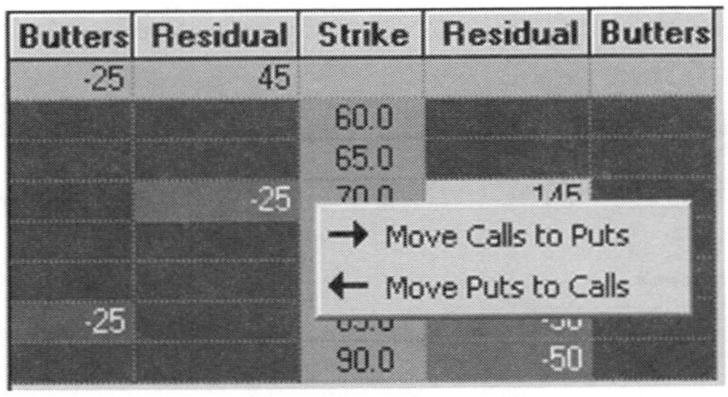

(Courtesy *First Traders Analytical Solutions, LLC*)

By dragging the –25 70 calls to the 75 call butters (butterfly) column, the user is able to create butterflies.

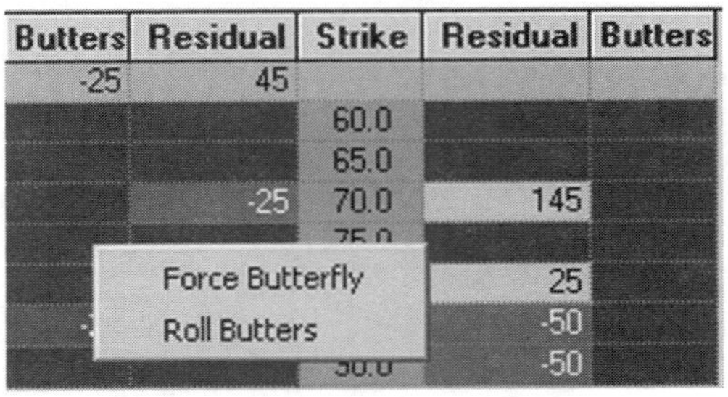

(Courtesy *First Traders Analytical Solutions, LLC*)

Once butterflies are created, they can be returned by dragging them into the residual column or by right clicking and selecting "Return Butters," in the following menu.

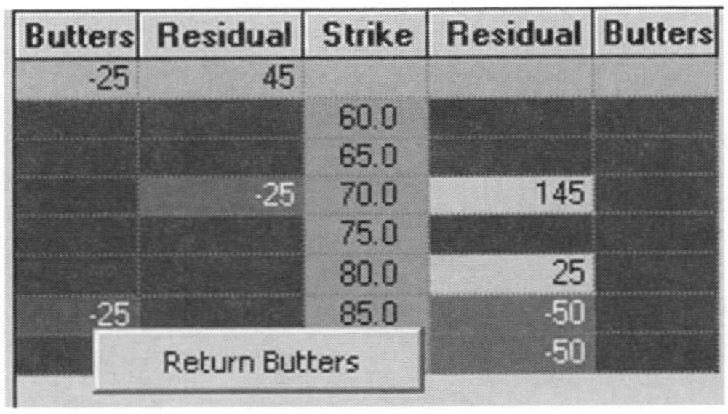

(Courtesy *First Traders Analytical Solutions, LLC*)

Boxes can be created by dragging a residual position to a different strike on the opposite side (e.g., drag 70 call residual to 80 put residual).

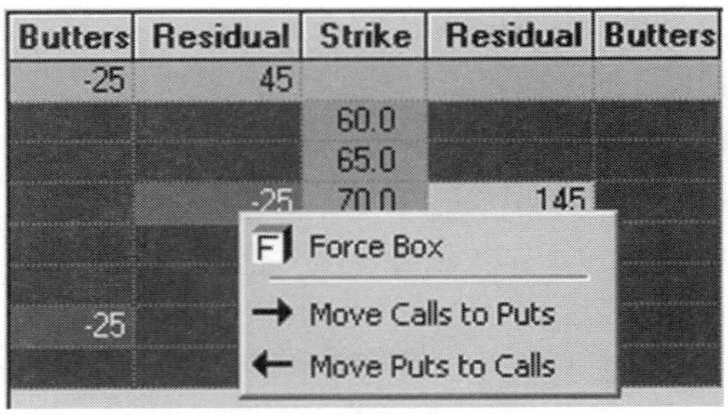

(Courtesy *First Traders Analytical Solutions, LLC*)

By right clicking on the aggregate row, the user can force in-the-money (ITM) options to OTM options (forcing conversions and reversals), or roll the entire month forward (forcing time spreads).

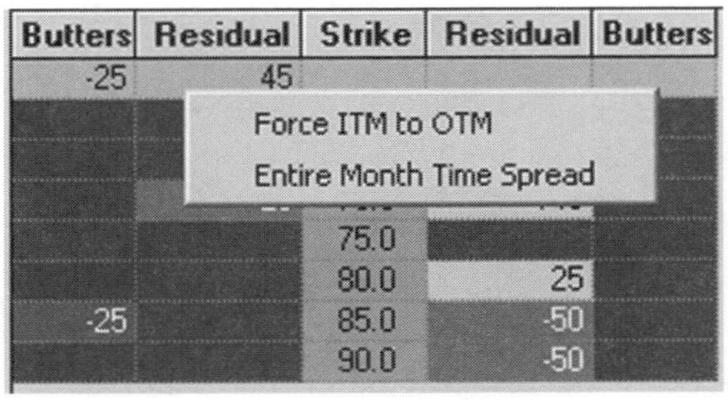

Butters
Residual
Strike
Residual
Butters
-25
45
Force ITM to OTM
Entire Month Time Spread
75.0
80.0
25
-25
85.0
-50
90.0
-50

(Courtesy *First Traders Analytical Solutions, LLC*)

The Hopper window shows all of the spreads for the selected symbol and contract list that have been extracted from a position.

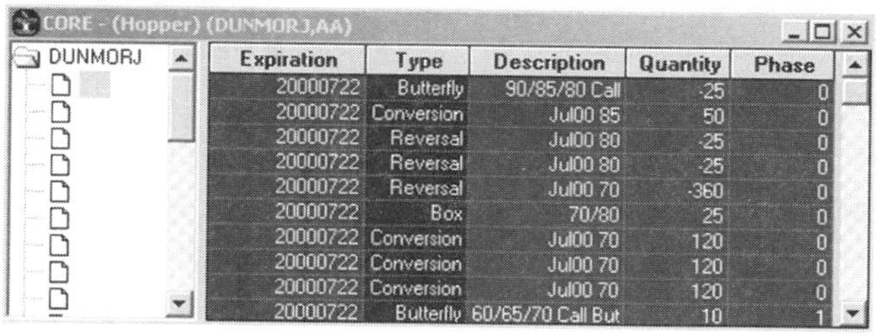

Expiration	Type	Description	Quantity	Phase
20000722	Butterfly	90/85/80 Call	-25	0
20000722	Conversion	Jul00 85	50	0
20000722	Reversal	Jul00 80	-25	0
20000722	Reversal	Jul00 80	-25	0
20000722	Reversal	Jul00 70	-360	0
20000722	Box	70/80	25	0
20000722	Conversion	Jul00 70	120	0
20000722	Conversion	Jul00 70	120	0
20000722	Conversion	Jul00 70	120	0
20000722	Butterfly	60/65/70 Call But	10	1

(Courtesy *First Traders Analytical Solutions, LLC*)

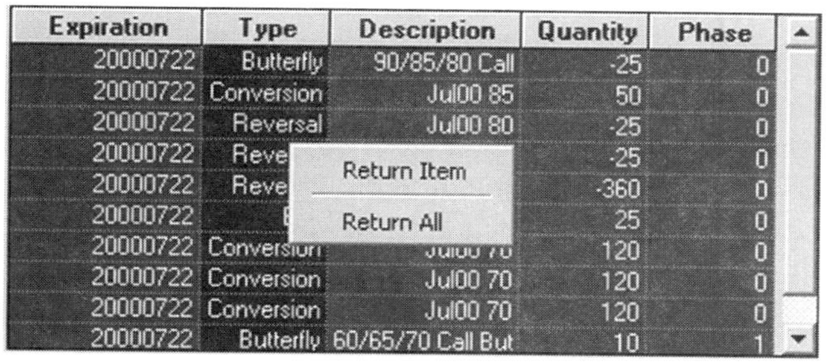

Expiration	Type	Description	Quantity	Phase
20000722	Butterfly	90/85/80 Call	-25	0
20000722	Conversion	Jul00 85	50	0
20000722	Reversal	Jul00 80	-25	0
20000722	Reve		-25	0
20000722	Reve		-360	0
20000722			25	0
20000722	Conversi		120	0
20000722	Conversion	Jul00 70	120	0
20000722	Conversion	Jul00 70	120	0
20000722	Butterfly	60/65/70 Call But	10	1

(Courtesy *First Traders Analytical Solutions, LLC*)

By right clicking on an item, the user can return it to the position, or return all of the displayed items to the position.

The Hopper Report window displays the same information as the Hopper window, only it provides aggregate rows by type of spread.

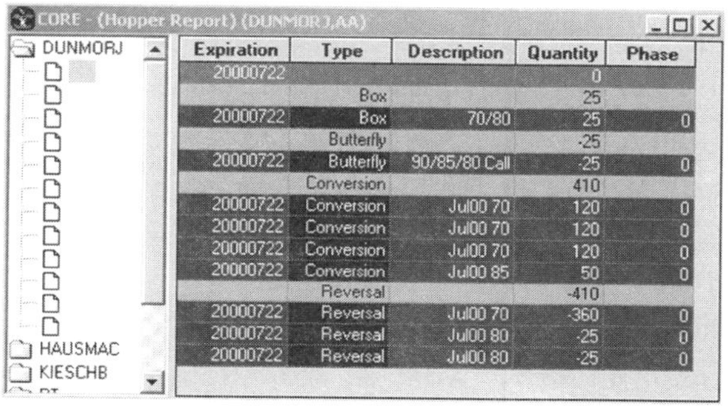

Expiration	Type	Description	Quantity	Phase
20000722			0	
	Box		25	
20000722	Box	70/80	25	0
	Butterfly		-25	
20000722	Butterfly	90/85/80 Call	-25	0
	Conversion		410	
20000722	Conversion	Jul00 70	120	0
20000722	Conversion	Jul00 70	120	0
20000722	Conversion	Jul00 70	120	0
20000722	Conversion	Jul00 85	50	0
	Reversal		-410	
20000722	Reversal	Jul00 70	-360	0
20000722	Reversal	Jul00 80	-25	0
20000722	Reversal	Jul00 80	-25	0

(Courtesy *First Traders Analytical Solutions, LLC*)

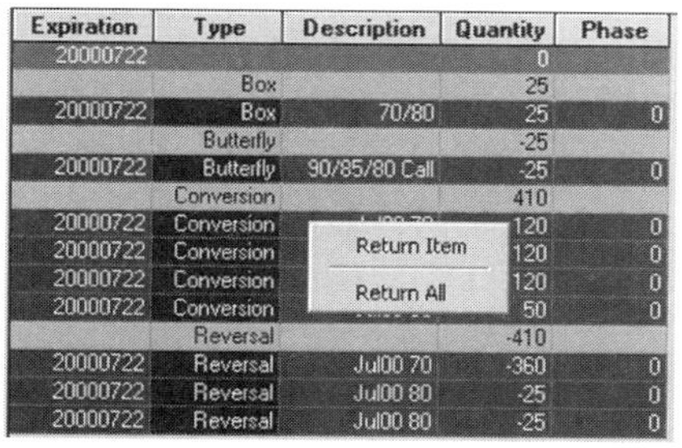

Expiration	Type	Description	Quantity	Phase
20000722			0	
	Box		25	
20000722	Box	70/80	25	0
	Butterfly		-25	
20000722	Butterfly	90/85/80 Call	-25	0
	Conversion		410	
20000722	Conversion		120	0
20000722	Conversion		120	0
20000722	Conversion		120	0
20000722	Conversion		50	0
	Reversal		-410	
20000722	Reversal	Jul00 70	-360	0
20000722	Reversal	Jul00 80	-25	0
20000722	Reversal	Jul00 80	-25	0

(Courtesy *First Traders Analytical Solutions, LLC*)

Again, spreads can be returned by right clicking on an item.

Plots 2000. Plots 2000 has been developed to allow the trader and/or risk manager to assess both risk and profit potential through a graphical format. The user is provided the ability to manipulate the inputs for each plot run. In addition to the typical profit and loss

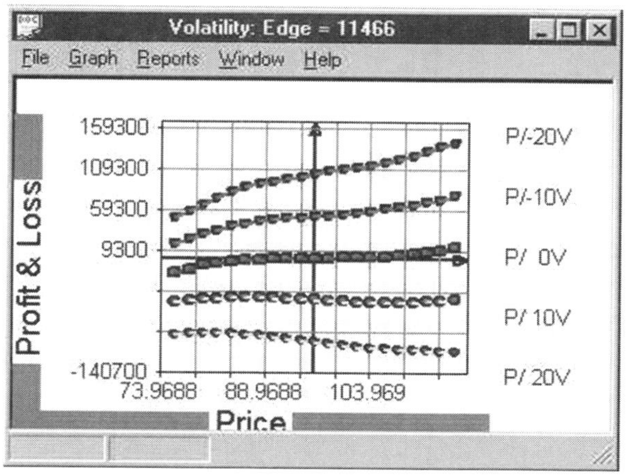

(Courtesy *First Traders Analytical Solutions, LLC*)

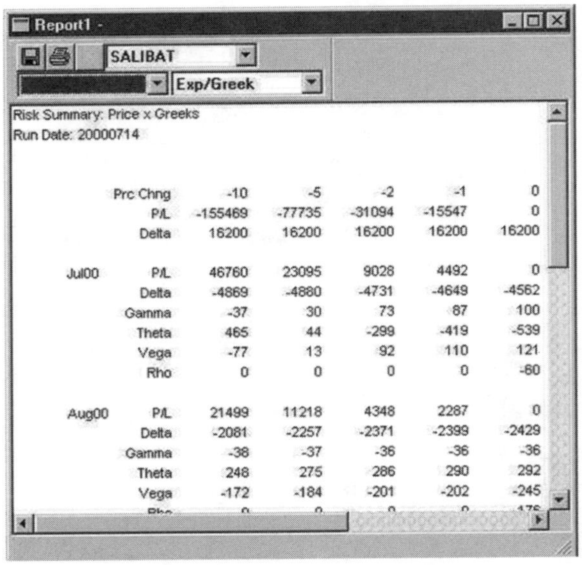
Report1 -
SALIBAT
Exp/Greek
Risk Summary: Price x Greeks
Run Date: 20000714

	Prc Chng	-10	-5	-2	-1	0
	P/L	-155469	-77735	-31094	-15547	0
	Delta	16200	16200	16200	16200	16200
Jul00	P/L	46760	23095	9028	4492	0
	Delta	-4869	-4880	-4731	-4649	-4562
	Gamma	-37	30	73	87	100
	Theta	465	44	-299	-419	-539
	Vega	-77	13	92	110	121
	Rho	0	0	0	0	-80
Aug00	P/L	21499	11218	4348	2287	0
	Delta	-2081	-2257	-2371	-2399	-2429
	Gamma	-38	-37	-36	-36	-36
	Theta	248	275	286	290	292
	Vega	-172	-184	-201	-202	-245

(Courtesy *First Traders Analytical Solutions, LLC*)

plots, a strategy interface allows the user to simulate a position and view its risk before trading it.

Plots 2000 has been developed with a reporting feature that allows the operator to produce reports using predefined or user-defined parameters.

Volatility management. VolMan™ is an advanced volatility management tool that has been designed by long-time volatility traders. With this utility, the trader is able to manage its volatility curves so that the trader's companion workstation can produce theoretical pricing based on custom settings. VolMan is useful purely as an analysis tool because it can read the current volatility values from the trader's workstation and fit a curve to those values. The VolMan utility can be used throughout the trading day to adjust volatility for a given option chain. Endless "what if" scenarios can also be generated.

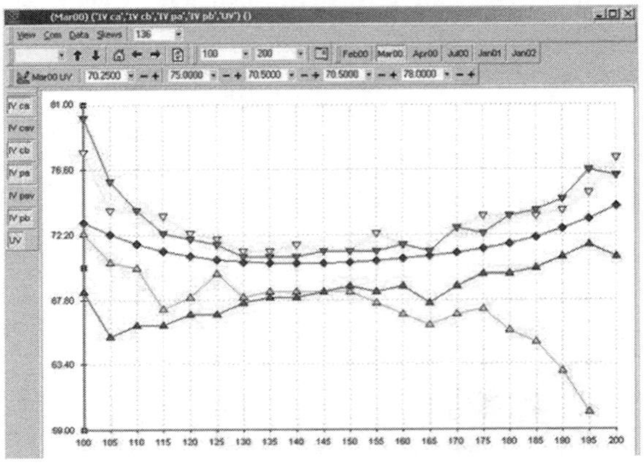

(Courtesy *First Traders Analytical Solutions, LLC*)

The trader selects the fields to view such as "IV" ca or "UV," the expirations for view such as Jan00 or Mar00, or the strike range.

THE 21ST CENTURY TRADER REVISITED

So far the focus of this chapter has been on the past and the present. Starting with the open outcry system that dates back to the earliest trading systems and progressing through the current state-of-the-art systems, a survey of the environment has been presented. Even today a significant number of firms continue using the telephone for routine trades. Though the Teletype machines are just about gone, many of the business processes have yet to modernize. With the advent of electronic communications networks (ECNs) and electronic exchanges coming online in the United States, it is clear that the quick adoption of technology may be a necessary survival initiative. Before discussing changes that are surely on their way, it might be interesting to take a glimpse at what one particular trading group is doing—STC, LLC, of Chicago, Illinois, (an affiliate hybrid trading operative founded by Anthony Saliba and The Charles Schwab Company).

A Hybrid Approach

STC found a novel way to maximize the open outcry system in the United States within the domain of the digital age. Their patent-applied-for approach fosters greater efficiency in the marketplace by yielding better prices for customers who are buying and selling options. STC partners with brokerage firms and liquidity providing organizations (LPO) to receive customer order flow information and third party liquidity information.

STC receives a copy of the order's vital information rather than the customer's order. When the order (copy) is eligible in the market, an LPO sends an electronic contra order to their floor broker "meeting" the order on the exchange. STC, and therefore its representative broker, steps up and matches the order, potentially at a better price than the current market.

For example, a customer order is routed to the floor of a particular exchange to buy 20 of the XYZ JUL 50 puts at $4.20. When the coincident STC copy of the order arrives at STC's trading facility, a contra ticket is generated and sent to the appropriate exchange to provide the other side of the order, the selling side in this example. The broker with the contra order (generated from the copy) may step up in the pit and better the market, selling to the customer at $4.10 or maybe even at $4.

Whatever the STC system/trader determines to do with that order is exactly what is communicated electronically to the floor broker representing STC. This is done instantaneously without disrupting the customer's path to execution.

This is a prime example of an innovative approach maximizing the efficiencies of the open outcry paradigm while taking advantage of the prevalent computing power and networking infrastructure available today.

The Future

Technology can be a catalyst for market swings. When information changes hands at a faster clip, markets can multiply the effects. In the future, traders will be required to be equipped with state-of-the art tools. Fortunately, the cost of hardware continues to slide while the quality of software increases.

The fierce competition in the data vendor market will result in a greater capability for the nonprofessional. These vendors continually strive to expand the reach of their product lines, and the retail market is always an attractive territory. The professional market in trading, similar to many industries, drives the software functionality provided to the general, or retail, trading market.

Stakes are high in trading, so the use of proprietary models and strategies are the rule, not the exception. Beyond the textbook functionality of pricing, execution, and risk management, trading firms are unwilling to share their thoughts and ideas in the public domain. Therefore, the generic features of a trading workstation are available by default from the trading software vendors. Proprietary enhancements are specified, integrated, and delivered at a charge. One can look at trading software as a set of integrated components. Each component can be tied to other components and new ones can be introduced to the system.

Novice traders should consider that the technology available to them falls short of that available to the professional. It is prudent to have a personal strategy to help you win in the markets. For example, mismatched prices in the market are opportunities best left to the professionals who have the technology and lower transaction costs on their side. A decision to compete at this level requires an analysis of the execution cost structure, account maintenance, and the implementation of sophisticated software to take full advantage of your strategies.

Future possibilities are exciting. Imagine instantaneously scanning thousands of underlying instruments and their associated derivatives for matches with your personal strategy. For example, you will be able to specify the way that the data is displayed so you can fly over the data as if it were terrain; the peaks representing trading opportunities. Maybe the view of walking through "dots" of opportunity is more appropriate, or depicting your risk as a heat map. All of these metaphors have the ability to present data in a way that fits your personal preferences. These functions are available today.

Our minds work in patterns and images. We match patterns to help us make decisions and evaluate our environment. Reading a sheet of numbers is a slow, cumbersome way to evaluate information. A chart representing the numbers is far more useful in a fast-moving trading environment. If processing power were unlimited, real-time display of the important trading elements would be prevalent. The most important aspect of trading is not a four-digit price quote, but the meaning of the quote's value. A trend or event can be detected and an alert triggered. Processing power will increase exponentially, but so will the demands for that power. The key is to thoroughly understand trading and to become adept at using a set of technological tools to complement your trading.

APPENDIX A

The Options Workbook

Final Examination

This examination has been prepared in an effort to assess your level of understanding of the options strategies covered in this workbook. For those who have Internet access, visit <www.itichicago.com> to take the exam electronically (coming soon). For those who wish to use this hard copy, simply complete the answer sheet that follows and mail it back to us. Our address is found on the top of the answer sheet. Unless otherwise noted, assume all questions refer to American-style options. (Select or fill in all answers that apply.)

1. American-style options can be exercised on or before an expiration date.
   a. True
   b. False

2. Delta is an expected change in ___________ compared with movement in the underlying price.

3. Gamma is defined as the rate of change of an option's __________.

4. Theta is the portion of an option's premium that
   a. decreases the extrinsic value.
   b. increases the intrinsic value.
   c. decreases the intrinsic value.
   d. increases the extrinsic value.

5. A bull spread is a vertical spread where an increase in the price of an underlying will result in a theoretical profit for the spread. Using the following strikes, construct a bull call spread and a bull put spread (use "L" for long and "S" for short)

	9175	**9200**
a. Bull Call Spread:	____C	____C
b. Bull Put Spread:	____P	____P

6. A bear spread is a vertical spread where a decrease in the price of the underlying will result in a theoretical profit for the spread. Using the following strikes, construct a bear put spread and a bear call spread (use "L" for long and "S" for short)

	9175	**9200**
a. Bear Put Spread:	____P	____P
b. Bear Call Spread:	____C	____C

7. Create an example of a long straddle by writing "+1" (wherever appropriate) in the spaces adjacent to the strike prices below.

CALLS	Strike Price	**PUTS**
_____	9200	_____
_____	9225	_____

8. Create an example of a short strangle by writing "–1" (wherever appropriate) in the spaces adjacent to the strike prices below.

CALLS	Strike Price	**PUTS**
_____	9200	_____
_____	9225	_____

9. Match the following definitions with the options vocabulary below.

A. ___ Notifies the seller of an option that the option has been exercised by the buyer.

B. ___ To use the right conferred by an option.

C. ___ The amount paid by the buyer of an option to the seller of the option.

D. ___ The price at which the underlying asset changes hands after the option is exercised.

E. ___ The commodity to be delivered in the event that the option is exercised.

a. Underlying	f. Deliverable
b. Premium	g. Strike Price
c. Exercise	h. Execution
d. Last day of notice	i. Out trade
e. Assignment	j. Expiration

10. Options buyers have (select all that apply)
    a. limited risk.
    b. limited reward.
    c. to collect premium.
    d. unlimited risk.
    e. unlimited reward.
    f. to pay premium.

11. The passage of time works for options sellers.
    a. True
    b. False

12. Options sellers have (select all that apply)
    a. limited risk.
    b. limited reward.
    c. to collect premium.
    d. unlimited risk.
    e. unlimited reward.
    f. to pay premium.

13. Buyers of options are
    a. long premium.
    b. short premium.

14. A call buyer has the right, but not the obligation, to buy the underlying at a specified price on or before an expiration date.
    a. True
    b. False

15. A call seller has the responsibility to deliver the underlying contract at a specified price on or before the expiration date if assigned.
    a. True
    b. False

16. A put buyer has the right, but not the obligation, to sell/short the underlying at a specific price on or before an expiration date.
    a. True
    b. False

17. A put seller has the responsibility of _______ the underlying at a specific price if assigned.
    a. buying
    b. selling

18. A put option has value on expiration only if the underlying contract is trading ________ the strike price.
    a. above
    b. below

19. A call option has value on expiration only if the underlying contract is trading ________ the strike price.
    a. above
    b. below

20. To reduce delta risk, long calls can be hedged against (select all that apply)
    a. long stock.
    b. short stock.
    c. long puts.
    d. short puts.
    e. another long call.
    f. short calls.

21. To reduce delta risk, short puts can be hedged against (select all that apply)
    a. long stock.
    b. short stock.
    c. long puts.
    d. short puts.
    e. another long call.
    f. short calls.

22. European-style options can be exercised at expiration only.
    a. True
    b. False

23. If perceived market volatility increases while other market parameters remain unchanged, both put and call prices can be expected to decrease.
    a. True
    b. False

24. An option that is in-the-money has no intrinsic value.
    a. True
    b. False

25. An option's exercise price may fluctuate over time.
    a. True
    b. False

26. An option's delta may change over time.
    a. True
    b. False

27. A put option is in-the-money when the price of the underlying is
    a. above the strike price.
    b. at the strike price.
    c. below the strike price.

28. A call option is in-the-money when the price of the underlying is
    a. above the strike price.
    b. at the strike price.
    c. below the strike price.

29. If a stock is at 50 and a call has a strike price of 45 with a premium of $8, what portion of the premium is considered intrinsic value?
    a. The entire $8
    b. $5
    c. $3

30. As expiration approaches, intrinsic premium will
    a. fluctuate with changes in implied volatility.
    b. erode, eventually to zero.
    c. increase or decrease, depending on the price of the stock.

31. XYZ is trading at 40.125. If the stock rises to 44.875, the greatest amount of extrinsic premium will be in the ____ calls.
    a. 40
    b. 45
    c. 50

32. The excess value of an option over and above the difference between the underlying stock price and the strike price for an option is known as
    a. extrinsic premium.
    b. rebate.
    c. intrinsic value.

33. With XYZ stock at 120, an in-the-money Oct 110 call with a price of 13.125 has extrinsic premium of
    a. 13.125.
    b. 10.
    c. 3.125.

34. ITI futures are trading at 9,050. Strike price: 9,000 9,025 9,050 9,075 9,100. Identify these strikes (list all):

a. OTM calls ______	d. OTM puts ______
b. ATM calls ______	e. ATM puts ______
c. ITM calls ______	f. ITM puts ______

35. OTM option premium can be made up of
    a. intrinsic and extrinsic value.
    b. extrinsic value only.
    c. intrinsic value only.

36. ATM options have the highest time value.
    a. True
    b. False

37. A trader who has short straddle position wants the market to sit still.
    a. True
    b. False

38. A bull call spread has limited loss potential, but unlimited profit potential.
    a. True
    b. False

39. When buying a butterfly, which transactions would be accurate?
    a. Buy an ITM, sell an OTM, buy two ATM
    b. Buy two call verticals
    c. Buy a put vertical and sell a put vertical

40. When buying a butterfly, the maximum profit at expiration is
    a. at the middle strike price.
    b. outside the wings.
    c. on the upside only.

41. An option with a delta or hedge ratio of 33 means that the option should theoretically move about
    a. 0.33.
    b. 33 percent of the time.
    c. ⅓ of the amount of the movement of the underlying.

42. Some major influences on the price of listed exchange traded stock options are (circle *all* that apply)
    a. strike.
    b. implied volatility.
    c. interest rate.
    d. time until expiration.
    e. volatility skews.
    f. liquidity.

43. The owner of a put on an exchange-traded futures contract has the right but not the obligation to
    a. buy a futures contract at the strike price of the put at any time from purchase of the put until expiration.
    b. sell a futures contract at the put strike price at any time from purchase to expiration.
    c. sell the physicals or actuals specified by the options futures.
    d. put the obligation onto writers of calls to be short a futures contract at the strike price.

44. The seller of a put retains the premium paid whether the option is exercised or left to expire.
    a. True
    b. False

45. Buyers of options can have margin calls if their position goes against them.
    a. True
    b. False

46. Theoretically, premium will erode at a more rapid pace
    a. 90 days prior to expiration.
    b. 60 days before expiration.
    c. 10 days before expiration.

47. If two call options have the same underlying contract and same amount of time to expiration and option A has an implied volatility of 12 percent and option B has an implied volatility of 14 percent, then
    a. the dollar price of option A will always be less than the dollar price of option B.
    b. the dollar price of option B will always be less than the dollar price of option A.
    c. in theoretical terms, option A is cheaper than option B.
    d. in theoretical terms, option B is cheaper than option A.

48. Which of the following will not help a trader who is long strangles? (Select all that apply.)
    a. The underlying market moves up sharply.
    b. Implied volatility begins to fall.
    c. The market moves down sharply.
    d. The underlying market trades in a small range between the strikes.

49. The greatest amount of extrinsic premium will be in which strike price?
    a. In-the-money
    b. At-the-money
    c. Out-of-the-money

50. When implementing a ratio spread; for example, XYZ @ 27.75 (buy 1 Sep 25 call @ 3.75, sell 3 Sep 30 calls @ 1.25 each), the risks are the (select all that apply)
    a. stock stays between 25 and 30.
    b. stock is taken over above 35.
    c. stock drops to 25.
    d. implied volatility increases.

51. Buying a straddle is often done (select all that apply)
    a. if anticipating that the underlying is going to be choppy (small moves up and down).
    b. in anticipation of an increase in implied volatility.
    c. if one wants to get long on upside or short on downside.

52. If you were to sell a strangle (e.g., sell Aug 85 put, sell Aug 95 call) and receive a 7.5 credit for the sale, you would lose money if, at expiration, the underlying was
    a. @ 86.
    b. @ 96.
    c. @ 106.

53. ITM options can be expected to move dollar-for-dollar with the underlying when ____________________________.

54. An option's theoretical value has as a component in the pricing model of which type of volatility?
    a. Historical
    b. Implied
    c. Future

55. If on Monday ED futures are trading 9051, the 9050 call premium is 0.06, and on Tuesday (all things being equal) the ED futures are trading 9050 but the 9050 call premium is 0.10, a trader would assume that current implied volatility is
    a. higher than Monday's.
    b. lower than Monday's.

56. A motive for putting on a backspread is anticipation of
    a. a stable market.
    b. a volatile market.
    c. a grinding trend.

57. When selling a butterfly (XYZ stock at 34.75, sell 1 July 30 call @ 5.125, buy 2 July 35 calls @ .75 each, sell 1 July 40 call @ .125), a loss will occur if, at expiration, XYZ is trading at
    a. 37.
    b. 34.
    c. 33.

58. A butterfly can be all calls, all puts, a combination of the two, or a combination of puts, calls, and underlying stock.
    a. True
    b. False

59. XYZ is trading at $59.25. The Oct 55 call is $6.5; the Oct 60 call is $3.75, and the Oct 65 call is at $2. Using the long butterfly, plot a 1:2:1 butterfly showing break-even points and maximum profit & loss at expiration (excluding transaction costs).

60. The concept of "undervalued" in relative price terms means
    a. current implied volatilities are lower than the average historical value.
    b. an option is being offered lower than a certain level creating the spreading opportunity.
    c. an option is cheap compared to the theoretical value model.
    d. an option is trading at a lower volatility at one strike compared to the options at other strikes.

61. A trader should increase the size of his or her trades when
    a. it has tracked the underlying stock movements, and knows the trend and all the players.
    b. there is greater degree of profit potential with the same or diminished risk.
    c. there is less liquidity.

62. If a trader spreads put options, buying 20 June 275 S&P puts (each with a premium of $2.40) and selling 10 June 280 puts (each with a premium of $4.30), how do we state the position and at what price?

63. With stock trading at 79, an in-the-money Oct 75 call with a price of $6.125 has extrinsic premium of
    a. $6.125. c. $2.125.
    b. $4. d. $75.

64. A trader puts on a long strangle in S&P 500 options because it anticipates a sudden but sharp movement up or down in the stock market. Assume: June futures = $283.50, June 285 calls = $3.10, June 280 puts = $3.00. (Note: each full point = $250; futures and options expire together.)
    a. What is the trader's maximum risk?
    b. What is the trader's maximum profit?
    c. How much money will the trader actually make or lose if June futures expire at 292.00?

65. Implied volatility is found by inputting current option prices to an options pricing model and is used to predict future volatility. True or false?

66. A high volatility ratio indicates that an option is underpriced. True or false?

67. Any out-of-the-money put is composed of intrinsic value only. True or false?

68. As the holder (owner) of a put you don't realize a profit until after the option's break-even point has been reached. True or false?

69. What is the synthetic of a short put?

70. Given the following market prices: Feb 500 call @ $6.625, Feb 520 call @ $1.50, construct a bearish call vertical. Did you buy or sell the spread and at what price?

71. In the case of a long put, time decay occurs at a steady rate right up to expiration. True or false?

72. The amount over parity for an in-the-money option is equal to the option's intrinsic value. True or false?

73. The synthetic of a short call equals short put and short underlying. True or false?

74. Write the synthetic positions of the following:

Short stock = _______

Long stock = _______

Long put = _______

Long call = _______

75. In the case of a synthetic long put, the call is the upside protection in case of an upward move. True or false?

76. What is your biggest risk with selling a synthetic put?

77. The underlying is trading at 118. The 115 call is trading at $4.00 with a delta of 65. The 120 call (assuming same expiration) is trading at 2.95 with a delta of 32. What is the delta of the 115/120 call spread?

78. Refer to the scenario in question 77, but substitute puts for calls?

79. Dividend risk is a consideration for a synthetic short call position. True or false?

80. Identify the synthetic that can be used as a hedge to the following positions:
a. 15 short puts (ITI stock)
b. 5 long calls
c. 12 short calls
d. Short 5,400 shares of ITI @ $10

81. If you sold a Jan 40 put for $0.72 and purchased a Jan 45 put for $3.025, did you buy or sell the spread?

82. You would sell a synthetic put if you think the stock will either increase or remain unchanged. True or false?

83. Calculate the credit received from the long iron butterfly based on the following prices:
May 450 call @ $1.35
May 450 put @ $5.65
May 455 call @ $0.75
May 445 put @ $3.00

The iron butterfly credit is ______?

84. You wish to buy the WXY Sep 50/55/60/65 put condor. Based on the prices below, answer the following questions:
Long 1 Sep 50 put @ $2.00
Short 1 Sep 55 put @ $4.50
Short 1 Sep 60 put @ $6.25
Long 1 Sep 65 put @ $9.85

a. What is your maximum profit?
b. What is your maximum loss?

FINAL EXAMINATION ANSWER SHEET

International Trading Institute Examinations
311 S. Wacker Dr., Suite 3800
Chicago, IL 60606

NAME: ____________________

DATE: ____________________

MAILING ADDRESS TO WHICH YOU WOULD LIKE YOUR PERFORMANCE PROFILE SENT: ____________________

FAX NUMBER: ____________________

E-MAIL ADDRESS: ____________________

1. ______

2. ______

3. ______

4. ______

5. 9175 9200

a. _____C _____C

b. _____P _____P

6. 9175 9200

a. _____P _____P

b. _____C _____C

7.

CALLS	Strike Price	PUTS
_____	9200	_____
_____	9225	_____

8.

CALLS	Strike Price	PUTS
_____	9200	_____
_____	9225	_____

9. A. ______

B. ______

C. ______

D. ______

E. ______

10. ______

11. ______

12. ______

13. ______

14. ______

15. ______

16. ______

17. ______

18. ______

19. ______

20. ______

21. ______

22. ______

23. ______

24. ______

25. ______

26. ______

27. ______

28. ______

29. ______

30. ______

31. ______

32. ______

33. ______

34. a. ______

b. ______

c. ______

d. ______

e. ______

f. ______

35. ______

36. ______

37. ______

38. ______

39. ______

40. ______

41. ______

42. ______

43. ______

44. ______

45. ______

46. ______

47. ______

48. ______

49. ______

50. ______

51. ______
52. ______
53. ______
54. ______
55. ______
56. ______
57. ______
58. ______
59. ______
60. ______
61. ______
62. ______
63. ______
64. a. ______
    b. ______
    c. ______
65. T F
66. T F
67. T F
68. T F
69. ______
70. ______
    ______
71. T F
72. T F
73. T F
74. ______
    ______
    ______
    ______
75. T F
76. ______
77. ______
78. ______
79. T F
80. ______
    ______
    ______
    ______
81. ______
82. T F
83. ______
84. ______
    ______

Below is a sample of the Final Exam Profile, should you wish to receive the results of your final examination.

International Trading Institute
Final Exam Profile

Totals for: John Doe

	Basics	Positions	Greeks	Arbitrage	TOTAL
Total Points Received	75	32	7	16	130
Total Points Possible	87	36	9	21	153
Score	86%	89%	78%	76%	**85.0%**

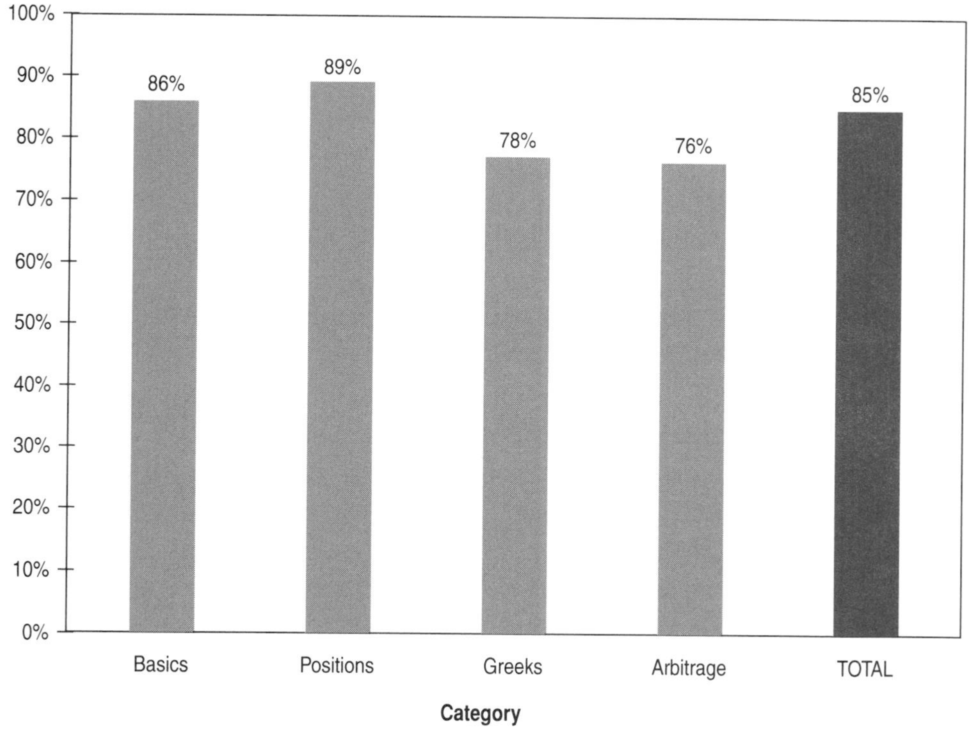

APPENDIX B

A Word with Tony Saliba

By Karen Johnson

One of the benefits of attending ITI is the opportunity it affords students to speak with and ask questions of founder Anthony (Tony) Saliba. A true pioneer in the options industry, Mr. Saliba is internationally recognized for his significant success in the options markets, as well as his personal commitment to the proliferation of options trading and education worldwide.

As is widely known by his option market contemporaries, Saliba, a long-time member of Chicago Board Options Exchange (CBOE), was very active in the shaping and formation of some of the fundamental rules that govern the way options business is transacted today. He played a large role in expanding options position limits. He was responsible for creating the Instant Exemption Process, which allows floor traders and upstairs traders to get exemptions from the onerous position limits (they were 500 contracts per side when Saliba began his efforts; they are now over 40,000 per side).

He was a founding member of the Market Performance Committee at the CBOE, whose efforts spawned the requirement of accountability for floor traders. A staunch proponent for firm quotes, Saliba suggested more than 15 years ago that all markets should be responsible for at least a minimum size for all market participants. This and other suggestions of his made it through the committee processes early on to become the foundation of today's methods of transacting business on the exchange.

Another instrumental contribution of Saliba's was his participation and input as a founding member of the Modified Trading System (MTS) committee. The MTS committee was established to explore a hybrid method of trading that combined the best of the specialist system and the market maker system. Saliba fought hard to bring flexibility into the rule structure so that the customers and members of the CBOE could enjoy the best of both systems. The fruits of this effort are today's Designated Primary Market Maker (DPM) system. The DPM system is now ensuring the sheer viability of the exchange.

Other areas of contribution included research into the feasibility of 24-hour trading for the exchange over a decade ago, and the attempt to launch various new products, one of which is the S&P 500 option in its current form.

Along with these and other institutional accomplishments including three years on the CBOE's board of directors, his trading success repeatedly reached new heights. He regularly traded over 20,000 contracts per day while in the S&P 500 options pit. The typical market maker at the time traded in the neighborhood of 5,000 contracts per day.

When the market suffered a near collapse as the Dow fell 508 points over the course of eight hours. During the chaos that followed, rumors of Saliba's demise began to circulate. However, when the smoke cleared, news spread quickly of his amazing success. Not only had he weathered the storm, his trading profits exceeded millions of dollars. This success cemented Saliba's reputation as a true Market Wizard.

This victory landed him a spot in Jack Schwager's best-seller, *Market Wizards,* as well as a cover story in *Success* magazine.

His trading style allowed him to take advantage of similar market events in 1989, 1991, 1995, 1998, and 2000. Not all of these market events were on the downside either. His success during the rallies of 1991, 1995, and 1998 (off the massive correction that autumn) were testimony that his strategy works in markets of either direction.

Many ask how Tony averted the disaster in 1987, unlike so many others. Did he know something that none of the other players did? In fact, Tony never cares anything about the market's direction. In this case, Tony's position was secure well before the market began its plunge. Months earlier Saliba had hedged himself with deep, out-of-the-money puts. While these puts were inexpensive when he purchased them (the stock's prices would have to fall considerably for the long puts to be in-the-money), the market meltdown made them quite valuable.

That his strategy contained a large percentage of at-the-money butterflies, his risk of a sideways market, thus rendering these puts worthless, was small. His finite risk in these butterflies was more than compensated for with the profits from the puts. His confidence that his position was free from open-ended risk allowed him to keep his wits about him in the frenzy.

Those not properly positioned were forced to respond reactively in a frantic situation where preparation was absolutely critical. In short, they were doomed. However, Tony's extraordinary degree of preparedness, a direct result of his vision and discipline, made all the difference.

His triumph inspired others and deepened his own commitment to the principles of hard work and determination that have made him a success. These principles are still very much the foundation on which all of Mr. Saliba's many endeavors are built.

In late 1989, seeing an opportunity to both introduce options to international markets and provide education and training for its participants, Tony founded International Trading Institute (ITI). The methods and principles taught at ITI are gleaned from his extensive trading experiences over the past 20 years.

Following are Mr. Saliba's answers to some of his former students' most frequently asked questions.

What potentially low risk options strategy would you recommend for an experienced trader in order to take advantage of today's highly volatile market?

Well, as you are asking me this question, implied volatilities have dropped to their lowest levels for most of the active stocks in over five years. With that as a backdrop, I would recommend purchasing a straddle on a stock or index. In times when front month volatilities are high (nearest term expiration), I would look to sell a straddle and use the proceeds to purchase strangles having a further out expiry on a ratio. In other words, I would use the proceeds from selling one front month straddle to purchase two or three next month strangles. This way I have financed added leverage, limited risk, and unlimited profit potential.

Your name is synonymous with the butterfly strategy. What do you find so intriguing about it?

In one word, flexibility! As a trading strategy, the butterfly is the most versatile. It allows me as a professional trader to formulate multiple secondary strategies. For the nonprofessional, the butterfly brings a strategy that the part-time trader can walk away from and not worry about the risk in the position. When I say this I mean that a properly timed butterfly strategy does not require the attention and risk management that other options strategies (particularly straight long or short call or put positions) require. The butterfly has multiple ways to enter and exit the position.

Why did the derivatives industry, specifically options, shoulder so much of the blame associated with the crash of '87?

Common wisdom tells us that a certain type of hedging strategy called "portfolio insurance" was quite popular at the time and up to the '87 meltdown. This strategy involved selling S&P 500 futures against your stock portfolio, when and only when certain price targets were reached on the downside. In theory the strategy worked, because it allowed equity portfolio managers to let their positions run to a greater degree, thinking that if prices got soft they could sell the futures contract to hedge themselves, but in practice, ran for the exits at the same time and tried to sell the futures contract. The liquidity in the futures pits couldn't handle the order flow. This created panic in and of itself, which exacerbated the selling pressure on stocks.

I could write an entire chapter about this subject and my opinion about it. In fact, chapters have been written, but suffice it to say that the reasons derivatives got the bad rap was purely political—purely a matter of perception, an issue of grabbing and controlling the spin in a day long before spin was popularized. The equity markets (stock exchanges and Nasdaq over-the-counter dealers) for the most part walked away from their obligation to maintain a fair and orderly market. This is what caused the gap in the stock prices, not the futures and options markets.

I have heard that in your interview in Market Wizards, *you stress the importance of discipline in becoming a great trader. Does this still apply as a trader in an electronic market?*

Even more so! Because in today's electronic market things happen instantaneously. It is much easier to take on considerable size with a click of a button. In the trading pit you need to find an order or hit a counter party's bid, whereas on a screen everything is available at your fingertips. It takes much more discipline to control the natural urge to overtrade.

What advice would you give to an amateur trader looking to incorporate options into an investment portfolio?

Approaching options from the standpoint of using them as combinations, or as spreads, is a way to take advantage of the opportunities options offer. More and more brokerage firms are enhancing their capabilities to execute spreads with greater efficiency and at lower costs. Spreads can reduce risk and more accurately focus on investment goals. They allow the flexibility to modify the risk/reward profile when the goals are redefined.

Bull spreads yield similar results to long calls, with less risk. Unless you are looking at hitting a home run, where you risk everything, a series of bull spreads over the long run will prove to be equally profitable, with less risk.

Why has America, the world leader in trading, lagged behind the rest of the world in the move toward electronic trading?

Actually that's not true. We are far ahead of any other nation in terms of electronic access for end-users of options. If you are speaking about professionals, the business case is debated at the highest levels today and the largest players are hedging their bets. The electronic access to the major outcry exchanges is more than adequate for the end-user today and will not change dramatically if and when they do go to a fully electronic platform for the professionals.

APPENDIX C

Contributor Profiles

The curriculum presented in this workbook was a collaborative writing effort among the following staff members of International Trading Institute (ITI) and Anthony Saliba.

Karen Johnson

Formerly President of International Trading Institute, Karen presently serves on the Board of Directors. Karen joined ITI in 1992 and is credited with helping to make it the premier venue for derivatives training worldwide. In addition to her role at ITI, over the past eight years she has been actively involved with other affiliated start-up companies of Anthony Saliba's, including First Traders Analytical Solutions, STC LLC (a partnership between Charles Schwab Co. and Anthony Saliba), and Saliba Asset Management.

Chris Hausman

Chris began his trading career in 1996 as a market maker in the S&P 500 options pit at the Chicago Mercantile Exchange. He also traded Microsoft at the Pacific Stock Exchange in San Francisco. Since 1995, Chris has consulted ITI in the areas of curriculum development and instruction. Presently, he is Senior Trader for STC, LLC, and holds the position of Lead Instructor at ITI.

Denise Hubbard

Denise's career has encompassed many aspects of the trading industry. She began as a pit trader on the Chicago Mercantile Exchange. From 1992 to 1999, Denise instructed and consulted for ITI, delivering workshops to the derivative desks globally. At present, she is Director of Trader Development for a multinational risk arbitrage firm.

Scott Mollner

Scott has spent the majority of his trading career as a market maker at the Chicago Board Options Exchange. He spent one year in the Boeing pit and four years assisting with the management of Saliba Partners' DPM (Designated Primary Market Maker). Recently Scott began his own CTA operation, Mariah Trading Company, LLC. Since 1993 Scott has assisted with instruction, curriculum development, staff training, and systems development at ITI and its affiliated companies. Presently Scott is Lead Lab Instructor for ITI's advanced options workshops.

Terri Raisch

Terri joined ITI in 1996 as Director of Operations and has been instrumental in making ITI the success that it is today.

Gavin Roe

Gavin has been a market maker in various equity pits on the floor of the Chicago Board Options Exchange since 1997. He formerly managed a DPM for Saliba Partners. He has consulted for ITI since 1995 in the areas of curriculum development and instruction.

James Kallimani

James is the Managing Director of First Traders Analytical Solutions, a software products development company serving the trading industry. Prior to First Traders, his career included positions in engineering, sales, and marketing for several technology start-ups. Additionally, he and his consulting firm provided product development expertise to several trading companies. In his role with First Traders, James manages company operations and takes an active role in all aspects of product formulation and marketing strategy.

Additional Contributors

In addition to the writing effort, the following individuals were responsible for assisting with research, graphics, and editing:

- Robert Bockel
- Joe Corona
- Chris Fisher
- Matt Gray
- Lori Helgren
- Jill Johnson
- Kristine Kallimani
- Brandon Kieschnick
- Robert Komm
- Mike McNamara
- Todd Miller
- Dave Schmueck and the staff of STC
- William Winger
- Luis Wooley

A special thanks to Patricia Turner for helping us edit the second edition.

APPENDIX D

Saliba's Top Four Favorite Sites for Options Trading and Trading Tools

There are an increasing number of online brokerage firms that offer assistance for your options trading needs. Volume data, volatility history and comparisons, probabilities and advanced combinations, and spread trading assistance are now becoming mainstream.

Site-specific criteria were considered prior to selection of these sites—namely, the ease of access, variety of information, kinds of specialty services (spread trading) allowed, the cost or fees associated with their services, and general user friendliness of interface.

I thought these four sites had unique offerings that warranted their inclusion on everyone's favorite list.

IVOLATILITY.COM

IVolatility.com

<www.ivolatility.com>

Professionals spend more time and money on determining volatility levels, past, present, and future than any other aspect of options pricing. IVolatility.com presents both the basic and the advanced in an organized, concise, and easy-to-use format. As you read this book and climb the learning curve, the tools on this site will become more valuable and integrated into your daily trading activities.

The home page immediately shows rankings of top and bottom stocks with volatility disparity—those issues where the historical volatility (that of the underlying stock) and implied volatilities (those volatilities where the options are currently trading) are at their greatest differences. Also, the user gets the top and bottom stocks tracking the site's Implied Volatility index.

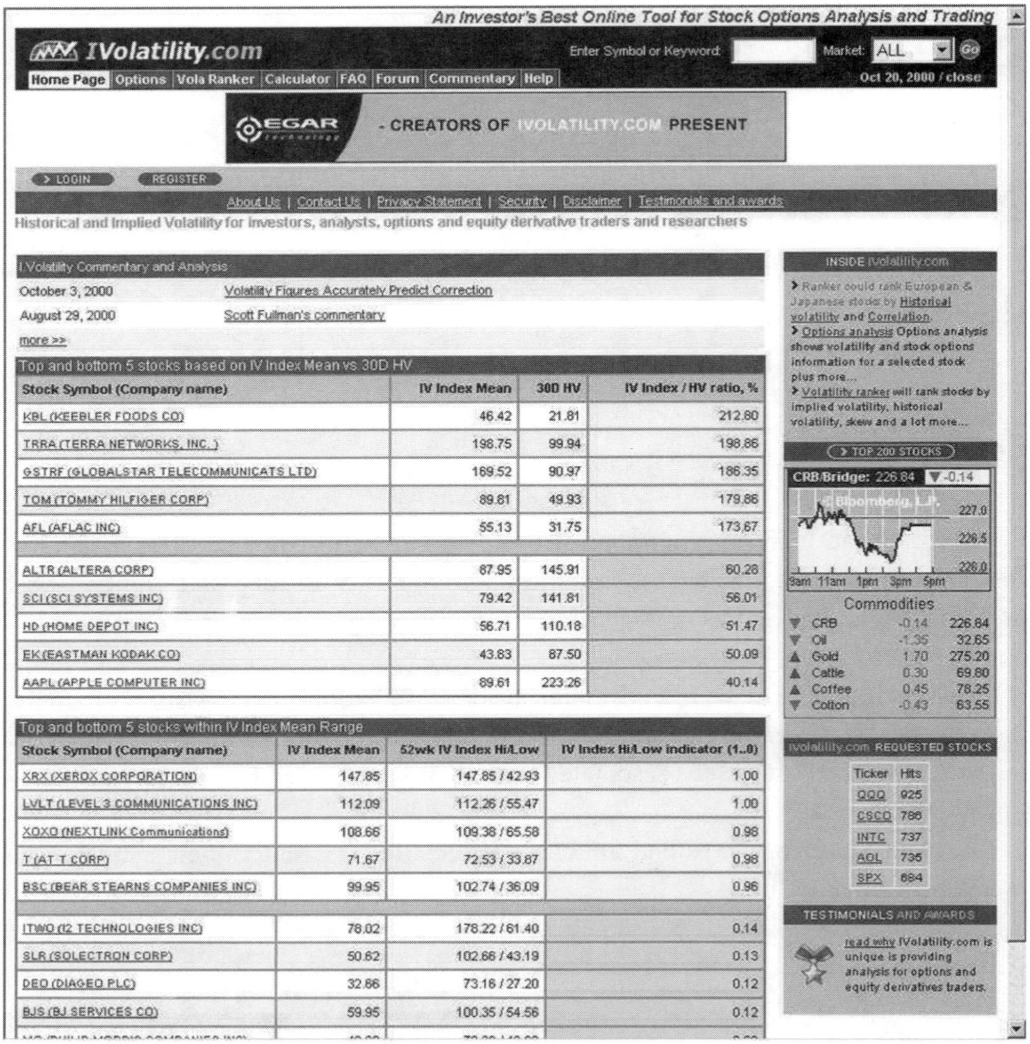

The user can get into the specifics of an individual underlying stock and its listed options. Three different moving averages and their values at three different points in time make for a well-rounded snapshot of the vital calculations. Details of when highs and lows occurred and fundamental volume metrics are presented uniformly.

IVolatility.com also has direct links to major news services, and instant access headlines for the stories on the stocks being researched are presented. The user can observe news while performing necessary research.

The user gets a unique search tool that allows for sorting and ranking stocks for their historical and implied volatilities. The tool is easy to understand, fast, and precise—aspects required by an active options trader.

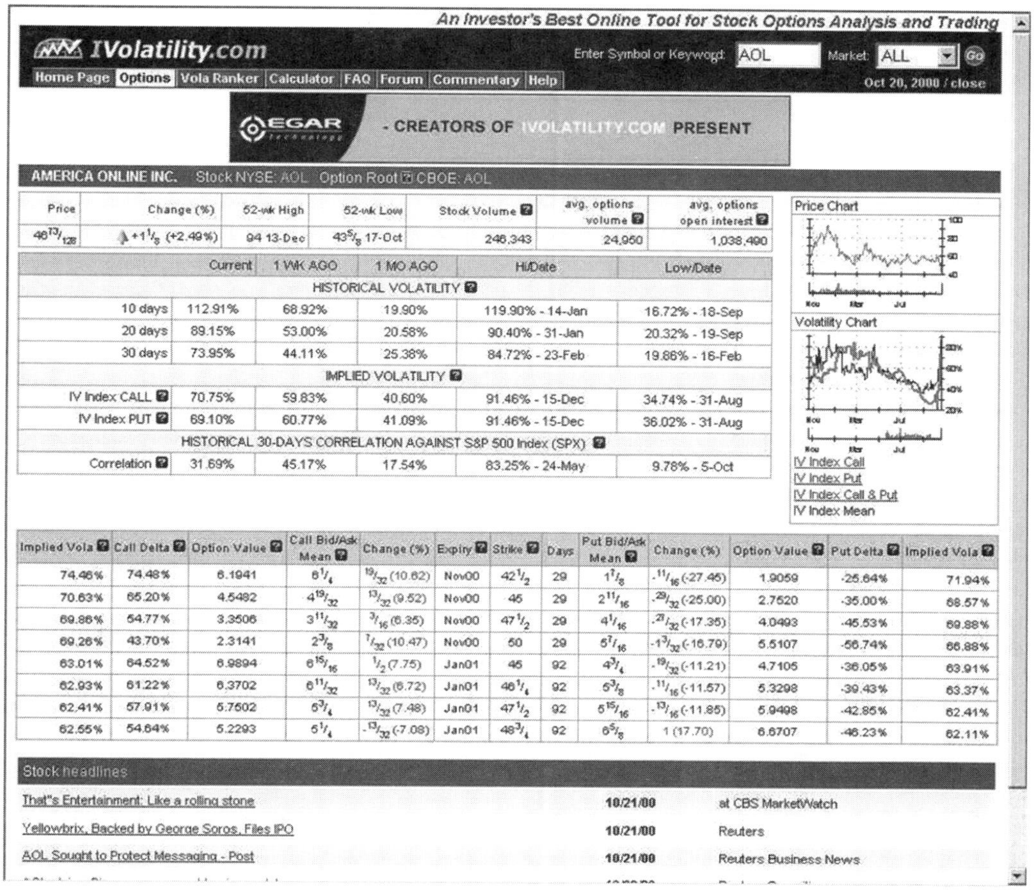

An Investor's Best Online Tool for Stock Options Analysis and Trading

IVolatility.com — Enter Symbol or Keyword: AOL — Market: ALL — Go

Home Page | Options | Vola Ranker | Calculator | FAQ | Forum | Commentary | Help

Oct 20, 2000 / close

EGAR Technology - CREATORS OF IVOLATILITY.COM PRESENT

AMERICA ONLINE INC. Stock NYSE: AOL Option Root CBOE: AOL

Price	Change (%)	52-wk High	52-wk Low	Stock Volume	avg. options volume	avg. options open interest
$46\frac{13}{128}$	$+1\frac{1}{8}$ (+2.49%)	94 13-Dec	$43\frac{5}{8}$ 17-Oct	246,343	24,950	1,038,490

	Current	1 WK AGO	1 MO AGO	Hi/Date	Low/Date
HISTORICAL VOLATILITY					
10 days	112.91%	68.92%	19.90%	119.90% - 14-Jan	16.72% - 18-Sep
20 days	89.15%	53.00%	20.58%	90.40% - 31-Jan	20.32% - 19-Sep
30 days	73.95%	44.11%	25.38%	84.72% - 23-Feb	19.86% - 16-Feb
IMPLIED VOLATILITY					
IV Index CALL	70.75%	59.83%	40.60%	91.46% - 15-Dec	34.74% - 31-Aug
IV Index PUT	69.10%	60.77%	41.09%	91.46% - 15-Dec	36.02% - 31-Aug
HISTORICAL 30-DAYS CORRELATION AGAINST S&P 500 Index (SPX)					
Correlation	31.69%	45.17%	17.54%	83.25% - 24-May	9.78% - 5-Oct

Price Chart

Volatility Chart

IV Index Call
IV Index Put
IV Index Call & Put
IV Index Mean

Implied Vola	Call Delta	Option Value	Call Bid/Ask Mean	Change (%)	Expiry	Strike	Days	Put Bid/Ask Mean	Change (%)	Option Value	Put Delta	Implied Vola
74.46%	74.48%	6.1941	$6\frac{1}{4}$	$\frac{19}{32}$ (10.62)	Nov00	$42\frac{1}{2}$	29	$1\frac{1}{8}$	$-\frac{11}{16}$ (-27.46)	1.9059	-25.64%	71.94%
70.63%	65.20%	4.5482	$4\frac{19}{32}$	$\frac{13}{32}$ (9.52)	Nov00	45	29	$2\frac{11}{16}$	$-\frac{29}{32}$ (-25.00)	2.7620	-35.00%	68.57%
69.86%	54.77%	3.3506	$3\frac{11}{32}$	$\frac{3}{16}$ (6.35)	Nov00	$47\frac{1}{2}$	29	$4\frac{1}{16}$	$-\frac{27}{32}$ (-17.35)	4.0493	-45.53%	69.88%
69.26%	43.70%	2.3141	$2\frac{3}{8}$	$\frac{7}{32}$ (10.47)	Nov00	50	29	$5\frac{7}{16}$	$-1\frac{3}{32}$ (-16.79)	5.5107	-56.74%	66.88%
63.01%	64.52%	6.9894	$6\frac{15}{16}$	$\frac{1}{2}$ (7.75)	Jan01	45	92	$4\frac{3}{4}$	$-\frac{19}{32}$ (-11.21)	4.7105	-36.05%	63.91%
62.93%	61.22%	6.3702	$6\frac{11}{32}$	$\frac{13}{32}$ (6.72)	Jan01	$46\frac{1}{4}$	92	$5\frac{3}{8}$	$-\frac{11}{16}$ (-11.57)	5.3298	-39.43%	63.37%
62.41%	57.91%	5.7502	$5\frac{3}{4}$	$\frac{13}{32}$ (7.48)	Jan01	$47\frac{1}{2}$	92	$5\frac{15}{16}$	$-\frac{13}{16}$ (-11.85)	5.9498	-42.85%	62.41%
62.55%	54.64%	5.2293	$5\frac{1}{4}$	$-\frac{13}{32}$ (-7.08)	Jan01	$48\frac{3}{4}$	92	$6\frac{5}{8}$	1 (17.70)	6.6707	-46.23%	62.11%

Stock headlines

That"s Entertainment: Like a rolling stone	10/21/00	at CBS MarketWatch
Yellowbrix, Backed by George Soros, Files IPO	10/21/00	Reuters
AOL Sought to Protect Messaging - Post	10/21/00	Reuters Business News

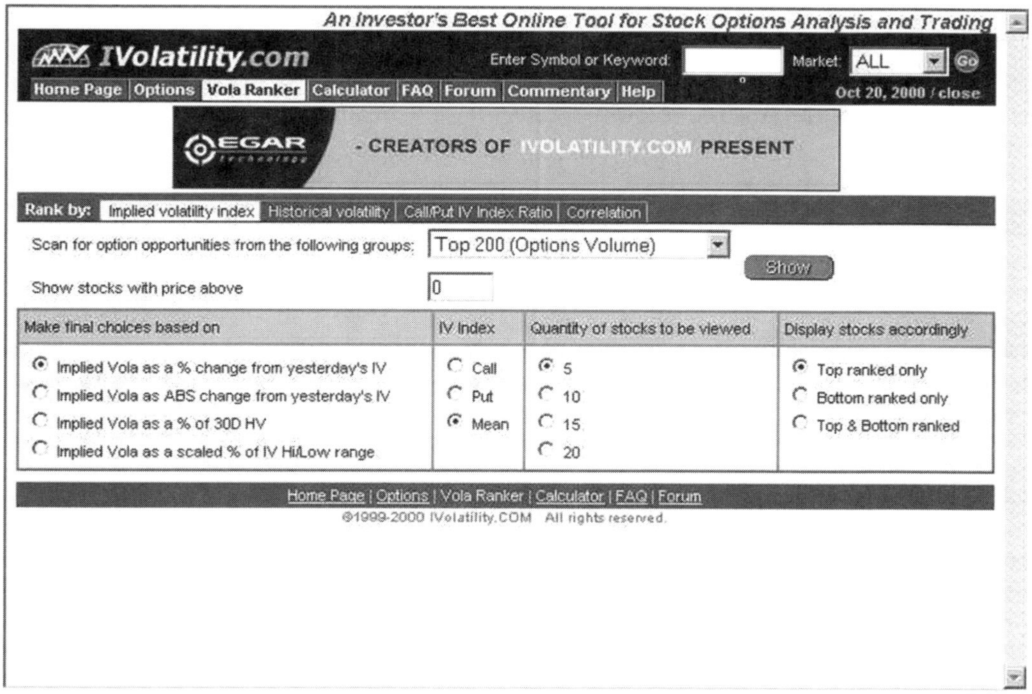

An Investor's Best Online Tool for Stock Options Analysis and Trading

IVolatility.com — Enter Symbol or Keyword: — Market: ALL — Go

Home Page | Options | Vola Ranker | Calculator | FAQ | Forum | Commentary | Help

Oct 20, 2000 / close

EGAR Technology - CREATORS OF IVOLATILITY.COM PRESENT

Rank by: Implied volatility index | Historical volatility | Call/Put IV Index Ratio | Correlation

Scan for option opportunities from the following groups: Top 200 (Options Volume)

Show stocks with price above 0 — Show

Make final choices based on	IV Index	Quantity of stocks to be viewed	Display stocks accordingly
(•) Implied Vola as a % change from yesterday's IV	( ) Call	(•) 5	(•) Top ranked only
( ) Implied Vola as ABS change from yesterday's IV	( ) Put	( ) 10	( ) Bottom ranked only
( ) Implied Vola as a % of 30D HV	(•) Mean	( ) 15	( ) Top & Bottom ranked
( ) Implied Vola as a scaled % of IV Hi/Low range		( ) 20	

Home Page | Options | Vola Ranker | Calculator | FAQ | Forum

©1999-2000 IVolatility.COM All rights reserved.

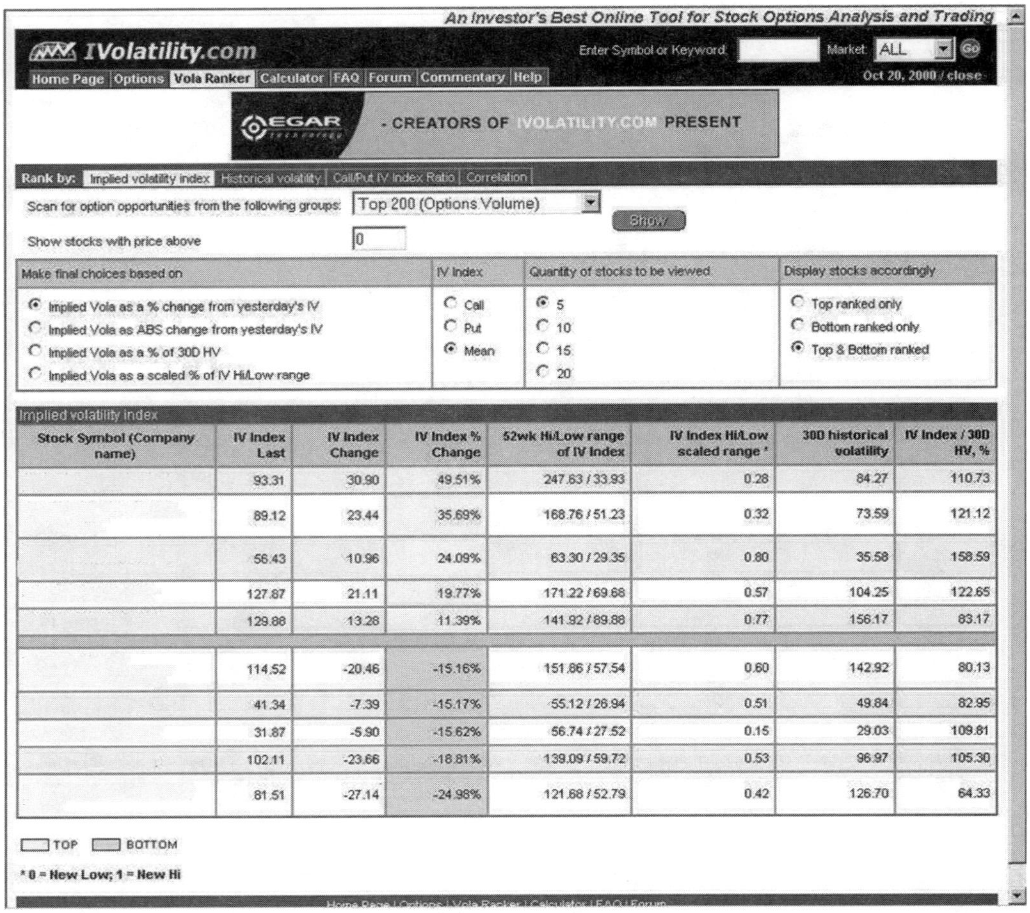

Stock Symbol (Company name)	IV Index Last	IV Index Change	IV Index % Change	52wk Hi/Low range of IV Index	IV Index Hi/Low scaled range *	30D historical volatility	IV Index / 30D HV, %
	93.31	30.90	49.51%	247.63 / 33.93	0.28	84.27	110.73
	89.12	23.44	35.69%	168.76 / 51.23	0.32	73.59	121.12
	56.43	10.96	24.09%	63.30 / 29.35	0.80	35.58	158.59
	127.87	21.11	19.77%	171.22 / 69.68	0.57	104.25	122.65
	129.88	13.28	11.39%	141.92 / 89.88	0.77	156.17	83.17
	114.52	-20.46	-15.16%	151.86 / 57.54	0.60	142.92	80.13
	41.34	-7.39	-15.17%	55.12 / 26.94	0.51	49.84	82.95
	31.87	-5.90	-15.62%	56.74 / 27.52	0.15	29.03	109.81
	102.11	-23.66	-18.81%	139.09 / 59.72	0.53	96.97	105.30
	81.51	-27.14	-24.98%	121.68 / 52.79	0.42	126.70	64.33

There is a forum where experts share their takes on various volatility related topics and frequently asked questions, and commentaries are provided monthly. The discussion revolves around volatility observations, but includes some market commentary, too.

The site is free for all of the above-mentioned features. There also is an advanced section that provides information on foreign issues, greater granularity of analysis, and downloadable data for portfolios.

I like the way the site is tightly laid out and facilitates quick maneuvering. Because the site is relatively new, there are a lot of directions in which they can take it. I look forward to seeing how it grows in usefulness for both the novice and the professional trader.

ONLINESPREADS.COM

<www.iSpreads.com>

Designed for easy integration, iSpreads™ not only simplifies your order entry process, but also enhances it. From providing educational content, calculation of theoretical spread prices, and display of improved spread price indications, to easy integration into your order entry process, iSpreads' technology is truly unique in options trading.

iSpreads employs two major components: floor-based order monitoring technology, and broker-integrated Web sites. The floor-based component facilitates a positive order execution experience for the broker's clients. Orders that are entered via the iSpreads technology are tracked and monitored by a custom software system for use on the trading floor. This system provides real-time information and alerts to the trading floor operation, which facilitates prompt attention to your spread orders. The broker-integrated Web site component contains the features and functionality of iSpreads within the broker's Web environment.

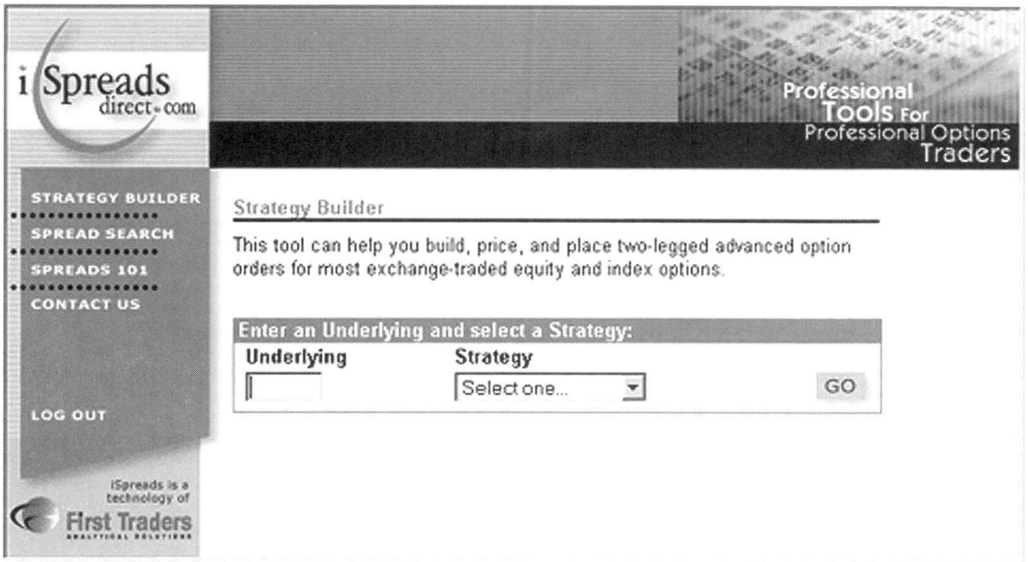

The iSpreadsDirect.com site shown above is a good venue to discuss some of the features of the iSpreads Technology. Though iSpreadsDirect.com is an iSpreads integration that can only be used by professional financial consultants, the user experience is similar to that of the iSpreads professional and retail integration affiliate sites. This site offers users price indications for full spread execution. Depending on the executing service you use, you can directly trade one of the spreads shown in the spread window by simply clicking on the side you prefer, which issues in a prepopulated order ticket. However, the indicative prices are not firm quotes and may not be available when an order is sent for execution.

The values on either side of the strike range column (center) show the inside price indications that these professionals have posted.

The values shown in the far left and right columns calculate the amount these price indications improve a theoretical value for the spread based upon the exchanges' net and posted prices for the individual legs of the spread.

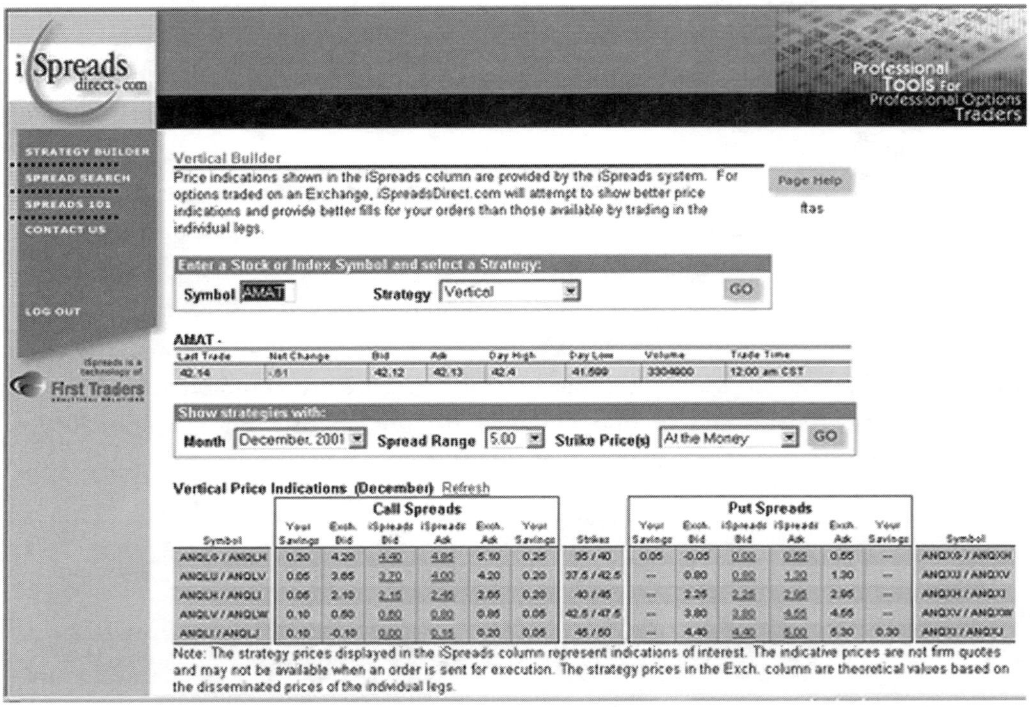

Once you have a feel for the risk characteristics of these spreads, a tool that will help you find indicative prices and risk/reward profiles is the spread search. The spread search feature will enable you to quickly sort through hundreds of spread opportunities.

You use the tool by defining the parameters upon which your search will be constrained. First, you select the symbol, spread type, and expiration month(s) that are of interest. Next, you define your risk/reward in terms of money-to-money, risk/reward ratio, or percentage return on your investment.

By defining the percentage move in the underlying price and the amount that you are investing, the search tool can return a specific set of strategies that meet the specific criteria. These strategies can then be traded immediately because the search return is a prepopulated ticket, ready to go to your point of execution. Indicative prices may not be available when order is sent for execution.

The alert feature on this site allows you to store away your favorite spread strategies and your target prices for each. When the spread reaches your target price, an alert is sent to you on the site (if you are browsing the site) and an email is sent to you alerting you to the fact that the specific price has been achieved.

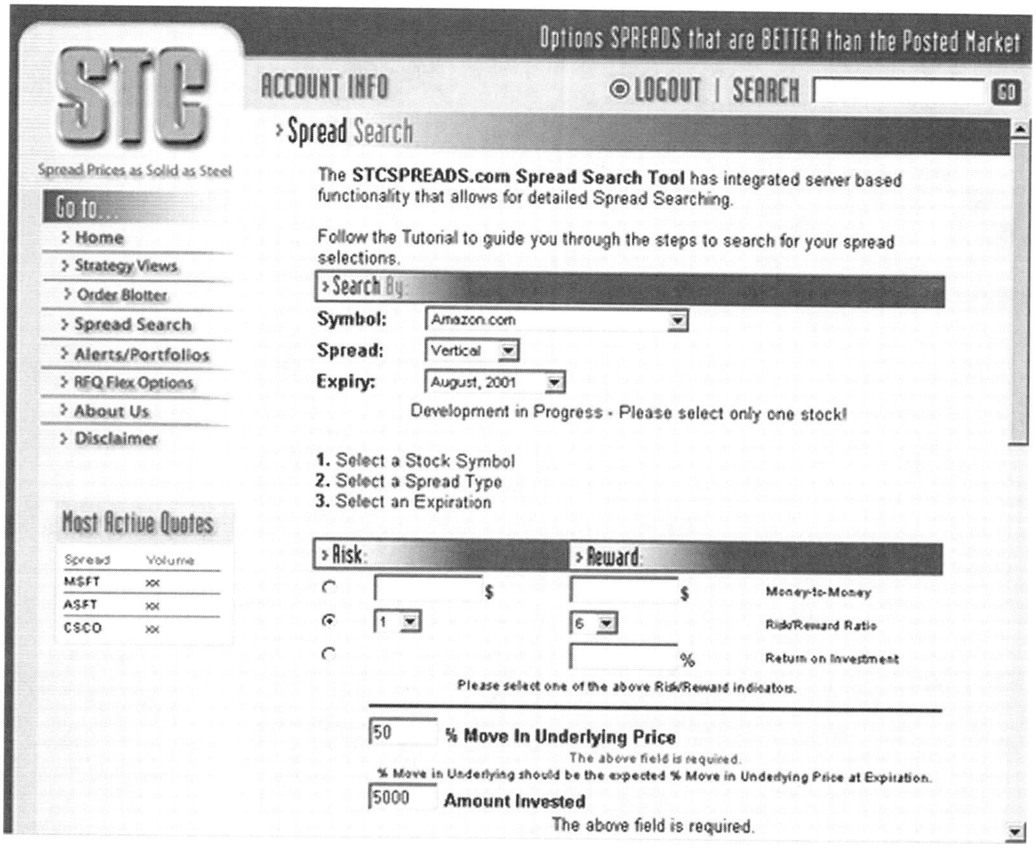
Options SPREADS that are BETTER than the Posted Market
STC
Spread Prices as Solid as Steel
ACCOUNT INFO
LOGOUT | SEARCH
GO
Spread Search
The STCSPREADS.com Spread Search Tool has integrated server based functionality that allows for detailed Spread Searching.
Follow the Tutorial to guide you through the steps to search for your spread selections.
Search By:
Symbol: Amazon.com
Spread: Vertical
Expiry: August, 2001
Development in Progress - Please select only one stock!
1. Select a Stock Symbol
2. Select a Spread Type
3. Select an Expiration
Go to...
Home
Strategy Views
Order Blotter
Spread Search
Alerts/Portfolios
RFQ Flex Options
About Us
Disclaimer
Most Active Quotes
Spread Volume
MSFT xx
ASFT xx
CSCO xx
Risk:
Reward:
Money-to-Money
Risk/Reward Ratio
Return on Investment
Please select one of the above Risk/Reward indicators.
50 % Move in Underlying Price
The above field is required.
% Move in Underlying should be the expected % Move in Underlying Price at Expiration.
5000 Amount Invested
The above field is required.

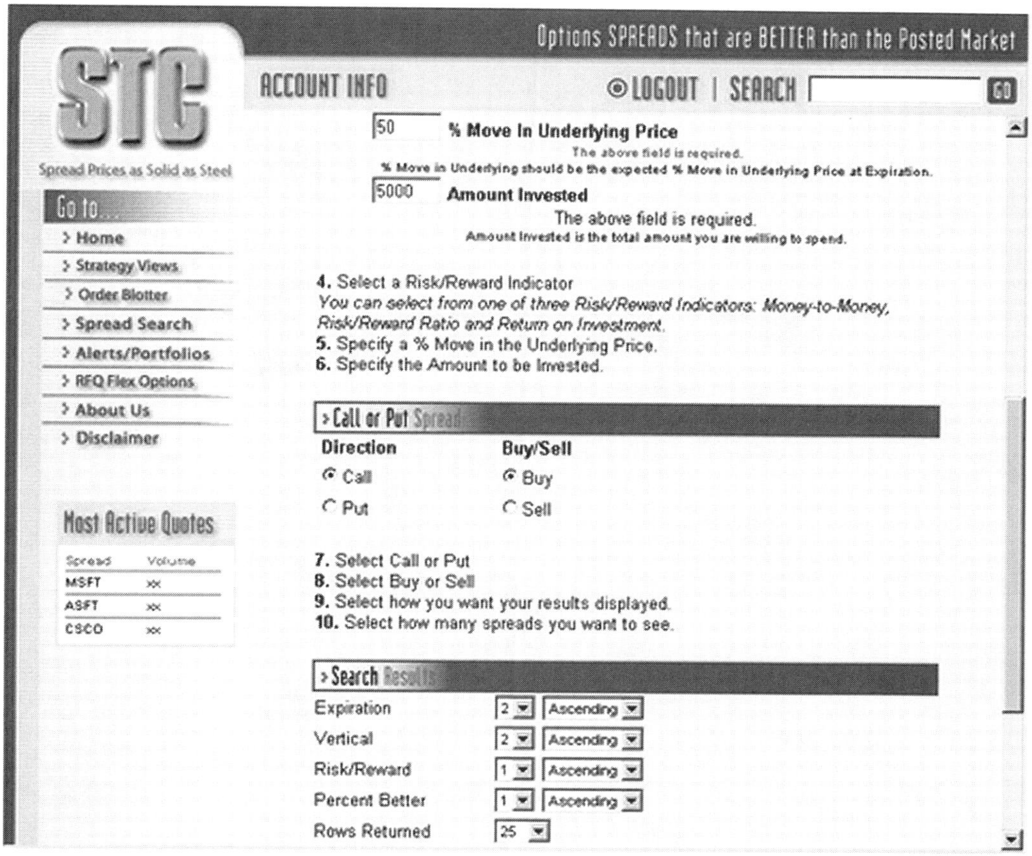
Options SPREADS that are BETTER than the Posted Market
STC
Spread Prices as Solid as Steel
ACCOUNT INFO
LOGOUT | SEARCH
GO
50 % Move in Underlying Price
The above field is required.
% Move in Underlying should be the expected % Move in Underlying Price at Expiration.
5000 Amount Invested
The above field is required.
Amount Invested is the total amount you are willing to spend.
4. Select a Risk/Reward Indicator
You can select from one of three Risk/Reward Indicators: Money-to-Money, Risk/Reward Ratio and Return on Investment.
5. Specify a % Move in the Underlying Price.
6. Specify the Amount to be Invested.
Go to...
Home
Strategy Views
Order Blotter
Spread Search
Alerts/Portfolios
RFQ Flex Options
About Us
Disclaimer
Call or Put Spread
Direction
Call
Put
Buy/Sell
Buy
Sell
Most Active Quotes
Spread Volume
MSFT xx
ASFT xx
CSCO xx
7. Select Call or Put
8. Select Buy or Sell
9. Select how you want your results displayed.
10. Select how many spreads you want to see.
Search Results
Expiration 2 Ascending
Vertical 2 Ascending
Risk/Reward 1 Ascending
Percent Better 1 Ascending
Rows Returned 25

OPTIONETICS

<www.optionetics.com>

This is an informational site stuffed with commentary and resources for the options trader. Although there is an area to maintain your portfolio listing, which updates results, the prime benefit I see in the site is their Options Analysis tools. They have a ranking system for cheap and expensive options that is easy to use.

Here the site offers the rankings of individual options against each other, regardless of their underlying stock. Rankings are by Implied Volatilities, Bollinger Band Volatility, Open Interest, Volume, and Price Change. This is very useful when scan-

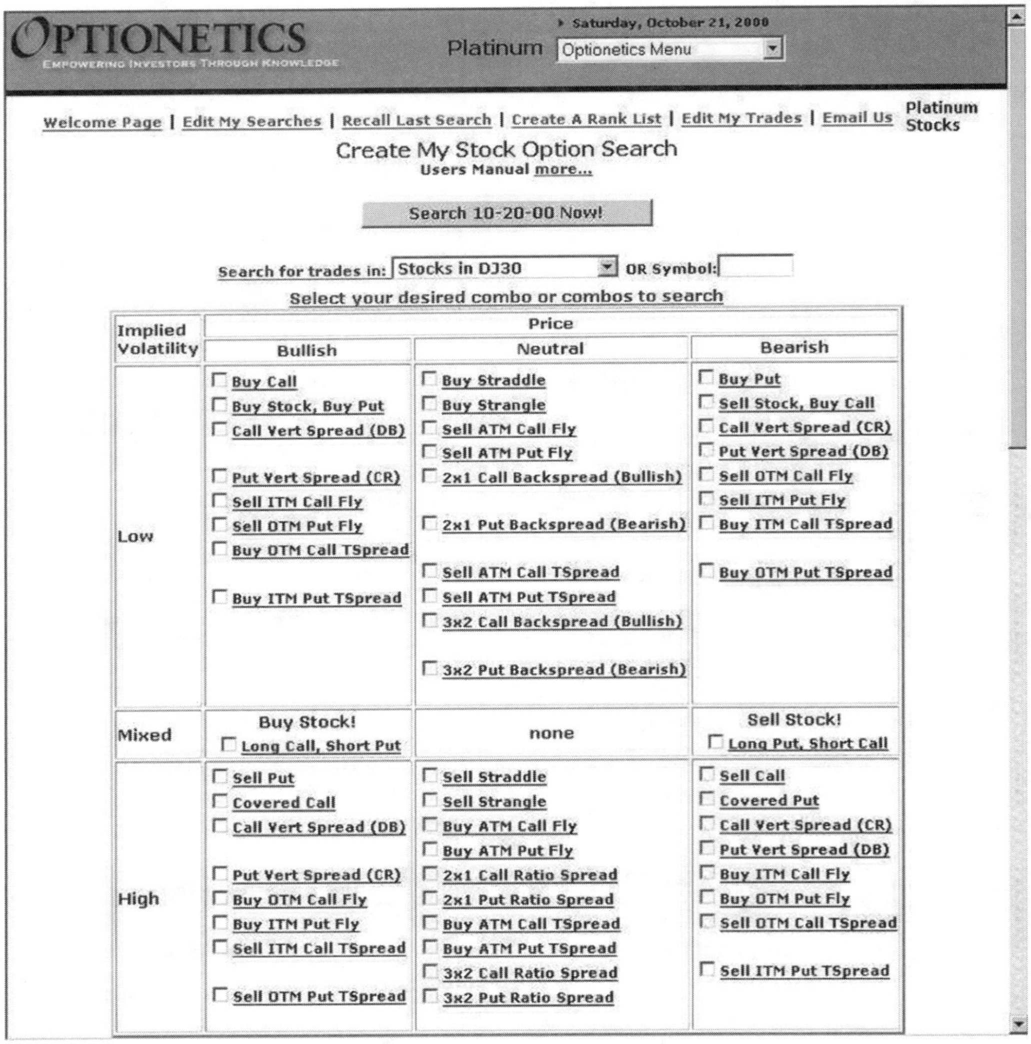

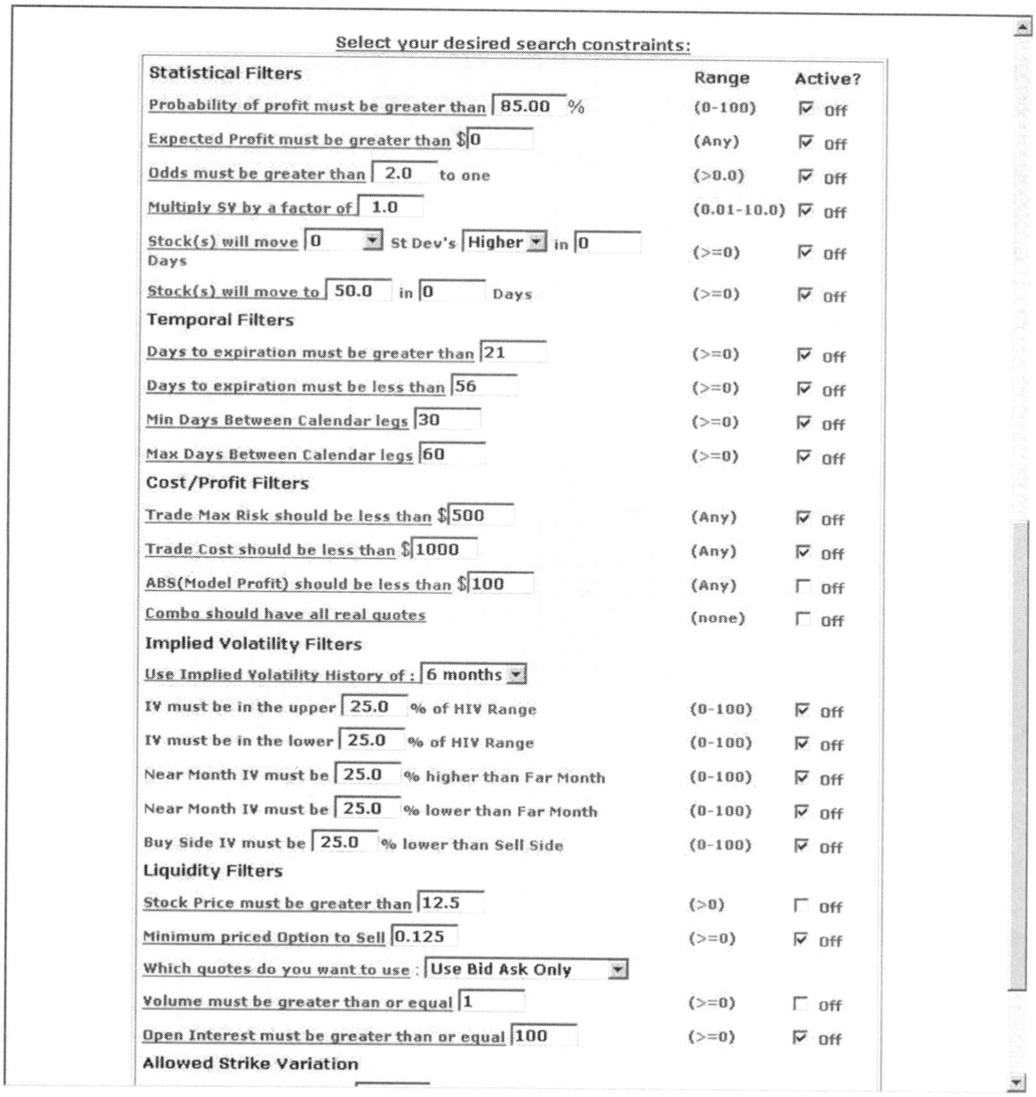

Select your desired search constraints:

Statistical Filters	Range	Active?
Probability of profit must be greater than 85.00 %	(0-100)	☑ Off
Expected Profit must be greater than $0	(Any)	☑ Off
Odds must be greater than 2.0 to one	(>0.0)	☑ Off
Multiply SV by a factor of 1.0	(0.01-10.0)	☑ Off
Stock(s) will move 0 St Dev's Higher in 0 Days	(>=0)	☑ Off
Stock(s) will move to 50.0 in 0 Days	(>=0)	☑ Off
Temporal Filters		
Days to expiration must be greater than 21	(>=0)	☑ Off
Days to expiration must be less than 56	(>=0)	☑ Off
Min Days Between Calendar legs 30	(>=0)	☑ Off
Max Days Between Calendar legs 60	(>=0)	☑ Off
Cost/Profit Filters		
Trade Max Risk should be less than $500	(Any)	☑ Off
Trade Cost should be less than $1000	(Any)	☑ Off
ABS(Model Profit) should be less than $100	(Any)	☐ Off
Combo should have all real quotes	(none)	☐ Off
Implied Volatility Filters		
Use Implied Volatility History of : 6 months		
IV must be in the upper 25.0 % of HIV Range	(0-100)	☑ Off
IV must be in the lower 25.0 % of HIV Range	(0-100)	☑ Off
Near Month IV must be 25.0 % higher than Far Month	(0-100)	☑ Off
Near Month IV must be 25.0 % lower than Far Month	(0-100)	☑ Off
Buy Side IV must be 25.0 % lower than Sell Side	(0-100)	☑ Off
Liquidity Filters		
Stock Price must be greater than 12.5	(>0)	☐ Off
Minimum priced Option to Sell 0.125	(>=0)	☑ Off
Which quotes do you want to use : Use Bid Ask Only		
Volume must be greater than or equal 1	(>=0)	☐ Off
Open Interest must be greater than or equal 100	(>=0)	☑ Off
Allowed Strike Variation		

ning or checking. Drill down allows for detailed analysis and display of the individual option. This part of the site is free.

They also offer an advanced service providing searches and "what-ifs" that is quite extensive. Many of the pertinent criteria for spread combinations are offered. Not only are pricing levels used, but volatility, volume, and open interest can be factored in.

Then you can sort and save your results for later review.

There is a factor to screen out potentially bad quotes, improving the probability that your trade is filled. This is very ingenious, and necessary until the exchanges go to "firm quotes" that are disseminated.

This service costs $750 per year for those desiring options services (it is less for their stock services). If you are an active trader using a discount broker, these services will probably save you at least the subscription price, not to mention help you fine-tune your risk profile.

CHICAGO BOARD OPTIONS EXCHANGE

CBOE
CHICAGO BOARD OPTIONS EXCHANGE

<www.cboe.com>

The "Mother of All Options Exchanges," the CBOE has led the securities industry with its technology and automation. The site is rich with real-time quotes, investor research, trader tools, and insight.

APPENDIX E

Option Strategies

Profit and Loss Snapshots

LONG UNDERLYING

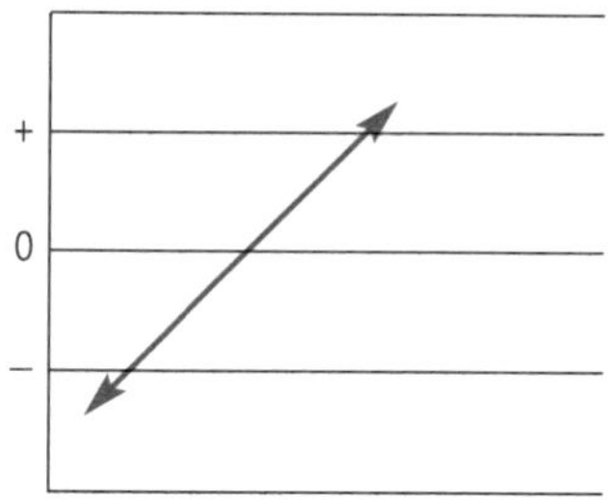

Strategy:	Buy shares of underlying
Directional bias:	Bullish market
Profit potential:	Unlimited to the upside
Loss exposure:	Substantial on the downside
Break-even:	Price of the underlying at initiation
Synthetics:	Long call, short put

SHORT UNDERLYING

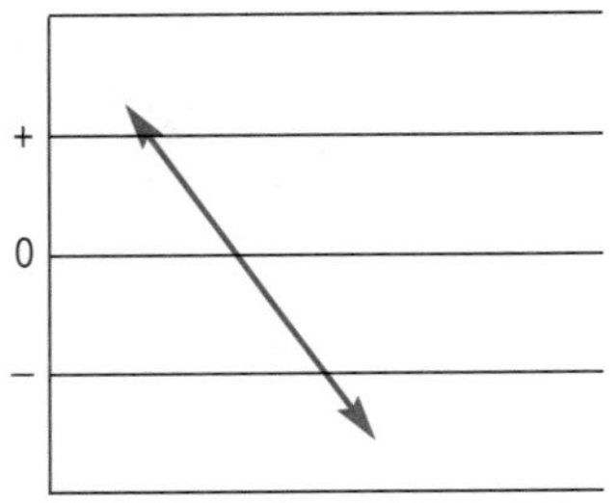

Strategy:	Sell shares of underlying
Directional bias:	Bearish
Profit potential:	Limited on the downside as the underlying falls to zero
Loss exposure:	Unlimited to the upside
Break-even:	Price of underlying at initiation
Synthetics:	Long put, short call

LONG CALL

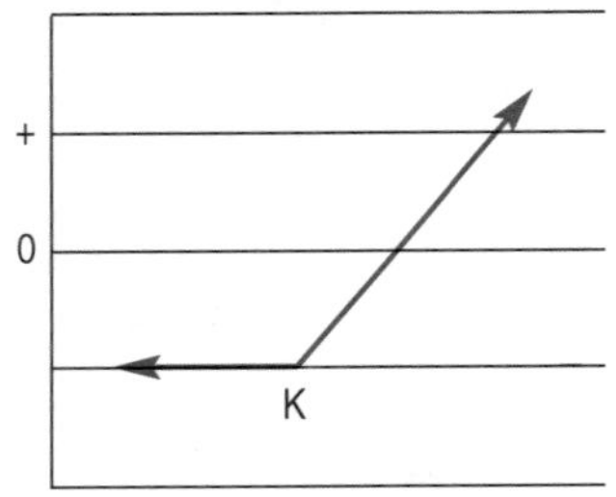

K = strike price; x axis = the underlying price at expiration

Strategy:	Buy a call option
Directional bias:	Bullish market
Profit potential:	Unlimited to the upside
Loss exposure:	Limited to the premium paid for the call option bought
Break-even:	Strike price + premium paid
Synthetics:	Long underlying, long put

SHORT CALL

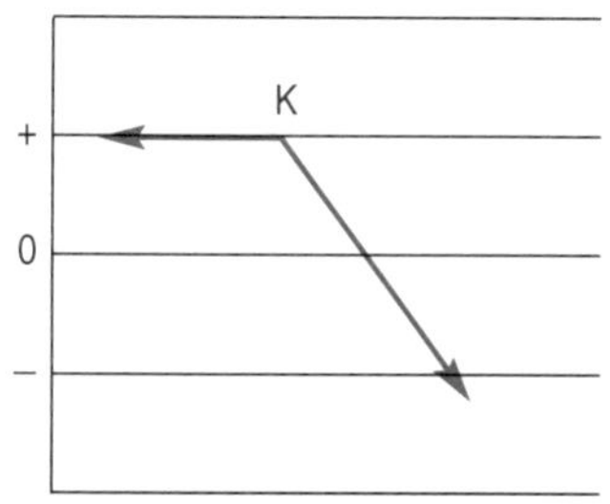

K = strike price; x axis = the underlying price at expiration

Strategy:	Sell a call option
Directional bias:	Neutral to bearish
Profit potential:	Limited to the premium received for the call option sold
Loss exposure:	Unlimited to the upside
Break-even:	Strike price + premium received
Synthetics:	Short underlying, short put

LONG PUT

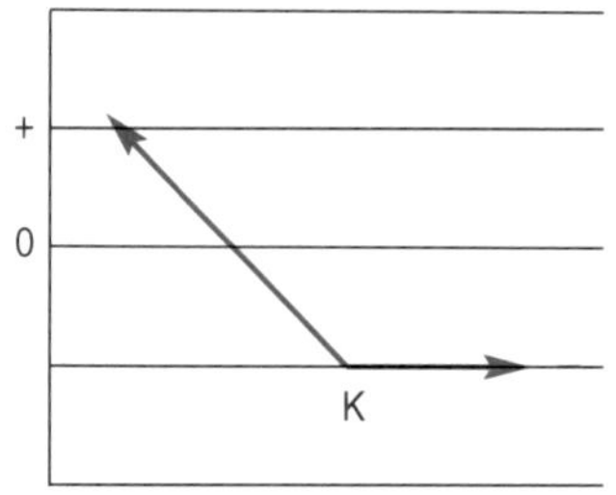

K = strike price; x axis = the underlying price at expiration

Strategy:	Buy a put option
Directional bias:	Bearish market
Profit potential:	Limited as underlying falls below break-even point to zero.
Loss exposure:	Limited to premium paid for the put option bought
Break-even:	Strike price – premium paid
Synthetics:	Short underlying, long call

SHORT PUT

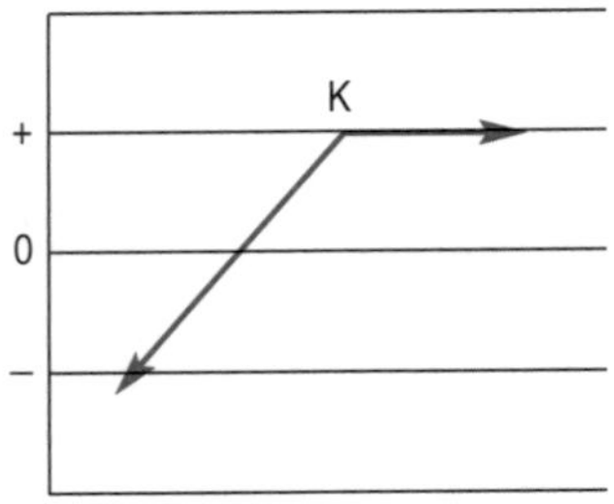

K = strike price; x axis = the underlying price at expiration

Strategy:	Sell a put option
Directional bias:	Neutral to bullish
Profit potential:	Limited to the premium received for the put option sold
Loss exposure:	Limited as the underlying price falls below break-even point to zero on the downside.
Break-even:	Strike price – premium received
Synthetics:	Long underlying, short call

BULL SPREADS USING CALLS (LONG CALL VERTICAL)

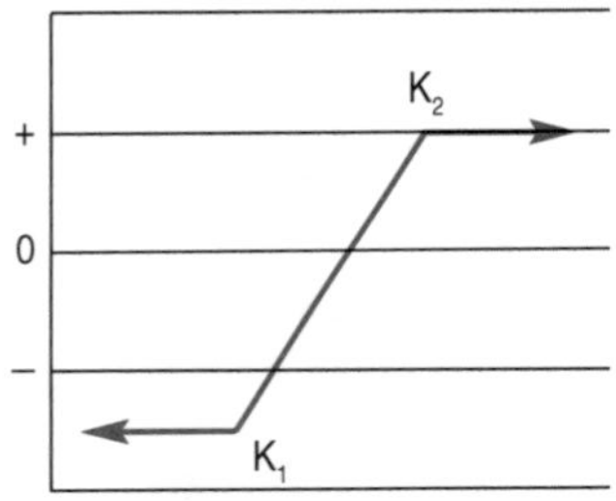

K = strike price; x axis = the underlying price at expiration

Strategy:	Buy (long) a lower strike (K_1) call and sell (short) a higher strike (K_2) call with the *same* expiration.
Directional bias:	Bullish market (modest)
Profit potential:	$(K_2 - K_1)$ – debit
Loss exposure:	Debit (net premium paid)
Break-even:	K_1 + debit

BULL SPREADS USING PUTS (SHORT PUT VERTICAL)

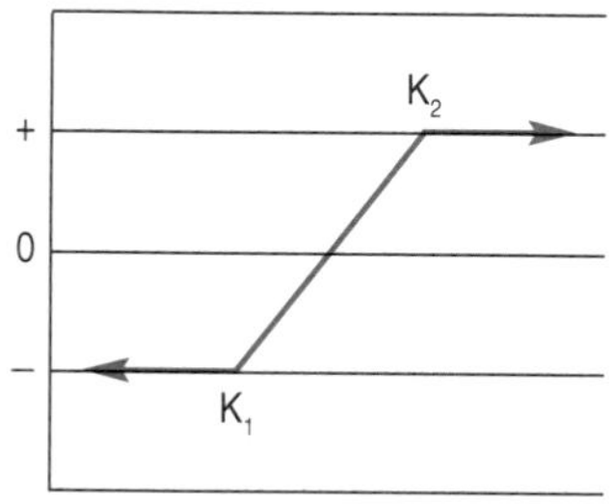

K = strike price; x axis = the underlying price at expiration

Strategy:	Buy (long) a lower strike (K_1) put and sell a higher strike (K_2) put with the *same* expiration.
Directional bias:	Bullish market (modest)
Profit potential:	Credit (net premium received)
Loss exposure:	$(K_2 - K_1)$ – credit
Break-even:	K_2 – credit

BEAR SPREADS USING CALLS (SHORT CALL VERTICAL)

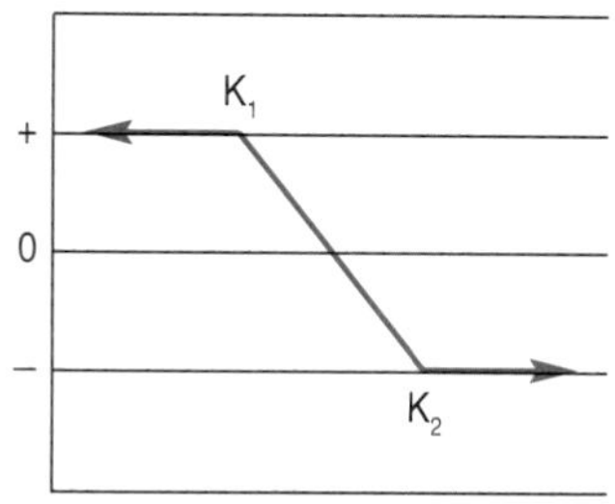

K = strike price; x axis = the underlying price at expiration

Strategy:	Sell (short) lower strike (K_1) and buy (long) higher strike (K_2) (same expiration).
Directional bias:	Bearish market (modest)
Profit potential:	Credit (net premium received)
Loss exposure:	$(K_2 - K_1)$ – credit
Break-even:	K_1 + credit

BEAR SPREADS USING PUTS (LONG PUT VERTICAL)

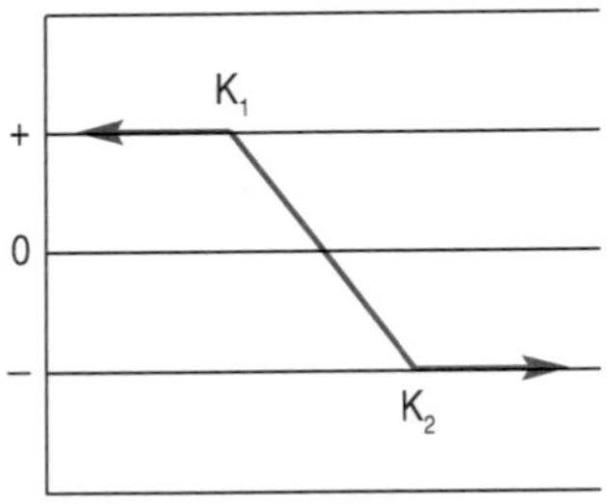

K = strike price; x axis = the underlying price at expiration

Strategy: Sell (short) lower strike (K_1) and buy (long) higher strike (K_2) (with same expiration).
Directional bias: Bearish market (modest)
Profit potential: $(K_2 - K_1)$ – debit
Loss exposure: Debit (net premium paid)
Break-even: K_2 – debit

LONG CALL BUTTERFLY

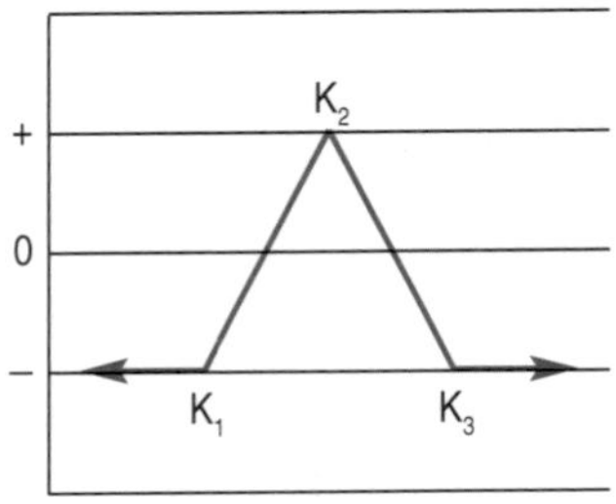

K = strike price; x axis = the underlying price at expiration

Strategy: Long 1 call at K_1; short (sell) 2 calls at K_2; long 1 call at K_3 (same expiration).
Directional bias: Stable
Profit potential: $(K_3 - K_1)/2$ – debit
Loss exposure: Debit (net premium paid)
Break-even: K_1 + debit; K_3 – debit

LONG PUT BUTTERFLY

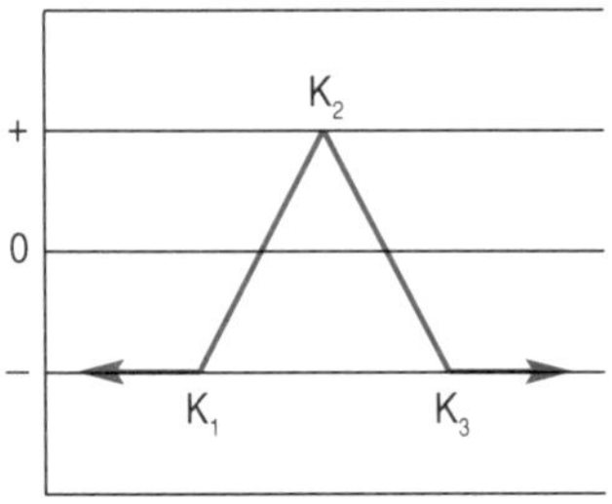

K = strike price; x axis = the underlying price at expiration

Strategy:	Long 1 put at K_1; short 2 puts at K_2; long 1 put at K_3 (with same expiration).
Directional bias:	Stable
Profit potential:	$(K_3 - K_1)/2$ – debit
Loss exposure:	Debit (net premium paid)
Break-even:	K_1 + debit; K_3 – debit

LONG STRADDLE

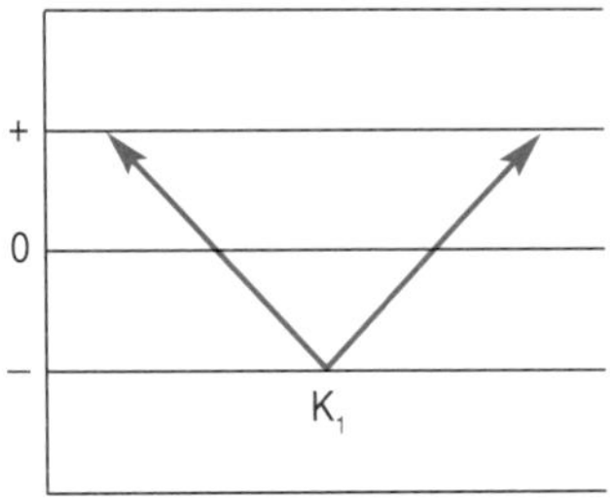

K = strike price; x axis = the underlying price at expiration

Strategy:	Long call at K_1; long put at K_1
Directional bias:	Volatile
Profit potential:	Unlimited to the upside; limited by price of underlyings to the downside
Loss exposure:	Debit (net premium paid)
Break-even:	K_1 – debit; K_1 + debit

SHORT STRADDLE

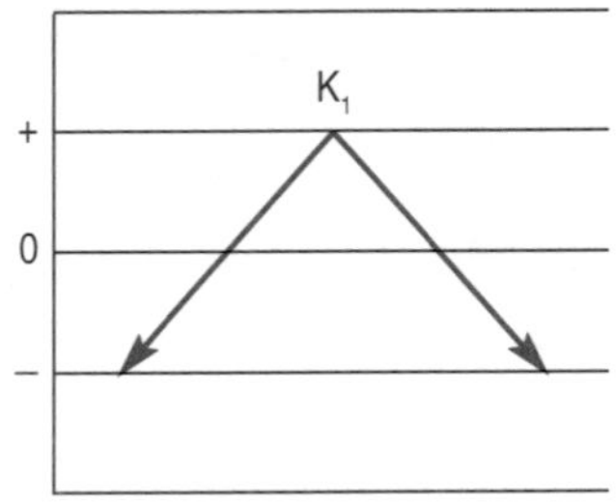

K = strike price; x axis = the underlying price at expiration

Strategy:	Short call at K_1; short put at K_1
Directional bias:	Stable
Profit potential:	Credit (net premium received)
Loss exposure:	Unlimited to the upside, substantial on the downside
Break-even:	K_1 – credit; K_1 + credit

CALL RATIO SPREADS

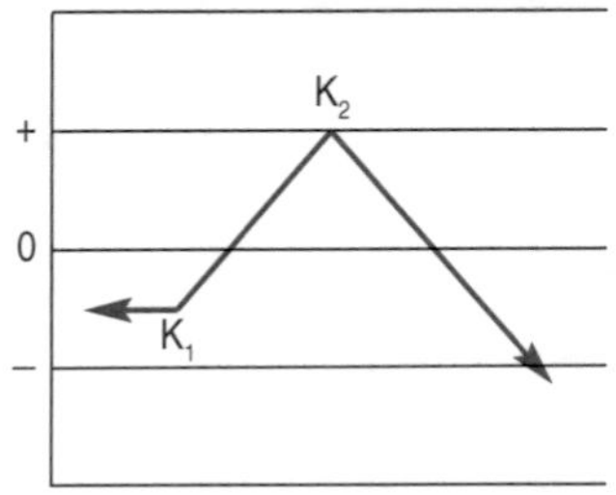

K = strike price; x axis = the underlying price at expiration

Strategy:	Short 2 calls at K_2 and long 1 call at K_1 (with same expiration)
Directional bias:	Stable—want underlying to be at the strike of sold option
Profit potential:	$(K_2 - K_1)$ + credit or – debit (to establish ratio spread)
Loss exposure:	Unlimited on the upside. Debit to establish on downside (if done for a debit)
Break-even:	Downside: K_1 + debit; upside: K_2 + maximum profit potential or {[(# long calls × difference in strike prices) + credit or – debit] / number of calls naked}

PUT RATIO SPREADS

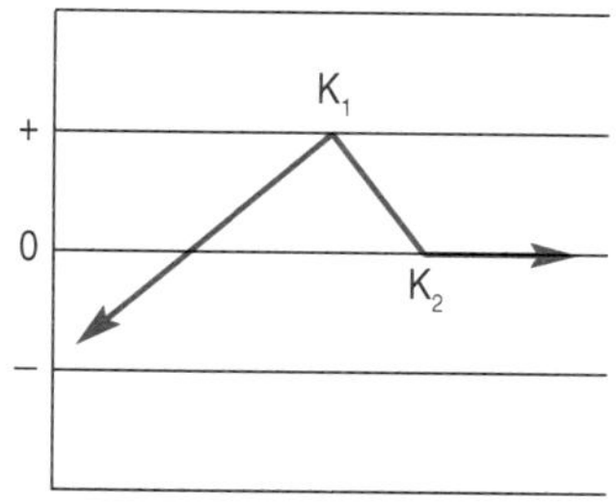

K = strike price; x axis = the underlying price at expiration

Strategy:	Short 2 puts at K_1 and long 1 put at K_2 (with same expiration)
Directional bias:	Stable—investor wants the underlying to be at the strike of the sold options
Profit potential:	$(K_2 - K_1)$ + credit or – debit (to establish ratio spread)
Loss exposure:	Substantial on the downside; upside limited to debit to establish (if done for a debit)
Break-even:	Upside: K_2 – debit; downside: K_1 – maximum profit potential, or {[(# long puts × difference in strike prices) + credit or – debit] / number of puts naked}

CALL BACKSPREADS

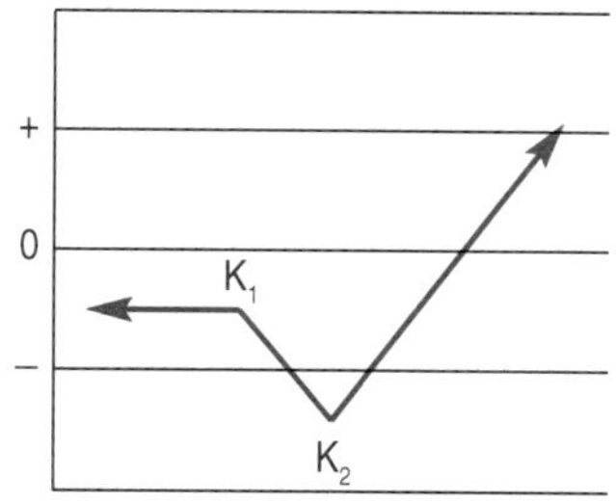

K = strike price; x axis = the underlying price at expiration

Strategy:	Long 2 calls at K_2 and short 1 call at K_1 (with same expiration)
Directional bias:	Volatile—prefer very bullish
Profit potential:	Unlimited to the upside; downside limited to debit to establish (if done for a debit).
Loss exposure:	$(K_2 - K_1)$ – credit or + debit (to establish backspread)
Break-even:	A) Upside: K_2 + maximum loss, or $[(K_2 - K_1)$ – credit or + debit] B) Downside: K_1 + credit or K_1 – debit

PUT BACKSPREADS

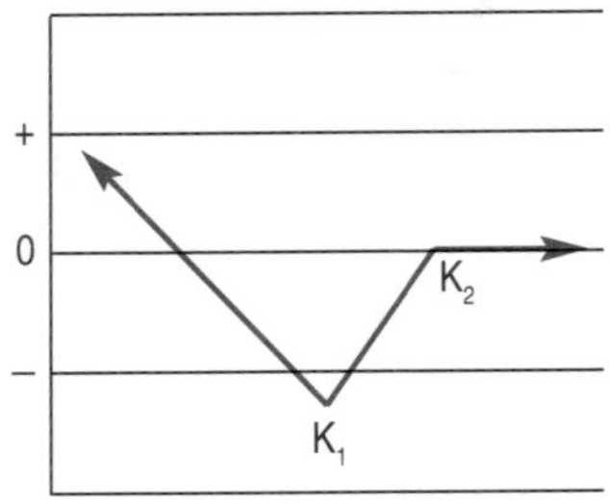

K = strike price; x axis = the underlying price at expiration

Strategy:	Long 2 puts at K_1 and short 1 put at K_2 (with same expiration)
Directional bias:	Volatile—prefer very bearish
Profit potential:	Limited to price of underlying on the downside (to zero); upside limited to credit received (if done for a credit)
Loss exposure:	$(K_2 - K_1)$ – credit or + debit (to establish backspread)
Break-even:	A) Upside: K_2 – credit or K_2 + debit B) Downside: K_1 – maximum loss, or $[(K_2 - K_1)$ – credit or + debit]

LONG IRON BUTTERFLY

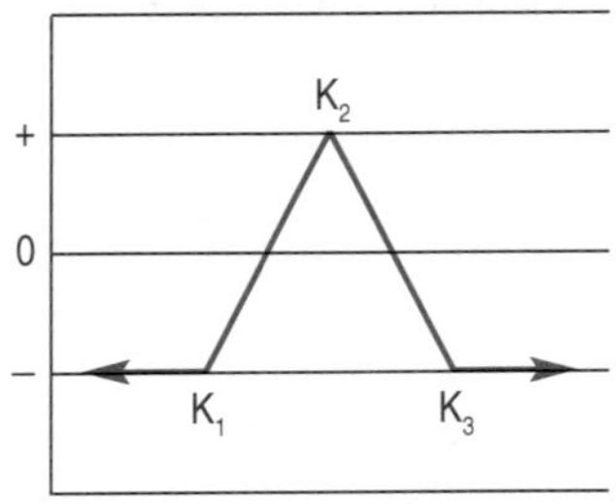

K = strike price; x axis = the underlying price at expiration

Strategy:	Short straddle at K_2 (1 short call and 1 short put) and long strangle at K_1 (put) and K_3 (call) with same expiration
Directional bias:	Stable
Profit potential:	Credit received
Loss exposure:	$(K_2 - K_1)$ – credit
Break-even:	K_2 – credit and K_2 + credit

LONG CALL CONDOR

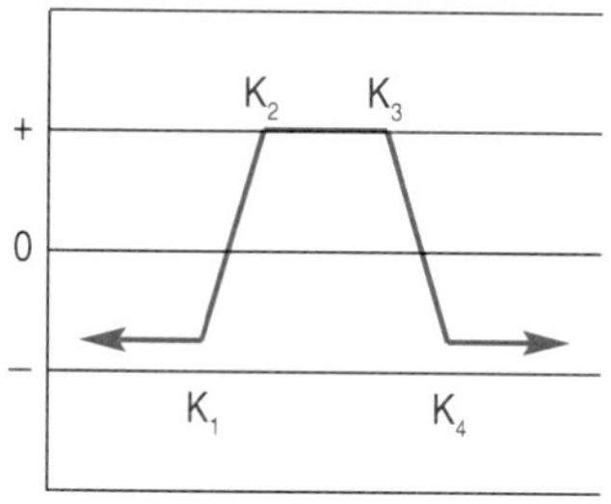

K = strike price; x axis = the underlying price at expiration

Strategy:	Long 1 call at K_1; short 1 call at K_2; short 1 call at K_3; long 1 call at K_4 (with same expiration)
Directional bias:	Stable
Profit potential:	$(K_2 - K_1)$ – debit
Loss exposure:	Debit
Break-even:	K_1 + debit and K_4 – debit

LONG PUT CONDOR

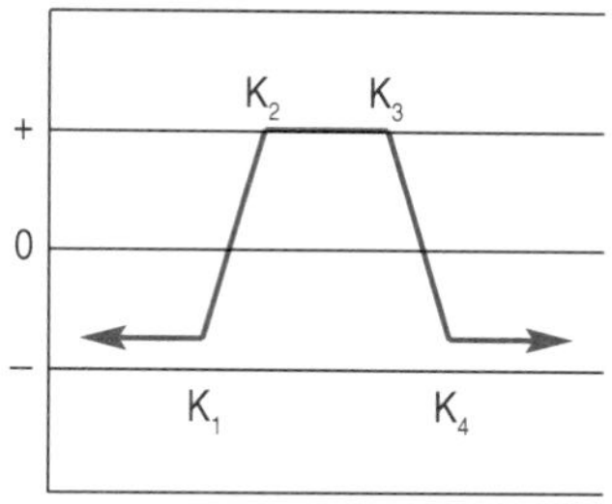

K = strike price; x axis = the underlying price at expiration

Strategy:	Long 1 put at K_1; short 1 put at K_2; short 1 put at K_3; long 1 put at K_4 (with same expiration)
Directional bias:	Stable
Profit potential:	$(K_2 - K_1)$ – debit
Loss exposure:	Debit
Break-even:	K_1 + debit; K_4 – debit

LONG STRANGLE

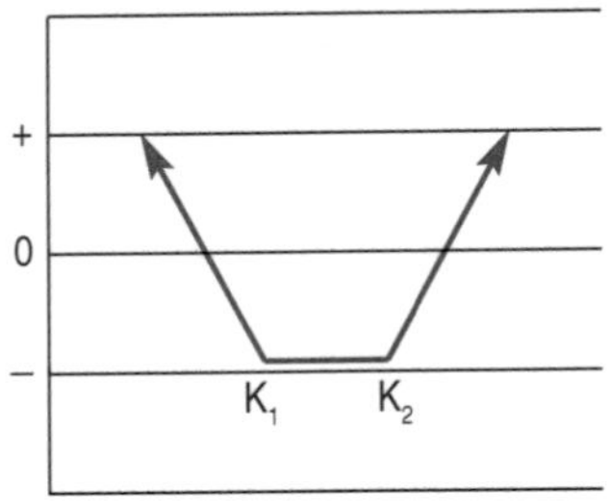

K = strike price; x axis = the underlying price at expiration

Strategy:	Long call at K_2, long put at K_1 (with same expiration)
Directional bias:	Either bullish or bearish, but more generally needs to be extreme.
Profit potential:	Unlimited to upside; limited by price of stock to downside
Loss exposure:	Debit paid
Break-even:	K_1 – debit; K_2 + debit

SHORT STRANGLE

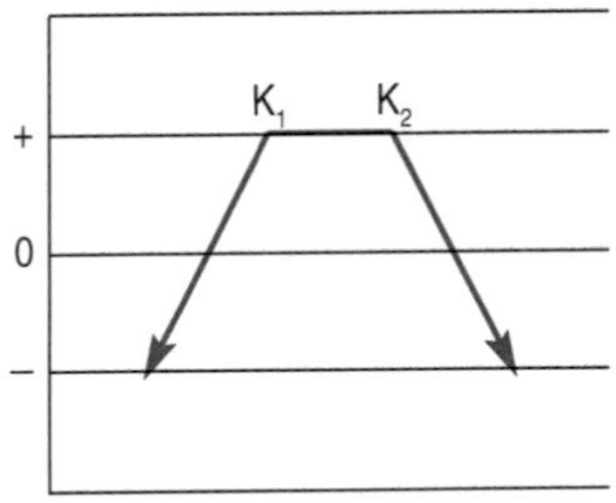

K = strike price; x axis = the underlying price at expiration

Strategy:	Short call at K_2, short put at K_1 (with same expiration)
Directional bias:	Want the market to sit still.
Profit potential:	Credit received
Loss exposure:	Unlimited to the upside; limited by price of stock to downside.
Break-even:	K_1 – credit and K_2 + credit

Index

T

U

V

W